CISTERCIAN FATHERS SERIES: N

AELRED OF RIEVAULX
THE LITURGICAL SERMONS

THE FIRST CLAIRVAUX COLLECTION
SERMONS ONE – TWENTY-EIGHT
ADVENT – ALL SAINTS

Translated

by

Theodore Berkeley, OCSO

and

M. Basil Pennington, OCSO

Cistercian Publications
Kalamazoo – Spencer – Coalville

© English translation, copyright Cistercian Publications Inc., 2001

A translation of part of *Aelredi Rievallensis Sermones I–XLVI*
Collectio Claraevallensis Primo et Secunda recensuit Gaetano Raciti
Corpus Christianorum Continuatio Medieualis IIa. Turnholt: Brepols, 1989.

Cistercian Publications
Editorial Offices and Customer Service
Institute of Cistercian Studies
WMU Station
1903 West Michigan Avenue
Kalamazoo, MI 49008–5415

available in the United Kingdom from
Cistercian Publications UK
Mount Saint Bernard Abbey
Coalville, Leics. LE67 5UL England

All rights reserved

The work of Cistercian Publications is made possible in part
by support from Western Michigan University to
The Institute of Cistercian Studies

Printed in the United States of America

CONTENTS

TABLE OF ABBREVIATIONS	7
Introduction by M. Basil Pennington OCSO	9
CONCORDANCE OF THE SERMONS OF AELRED OF RIEVAULX	51
A NOTE ON THE TRANSLATION	53

THE SERMONS OF AELRED OF RIEVAULX

SERMON ONE *For the Coming of the Lord*	57
SERMON TWO *For the Coming of the Lord*	77
SERMON THREE *For the Nativity of the Lord*	91
SERMON FOUR *For the Epiphany of the Lord*	106
SERMON FIVE *For the Purification of Saint Mary*	119
SERMON SIX *For the Feast of Saint Benedict*	129
SERMON SEVEN *For the Feast of Saint Benedict*	142
SERMON EIGHT *For the Feast of Saint Benedict*	147
SERMON NINE *For the Annunciation of the Lord*	155
SERMON TEN *For Palm Sunday*	170
SERMON ELEVEN *For the Feast of Easter*	182
SERMON TWELVE *For the Feast of Easter*	194
SERMON THIRTEEN *For the Ascension of the Lord*	205
SERMON FOURTEEN *For the Nativity of Saint John Baptist*	218
SERMON FIFTEEN *For the Feast of the Holy Apostles Peter and Paul*	227
SERMON SIXTEEN *For the Feast of the Holy Apostles Peter and Paul*	242
SERMON SEVENTEEN *For the Feast of the Holy Apostles Peter and Paul*	245

SERMON EIGHTEEN *For the Feast of the Holy Apostles Peter and Paul*	254
SERMON NINETEEN *For the Assumption of Saint Mary*	263
SERMON TWENTY *For the Assumption of Saint Mary*	275
SERMON TWENTY-ONE *For the Assumption of Saint Mary*	289
SERMON TWENTY-TWO *For the Nativity of Holy Mary*	306
SERMON TWENTY-THREE *For the Nativity of Holy Mary*	318
SERMON TWENTY-FOUR *For the Nativity of Saint Mary*	327
SERMON TWENTY-FIVE *For the Feast of All Saints*	346
SERMON TWENTY-SIX *For the Feast of All Saints*	354
SERMON TWENTY-SEVEN *For the of All Saints*	370
SERMON TWENTY-EIGHT *To the Clerics at the Synod*	380

Table of Abbreviations

CCCM	Corpus Christianorum Continuatio Medievalis series. Turnhout: Brepols
CCSL	Corpus Christianorum Series Latina series. Turnhout: Brepols.
CSEL	Corpus scriptorum ecclesiasticorum latinorum series. Vienna.
Hesbert	R.-J. Hesbert. *Corpus antiphonalium officii.* 6 volumes. Rome: Herder 1963, 1979
Interpretatio	Jerome, *Liber interpretationis hebraicorum nominum* (The Interpretation of Hebrew Names)
PL	J.-P. Migne, *Patrologia cursus completus series Latina*
SCh	Sources chrétiennes series. Paris: Cerf.

Scriptural passages are cited according to the enumeration of *The New Jerusalem Bible,* with the exception of psalms, which are cited first according to the Septuagint-Vulgate enumeration and then, in brackets, according to the Hebrew (NJB) enumeration.

INTRODUCTION

MOST OF THOSE who pick up this volume will, I suspect, already be quite familiar with Aelred of Rievaulx, so my introduction to this eminent abbot can be quite brief. We are fortunate to have a *Life* written by his admiring disciple, Walter Daniel, who was also his infirmarian in his last years. This is readily available in the fine edition of F. M. Powicke.[1] An excellent biographical study done by another admiring disciple, one of our own times, Father Aelred Squire, is also available.[2] His volume not only incorporates all the research done on Aelred until 1969, but it also reviews each of Aelred's known writings, placing them in the context of the great abbot's life.

Fortunately, the clerical celibacy mandated by the gregorian reform was not yet rigidly imposed in the twelfth century or the Church and the world would have not been blessed with this great Cistercian Father who was the son of an hereditary priest, Eilaf by name, the keeper of the shrine at Hexham. Eilaf had connections, for at an early age Aelred found himself in the court of David, king of Scotland, where he enjoyed a special intimacy with the royal heir, Henry, the future king of the Scots. Aelred, in his humility, often referred to himself as unlettered, because he never attended any of the well-known schools of his

---

1. *Walter Daniel's Life of Ailred (Vita Ailredi)*, ed. and trans. F. M. Powicke (London: Nelson, 1950), reprinted with revised notes and a new introduction by Marsha Dutton in the Cistercian Fathers Series, Number 57 (Kalamazoo-Spencer: Cistercian Publications, 1994).
2. *Aelred of Rievaulx. A Study* (London: SPCK, 1969 - Kalamazoo: Cistercian Publications 1981).

time, nor, as far as we know, any other school. Yet, as his literary output clearly shows, he received a good classical education either at home or at court, or at both. At some point he was given an office, and a significant one, that of royal dispenser. This he used as the basis on which to lay his claim that he was a man more familiar with pots and pans than literary devices.

Whatever his literary insecurities, he did not have to enter monastic life to have his abilities recognized. King David sent this promising young courtier on official missions and it was in the course of one of these, in the year of 1134, that he first visited the recently founded abbey at Rievaulx.[3] It was a moment of conversion. The twenty-four-year-old courtier turned monk.

Life at Rievaulx must have been somewhat austere in those primitive days. Under the guidance of Abbot William, Aelred evidently received a solid cistercian formation. Before many years had passed he was entrusted with important affairs, even while his monastic wisdom was readily recognized. Contrary to a popular misperception, the monastic way does not hide its followers' light under a bushel. The diplomatic abilities which had been recognized and nurtured in this young man at the scottish court were now put to use in the service of the King of kings, his Church, and the Cistercian Order.

In 1142 Aelred was sent to Rome to represent his Order's interests and what the Cistercians conceived of as the best interests of the Church of York. To all intents and purposes, Aelred's mission was successful, though the matter was to drag out over a long period. More important for the life of Aelred and for us was the opportunity the mission afforded Aelred

---

3. On the banks of the river Rye, Rievaulx was founded in 1132 on the lands of Walter Espec and not far from his castle at Helmsley. The founders came from Clairvaux under the leadeship of an Englishman, William, who had been secretary to abbot Bernard of Clairvaux.

to visit not only Cîteaux, the source and motherhouse of his Order, but also Clairvaux, where he came to know personally his Father Immediate, Abbot Bernard.[4] The appreciation that arose in these two men was mutual. Bernard's influence is not missing from the writings of the future abbot of Rievaulx. And it was the abbot of Clairvaux who propelled the young monk into his 'career' as an author. Indeed, so impressed by the monastic wisdom of the monk from the north was the abbot who incarnated the cistercian spirit that Bernard used his authority to require Aelred on obedience to write what was to be in fact a basic manual for cistercian novices. Arriving safely back at Rievaulx, the young novice master gathered up his notes and produced his *Mirror of Charity*.[5]

Aelred did not long remain novice master. Rievaulx sent out the third of its groups of founders to establish Revesby, in Lincolnshire, in 1143.[6] At their head went the novice master of Rievaulx. Nor did Aelred remain long in this post. In 1147, Maurice, the second abbot of Rievaulx,[7] resigned and the monks of Rievaulx summoned Aelred back to serve them as abbot. So began a long and fruitful abbatial reign of almost twenty years.

4. In the Cistercian Order the abbot of the house from which the founders of a new monastery come is traditionally called the 'father abbot' or Father Immediate. In accordance with the cistercian constitution, The Charter of Charity, he continues to have some responsibilities for the new monastery which his community inaugurated; most significantly, he is required to make regular canonical visitations and to report to the General Chapter, to administer the house in the absence of its own abbot (*sede vacante*) and to preside at the election of a new superior.
5. *The Mirror of Charity*, tr. Elizabeth Connor, CF 17 (Kalamazoo: Cistercian Publications, 1990).
6. Rievaulx sent monks to establish Wardon on the Bedfordshire property of Walter Espec in 1135, and in 1136 dispatched monks to Melrose, where King David had given them land. The Revesby property was given by William de Roumare.
7. William, the first abbot of Rievaulx, who had formed Aelred, died in 1145. Maurice, a former monk of Durham who had come to the Cistercians with a great reputation for learning, was elected his successor. He proved to be an unskilled administrator and resigned the pastoral office after only two years.

Although criticized by other abbots and even by the General Chapter of the Cistercian Order, Aelred was a successful abbot. Like Bernard of Clairvaux, he left behind him an enormous, flourishing, fervent community, a community marked above all by the love which the monks and the lay brothers had for one another and for their abbot. And he left as well a rich literary heritage, a varied body of works which contained, along with the usual monastic treatises, historical studies,[8] sermons on state and ecclesial occasions[9] and pieces of popular devotion.[10]

The first thing that comes to mind when one thinks of Aelred of Rievaulx is his friendships and his warm relationship with his monks. His wonderful treatise on *Spiritual Friendship*[11] is no doubt partly responsible for this reputation, but the image Walter Daniel conveys certainly supports it. Like Bernard, he knew a lot of sickness and used times of convalescence to enjoy his friends. One of the criticisms levelled at him by the General Chapter was his habit of making the special infirmary room he had built for himself a gathering place where the brethren could crowd in to be with their abbot.

After much suffering from severe arthritis, the holy and much-loved abbot died peacefully in the midst of his sons on 12 January 1167, in the fifty-seventh year of his life.[12]

---

8. *The Genealogy of the Kings of England, The Battle of the Standard*, and *The Life of Edward the Confessor*, to mention only the most significant works. These rather idealistic and somewhat mythological works hold up an ideal of christian chivalry to a future king. The study of them has its value, not only in giving us a fuller understanding of the context of Aelred's life but also in giving us insight into his personality. All of Aelred's historical works in english translation by Jane Patricia Freeland are forthcoming from Cistercian Publications.

9. Such as the Sermon to the clergy at the synod at Troyes which is to be found in this collection of sermons.

10. See, for example, *On Jesus at Twelve Years* and *Letter to his Sister*, in *Aelred of Rievaulx: Treatises I* ,CF 2 (1971).

11. Available in english translation by Mary Eugenia Laker ssnd, CF 5 (1974).

12. Walter Daniel, *The Life of Aelred of Rievaulx* 57; CF 57:138.

THE SERMONS

During his twenty years as abbot, Aelred preached many times: in his own monastery, in other monasteries, and at significant gatherings outside the cloister. Walter Daniel mentions hundreds of sermons. Relatively recent discoveries have enabled us to enjoy a fuller portion of this rich heritage.[13] A critical edition of the abbot of Rievaulx's sermons is now being published. In 1989 Gaetano Raciti published the first part of the first volume,[14] which includes, in fact, two collections of Aelred's sermons: the First and Second Collections of Clairvaux. It is the first of these that we offer here in volume one of *The Liturgical Sermons of Aelred of Rievaulx*.

The First Collection of Clairvaux is found in Manuscript 910 of the Municipal Library of Troyes, a manuscript that came from Clairvaux. It was copied in the latter part of the twelfth century, thus not long after the death of the abbot of Rievaulx. Included among other writings, the sermon collection is clearly marked as a work of Aelred.[15] The collection was undoubtedly copied for the use of the community at Clairvaux.

In those early days of the Cistercian Order, abbots were expected to speak to their monks in chapter every morning, commenting on the passage of Saint Benedict's *Rule for Monasteries*[16] that had just been read in the chapter house in which the monks

---

13. See Gaetano Raciti, 'Deux collections de Sermons de S. Aelred—une centaine d'inédits—decouvertes dans les fonds de Cluny et de Clairvaux' in *Collectanea Cisterciensia* 45 (1983) 165–184.

14. *Aelredi Rievallensis Sermones I-XLVI*, ed. Gaetano Raciti, Corpus Christianorum Continuatio Mediaevalis, IIA (Turnholt: Brepols, 1989).

15. At the head of the first sermon we find this inscription: *Domni Aeraudi* (a later hand has corrected this to *Aelredi*) *abbatis Rievallis sermo primus de Aduentu Domini*.

16. The best critical edition, with english translation, is *RB 1980: The Rule of Saint Benedict in Latin and English with Notes*, ed. Timothy Fry et al. (Collegeville, MN: Liturgical Press, 1981).

assembled immediately after the celebration of the office of Prime in church. In addition, they were required to preach to the whole community, including the lay brothers, on fifteen principal days of the liturgical year as well as on the anniversary of the dedication of the monastery's church. The collection we have here includes sermons for fourteen of these days:

— the inauguration of the liturgical year on the First Sunday of Advent and the inauguration of Holy Week on Palm Sunday;

— five feasts of our Lord: Christmas, Epiphany, the Annunciation, Easter, and his Ascension;

— three feasts of the Blessed Virgin Mary: her Purification, Assumption, and Nativity;

— and the Feast of All the Saints, as well as the feasts of Saint Benedict of Nursia, of the nativity of Saint John the Baptist, and of Saints Peter and Paul.

The order of sermons in the manuscripts follows the liturgical year with a couple of curious inversions. One of the Advent sermons finds its place as a sermon for Palm Sunday. This is somewhat understandable. At the time the portion of the Gospel read on the first Sunday of Advent did indeed recount Christ's triumphal entrance into Jerusalem on Palm Sunday. One would think, however, that a cistercian scribe, being fully aware of this, would not have misplaced the sermon. The other misplaced sermon is one of the Assumption sermons, which finds its place among those for the Feast of All Saints. If the scribe had attended to the internal evidence he would not have made this mistake. Previous editions of the sermons, those of Tissier[17] and Migne,[18] retained the order found in the manuscript. Father Raciti in this critical edition has restored the sermons to their proper places. Thus the numbering of

17. *Bibliotheca Patrum Cisterciensium*, volume 5, ed. B. Tissier (Bono-Fonte, 1662).
18. *Patrologia cursus completus, series latina*, ed. J.-P. Migne, volume 195 (Paris, 1860).

the sermons in the critical edition and in this translation differs for the most part from that found in Tissier and Migne. To assist those who are used to the Migne enumeration we have appended a concordance to this Introduction.

The First Collection of Clairvaux contains twenty-eight sermons. Some occasions are represented by more than one sermon; there are two for the first Sunday of Advent, two for Easter, three for the Assumption and for the Nativity of the Blessed Virgin Mary, three for Saint Benedict and for the Feast of All the Saints, and four for Saints Peter and Paul. There is also a sermon which Aelred preached to the clergy gathered in synod at Troyes. During the whole time Aelred was abbot, the bishop of Troyes was Henry of Carinthia, who had been a monk of Morimond and then its abbot. Henry probably took advantage of the famous abbot's presence in France for a General Chapter to invite him to speak to his clergy. The inclusion of this sermon may be explained by the provenance of the collection. Indeed, although it seems clear that this copy of the sermons was made for the monks of Clairvaux (which was situated in the diocese of Troyes), an outside copyist connected with the diocesan chancery may have executed the collection. This might perhaps make the curious inversions mentioned above more understandable.

THE MANUSCRIPT

Early in life Aelred was introduced into the court of King David I of Scotland, who was in fact an Englishman. Thus began his connections with the secular powers of England and Scotland, connections which he later cultivated through his historical writings.[19] While still a young man in his early thirties, he was sent on a mission to Rome in an affair that concerned the primary episcopal sees of both Scotland and England. And

---

19. See note 8.

thus he became known in high ecclesiastical circles. Soon after returning, he found himself abbot of Rievaulx's third daughter house and then three years later still, abbot of Rievaulx itself. He thus became a significant leader in british monasticism. Adding to his importance is the fact that Bernard of Clairvaux, the monk of the hour, never crossed the Channel to visit the islands. Aelred was seen as his endorsed disciple, his man in Britain, the 'Bernard of the North', as he was called.

Not only did his activities give Aelred more than the usual opportunities of a cistercian abbot to preach, but his prominence created a large audience ready to hear what he had to say. The many attractive personal qualities he brought to his preaching and the reputation for teaching abilities broadcast by his various literary works only increased the eagerness of his audience and its size.

All this undoubtedly contributed to the confusing number of collections of the sermons of Aelred of Rievaulx. At the bottom of the confusion, though, lies the fact that Aelred himself never, as far as we know, undertook the creation of an edition of his sermons as did his master, Bernard of Clairvaux,[20] or his fellow abbot, Guerric of Igny.[21] It is possible that one or another of the sermon collections of Aelred that have come down to us was prepared by him or under his supervision for transmission to one of his daughter houses,[22] to the

---

20. See Jean Leclercq and H. M. Rochais, *Sancti Bernardi Opera* 4 (Rome: Editiones Cistercienses, 1966) 132ff.

21. Although Guerric repented of this undertaking and on his deathbed commanded that his collection be burnt, a ruse on the part of his loving sons preserved for posterity a partially completed collection which gives a rich sampling of the monastic teaching of this contemporary of Aelred. See *The Liturgical Sermons of Guerric of Igny*, CF 8 and 32 (Spencer - Kalamazoo: Cistercian Publications, 1971).

22. Although Rievaulx had been founded only fifteen years by the time Aelred became abbot, it already had five daughterhouse, that is, communities which had been founded from Rievaulx and over which the abbot of Rievaulx had a

motherhouse at Clairvaux,[23] or to some other monastery. In Aelred's case this might well have been Reading, a cluniac abbey in the south of England which seemed to have a special interest in the writings of Aelred and which has provided more than its share of manuscripts of the holy abbot. We know, however, that there were collections of Aelred's sermons at such other monasteries as Durham (in the north) and Westminster (just outside London). It is also possible that Aelred had his own collection made in order to make repeated use of his sermons as he traveled within the Order and around England.

Whatever the reason, we are left with a rather confusing collection of collections of Aelred's sermons. Confusing, because it seems impossible to relate them one to another as successive redactions. Whole sermons are carried over from one collection to another, as are parts of sermons. In this day of word-processing, we are familiar enough with the habits of authors who lift passages from one article or sermon and fit them into another. But we do not usually think of our Cistercian Fathers doing it. Yet we find Aelred doing just that. The last eleven paragraphs of Aelred's First Sermon for Advent are used to complete his Second Advent Sermon, paragraphs 31–42.[24] In fact, two sermons did not even have to pertain to the same feast for such borrowings to occur. Twenty-two lines of his Sermon for the Annunciation of the Lord (Sermon Nine) turn up in his Sermon for the Feast for All Saints (Sermon Twenty-Six).[25] These two examples can be found within the same collection, our First Clairvaux Collection. There are numerous

---

certain supervisory role: Wardon, founded in 1135; Melrose, 1136; Dundrennan and Revesby, 1143; and Rufford, 1146. Although Rievaulx continued to grow at an extraordinary rate, no foundations were made during Aelred's long tenure. Perhaps he was too attached to his monks to send any of them off.

23. In cistercian usage, the monastery from which the founding monks come to start an abbey is called the motherhouse.

24. 1:47–58 = 2:31–42.

25. 9.1–2 = 26.1–2.

examples where the passages are carried over to sermons in other collections.[26]

In addition to this verbatim copying, there are cases where sermons are reproduced in other collections but in different redactions. The redactions may be of quite different length: one short and condensed, the other long and elaborate. More often, rather than being a question of length, the variation results from treating details differently. Sermons can have the same subject, develop the same ideas in the same order but still be different textually, and each can contain paragraphs which are exclusive to it. In sum, the differences are such that discerning which redaction depends on which other is impossible to say.

Sermon Twenty-Seven of this First Collection of Clairvaux, which is also found as Sermon Forty-two of the Second Collection, though it is incomplete in the latter, provides an example of this. Sermons 8, 13, 14, 18, 20, and 22 of this First Collection of Clairvaux are found in a collection produced about the same time but coming from the cluniac benedictine community at Reading.[27] Sermons 9 and 15 are found in a twelfth-century collection now at Cambridge.[28] Another redaction of Sermon Nine is found in a thirteenth-century collection coming again from Reading.[29]

While it is not possible to trace a gradual process whereby one sermon collection was edited into the different collections now extant, it is possible to conjecture on the relationship between them. Gaetano Raciti, the editor of the critical edition, sets out an interesting hypothesis. According to him, we may consider

---

26. Among a number of examples where passages from the First Clairvaux Collection are carried over into the Second Collection are 19.14 = 45.7; 20.2–3, 5, 34, 36 = 45.4–5, 6, 9, 16, 41, 43; 27.11–22 = 46.15–16.

27. Paris, Bibliothèque Nationale, new latin acquisitions MS 294, ff. 52–54, 66–69, 99–103, 134–137, 140–141.

28. Eton College, 38, folios 61–65 and 105–110.

29. Oxford, Trinity College, 19, folios 141–142, reproduced in C. H. Talbot, 'Ailred's Sermons: Some First Drafts' in *Sacris Erudiri* 13 (1962) 153–193.

some collections as *pre-écrit* and others as *post-orale*. The 'prewritten' sermons are not summaries or schemas or memory aids but rather complete texts written with a view of actual use and yet in the course of delivery they would be adapted to the capacity and interests of the audience and the inspiration of the moment. Father Gaetano would place the Reading-Cluny Collection, as well as the collection found in the Oxford, Trinity College, manuscript 19, in this class. On the other hand, the 'post-delivery' sermons are those which were copied down more or less faithfully and integrally by a scribe during the sermon's actual delivery. It is not impossible that Aelred himself reviewed and corrected these texts. The First and Second Collections of Clairvaux would fall into this category. Father Gaetano goes a step further and conjectures that the *Sermones inediti*, primarily the collection found in an Eton manuscript and published by Charles Talbot, represents *post-orale* sermons which were, in fact, re-preached or preached a second time.[30] Here, then, is a possibility of tracing some development in the thought of Aelred, an immense, interesting possibility for future aelredean studies.

Given all this, the editors of the critical edition of the sermons of Aelred prepared for publication in the Corpus Christianorum Continuatio Mediaevalis have decided to keep each of the known collections intact.[31] Each of the different collections has its own particular selection of sermons with its own particular coherence and homogeneity.

The First Collection of Clairvaux, as we have mentioned, is found essentially in manuscript 910 of the Bibliothèque municipale of Troyes, on the first ninety-eight folios. It is followed by the writings of a Cardinal Drogo, the *Opuscula sacra* 1, 2, and 4 of Boethius, and a short, anonymous treatise

---

30. Raciti, "Deux collections," pp. 174ff. C. H. Talbot, *Sermones Inediti B. Aelredi abbatis Rievallensis*. Rome 1952.
31. CCCM IIA, p. vi.

on the canon of the Mass. This is the only manuscript that gives us this particular aelredean collection. It is also the only one that indicates the name of the author. The inscription for the first sermon reads: '*Domni Aeraudi abbatis Rievallis sermo primus de Aduentu Domini*'. A later hand changed the *Aeruadi* to *Aelredi*. On folio 98 there is a table listing the *Capitula in sermonibus domni Aeraudi Rievallis abbatis* and in this instance the name has not been corrected.

The First Collection of Clairvaux includes twenty-seven liturgical sermons: sermons for the First Sunday of Advent, Christmas, Epiphany, the Purification of Saint Mary, the feasts of Saint Benedict, the Annunciation, Palm Sunday, Easter, the Ascension, the Nativity of Saint John Baptist, Saints Peter and Paul, the Assumption and the Nativity of the Blessed Virgin Mary, and All Saints. The only feast on which the *Consuetudines* required the abbot to preach that is missing here is Pentecost. And, indeed, it may not be totally missing. For the third sermon for the Feast of All Saints, Sermon Twenty-Seven in this collection, appears in the Second Collection of Clairvaux, though in an incomplete form,[32] as a Sermon for the Day of Pentecost, although in another redaction. Since the sermon correlates the gifts of Holy Spirit with the beatitudes, which are proclaimed in the Gospel for the Feast of All Saints, the matter of this sermon would be appropriate for both feasts.

Unlike the Reading-Cluny collection which includes many sermons for occasions on which a cistercian abbot would not ordinarily be called upon to preach, [33] the First Clairvaux Collection is a distinctly monastic collection. Its cloistered origin is

32. The sermon in the Second Collection ends with section 14 and a note inserted at the end: *deest de sermone*, the rest of the sermon is missing.
33. The Reading-Cluny Collection with ninety-five sermons contains discourses for many different saints, such as Gregory the Great, Mary Magdalene, Michael, Edward the Confessor, Martin, and Catherine. We could well imagine a popular abbot being called to preach at popular celebrations in honor of these saints. There are also sermons which represent days in the temporal cycle that

evident not only by the days to which the sermons pertain but also by the style of the sermons themselves. They have a certain simplicity about them much in accord with the monastic way of life. Aelred alludes to the presence of the lay brothers as a reason for not developing more intricate patristic themes.[34] In fact, he knew what he was doing and humbly denigrated himself while going about it:

> Someone who speaks the word of God to others ought to aim, not at vaunting his own knowledge, but at discerning how he can build up his hearers. And with a motherly compassion for weaker minds he ought, I might say, prattle to them, descending to the use of baby talk. But the limit of my gifts make it necessary that my hearers stoop down to the poverty of my words. (14.1)[35]

His Latin is simple enough, a popular sort of Latin. There is little artifice, yet the sermons have a richness and nobility. There is a power and a charm to them.

THE STYLE OF THE SERMONS

The sermons convey the very familiar tone we would expect in hearing Aelred speak to his monks: dearest brothers, my brothers, or simply, *carissimi* ('my dears'). He knows his men and speaks to them directly: 'How beautiful it is to see some of you, who in the world were so wise, so powerful, so proud and so cunning, become now so simple and plain as if you knew nothing' (1.36). He appreciates them for who they are and what they have done: 'For you have thrown down the branches of trees, that is, all the world's pomp, to worship and honor Christ.

---

did not usually merit an abbatial sermon in cistercian monasteries: Christmas Eve, Feast of the Circumcision, Holy Thursday, and Trinity Sunday.

34. Sermon 13.8.

35. In this Introduction Aelred's sermons are cited by sermon and then then section number.

What is more, you have despised your very bodies for him. Your very soul, which is going further still, you have spent in Christ's honor, for you have given up your own will, the will of your soul' (2.35). 'You have wisely gone out of Egypt and come three-days journey into solitude' (10.34).

He also knew sorrow, pain, and disappointment in regard to them:

> It is a grievous persecution to have the care of all, to suffer pain for all, to be saddened when someone is saddened, to be afraid when someone is tempted. Again, the persecution that sometimes befalls us is intolerable when one of those whom we feed and take care of and love as our own flesh and blood is vanquished by the devil, and so badly that he even departs from us or lives so perversely and prodigally that we have no choice but to expel him from our midst. Brothers, if you feel sorrow and great sadness when such things happen, you who are the brothers of those concerned, what sadness do you think is ours who are at once brother, father and guardian and have undertaken to render an account for them? Certainly, brothers, you should have great compassion for us and gladden us by your virtuous way of life, for so many other things cause us sadness. Yet blessed is the person who suffers this blackness for Christ (26.18–19).

As he goes on to say: 'The more he loves, the more he often grieves and feels sorrow for those whom he loves' (26.20).

In these sermons we find none of the richly autobiographical passages that we do in some of Aelred's treatises. Even so, there is a certain self-revelation. He is in touch with the pains and miseries of life:

> Who can count all the infirmities of this life: hunger, thirst, toil, pain, disease, languor, weariness? But these

concern the body. How many are the infirmities the soul! How much concupiscence, how many temptations! (1.10)

He is a man of compassion, fully conscious of his own weakness and, in that, sensitive to the needs of his monks:

> How I savor it when I see the Lord of all majesty showing himself as far as bodily exertion and human emotion are concerned not like the strong but the weak. What a comfort it is to me in my weakness! Truly this weakness of my Lord without doubt brings me strength and stability in my weakness. . . . I am entrusted with the care of my brother's body and soul— for I do not love the whole man if I neglect anything belonging to either—for it is very difficult for the mind not to be tempted when the flesh has too much to suffer. If I see him in distress, whether it be on account of the austerity of the food or because of work or the vigils—if, I say, I see that he is tormented in body and tempted in spirit, if I see him in such affliction and . . . do not on occasion accommodate myself to the infirmities of the weak I am not running in the fragrance of Christ's ointments but with the harshness of the pharisees. (3.33–34)

Aelred did not hesitate to wear his heart on the sleeve of his ample white cowl and reveal some of his feelings and emotions—as we have just seen with his brothers. He does the same in relation to Jesus and Mary.

> For me certainly your sadness, Lord Jesus, is more fragrant than all the world's gladness. To me the tears that you shed at the death of your friend [Lazarus] are sweeter than the stoic endurance of the philosophers who would have the wise one left unmoved by any emotion. More pleasant to me certainly is the smell of your food and drink in the midst of sinners and tax-gatherers than the rigid abstinence of the pharisees.

Certainly the *fragrance of your ointments surpasses all scents.*[36] How I savor it when I see the Lord of all majesty showing himself as far as bodily exertion and human emotion are concerned not like the strong but the weak. What a comfort it is to me in my weakness! Truly this weakness of my Lord without doubt brings me strength and stability in my weakness. (3.32–33)

Again and again he gives witness to his psychological insightfulness:

> ... if we are kept waiting some time for something that we much desire, when that which we love comes it seems sweeter to us. (1:4)

> If we take pleasure in things which we must lose, when the time comes for us to lose them we shall feel distress equal to our former pleasure. (1.14)

Despite Aelred's self-deprecation, the sermons are not wholly lacking in literary style. Aelred knew how to capture his audience with masterful openings in which he sometimes, in good classical style, proclaims his ineptness or unworthiness. He likes to use the triplicate, sometimes for emphasis, sometimes for bringing out various aspects of the reality under discussion. For example, in the first four paragraphs of Sermon Twenty-Six for the Feast of All Saints we find:

> ... because he knew that our memory was vitiated by forgetfulness, our intellect by error and our good intent by cupidity. ... that there might always be fresh in our memory the wonderful love, the wonderful goodness, the wonderful charity that he showed ... he suffered death for us once, at present he gives us forgiveness of sins, after this life he promises eternal happiness. We must recall to memory, dearest brothers, this

---

36. Sg 4:10.

liberation of ours, this hope of ours, this happiness of ours. . . . . . . from hearing of their life, their sufferings and their labors. . . .

They go on, these triplicates, a dozen or more at least, all through this sermon. They are indeed scattered throughout his sermons.

Another artifice he liked to use is the contrast. By it he challenges us at times in almost koan-like fashion to enter more deeply into the reality of God:

> You fear the Lord of the angels but love the little Child. You fear the Lord of majesty but love the One who is wrapped in swaddling clothes. You fear the One who reigns in heaven but love the One lying in the manger. (3.37)

Speaking on Saint Benedict's feast he said:

> So today our Father has passed from earth to heaven, from prison to the kingdom, from death to life, from misery to glory. (7.3)

Speaking of Jesus, he tells us:

> He who was wisdom willed to be, as it were, foolish. He who was strong willed to be weak. . . . bread hungers, the fountain thirsts, strength is tired and life dies." (12.19)

And he goes on to say:

> It is his hunger that feeds us, his thirst that inebriates us, his weariness that refreshes us, his death that brings us life. (12.20)

And speaking of what lies ahead for us, he tells us it is 'as far beyond as heaven is from earth, as death is from life, as misery is from happiness, as light is from darkness' (21.11).

> To this life belongs toil, to that life rest; to this life belongs temptation, to that life security; to this life poverty, to that life wealth; to this life struggle, to that life consolation; to this life hunger and thirst, to that life satiety. (26.10)

In his use of these literary devices Aelred is not unlike his master and friend, Bernard of Clairvaux, and indeed the whole patristic school.

Aelred was a man of his time and place. When he spoke of 'the whole world', (1.28, 25.2) or of 'all nations' (24.2) he was speaking of Christendom. He had little consciousness of the great islamic world, to say nothing of India and China, where the faith had been preached many centuries earlier with little lasting impact. His imagery is of castles, moats and the things which would have been familiar to his contemporaries (see 19.6). Yet his sermons have a relevance for all times for they are intimately connected with and flow from the perennial sources of christian life: the living Tradition as it is expressed in the prayer of the Church and the Scriptures.

These are liturgical sermons. They were preached on and about the festivals of the Church. Their texts were chosen from the liturgy of the day, most frequently the Gospel reading at the Mass of the day, though sometimes it is an antiphon which in his treatment becomes almost an antiphon for the sermon as it is repeated again and again. Aelred had a great appreciation for the power with which the liturgy with its feasts and its sacraments can make Christ and his mysteries present to us, 'what the sacrament of the season contains' (2.4):

> Because it is expedient for us always to be mindful of his benefits which he bestowed on us through his bodily presence and because he knew that our memory is impaired by forgetfulness, our intellect by error, our zeal by cupidity, he kindly provided for us. Not only do the Scriptures recount his benefits to us. These benefits are also re-presented for us by certain spiritual actions. Thus, when he gave his disciples the sacrament of his Body and Blood he told them: *Do this in memory of me*.[37]

37. Lk 22:19, 1 Cor 11:24.

> It is for this reason, brothers, that these feasts have been instituted by the Church. By re-presenting now his birth, now his passion, resurrection, ascension, that wondrous devotion, that wondrous sweetness, that wondrous charity, which he showed for us in all these, will always be fresh in our memory. These feasts should also be an occasion of great growth in our faith when we hear with our ears and almost see beneath our eyes what Christ suffered for us; also what he gives us in this life and what he promises us after this life. (9.1–2)

Aelred truly believed that he encountered Christ Jesus, Saint Mary, and the saints in the liturgy, that he truly experienced the saving events of Jesus' life, and anticipated something of the joys He promised. Each liturgical element had meaning for him:

> The songs are a symbol of the unending celebration in which the saints live because of the ineffable joy which is theirs in God; the hymns, a symbol of the indescribable praise which they are always giving to God. . . . The lights signify the everlasting light in which God's saints live (25.2).

Yet even while he cherished good liturgy, he remained truly a Cistercian:

> They do not celebrate these feasts well or reasonably, it seems to me, who seek excessive external pomp and ceremony. The result of such excess is that the outer self becomes so intent on the singing, the ornaments, the lights and suchlike trappings that one is scarcely able to think of anything but what is seen with the eyes, heard with the ears, or perceived with the other senses. . . . Let us turn our thoughts to and take pleasure in that true beauty in which the saints live free from all defilement. (25.5–6)[38]

---

38. Cf. Bernard of Clairvaux, *Apologia to Abbot William*, 28f, ET by Michael Casey ocso, in *Bernard of Clairvaux: Treatises I*, CF 1 (1970) 63–68 = now available as *Cistercians and Cluniacs: St Bernard's* Apologia to Abbot William, CF 1A.

In these sermons we find little of the meditation which Aelred advocated in his treatise *On Jesus at the Age of Twelve* or in his *Rule for a Recluse*, a meditation which applied the imagination to the literal sense of the Scriptures. Here his consideration of the mysteries of Jesus and Mary is less colorful and emotional, more Scriptural and more dependent on the allegorical, spiritual sense of Scripture. There can be no doubt that the sermons were the fruit of Aelred's own *lectio* and the *meditatio* that flowed from it. Sometimes the text gives expression to his *oratio* even while inviting the brethren to *contemplatio*.

Aelred was keenly aware of the different senses of Scripture. He repeatedly speaks of them explicitly (e.g., 4.17f; 11.4, 28; 13.8; 21.3, 4). He sometimes refers to them as the different 'faces' of Scripture:

> Its first face is history, the second morality, the third allegory, the fourth anagogy, that is, a sense of what is above. . . . Therefore, brothers, we have heard this Gospel and have considered its one face, the simple story, and it appears to us as sufficiently beautiful. For what Scripture is more beautiful than this which tells of the glory of our most sweet Lord and the devotion of a faithful people? But nonetheless, by means of this face it does not show us how this reading pertains to this time. Therefore, let us consider another face of the text and see whether that reveals to us something of the mystery of this time. (2.2–3)

Speaking of the experiences of Daniel and his companions in Babylon, Aelred quotes the Apostle Paul, 'All these things were done symbolically for us'.[39] Sometimes he develops the literal sense and sometimes he draws on the moral sense, but primarily it was the allegorical or mystical sense that attracted him and that he explored to the full.

39. 1 Co 10:6 in Sermons 24.36 and 8.1.

Within Tradition three kinds of contemplation have been differeniated. Direct contemplation plunges the contemplater directly into the Divine. Of this little can be said. As our Cistercian Fathers might say: someone who has experienced direct contemplation knows what I am talking about and someone who has not had the experience will need to have it before being able to know. Secondly, there is oblique contemplation: coming to the experience of God through his presence and image in his creation. At times Aelred shares this kind of experience with us. Finally there is circular contemplation: circling around the Reality, the person contemplating catches one glimpse after another, gradually coming to a fuller and fuller appreciation of the mystery of that Reality. This is the kind of contemplative experience that Aelred primarily shares with us in these sermons.

For him no detail in the inspired Word was too insignificant to invite an exploration aimed at a deeper meaning. Speaking of the Scriptures as bread for the journey, he tells us: 'This bread must be broken to be eaten, because these matters must be explained to be understood' (5.3). 'Everything, it would be seen, is full of mysterious significance' (20.16), and Aelred did not hesitate to give each detail its meaning. (See, for example, 5.6, 8.1, 11.30ff, 14.3.)

Following the patristic tradition of which he was very much a part, Aelred seems especially to delight in assigning various animals their particular significance. Sheep represent not only those shepherded by Christ but also good affections or thoughts (3.18), the senses (3.18), the virtues within us (18.13) and even Rachel and Mary (9:12). Goats can represent bad thoughts (3.21) as well as bad followers. Reptiles are, not unexpectedly, malicious spirits (24.9); the serpent, the devil (17.17). The deer finds itself representing Saint Peter because it kills serpents (15.24). *The lion that prowls around looking for someone to devour*,[40] who lies in wait, also represents the evil one

---

40. 1 P 5:8; Ps 9:29; the verse is used in the Divine Office each night at Compline.

(24.32, 3.17). The turtle dove, a chaste bird with the wings of purity and innocence, seeks solitude (14.15) and in its modesty sheds tears of shame (5.24), while the pigeon's tears come from being fearful (5.26). The bee can represent the flatterer or the secret detractor, for along with its sweetness it also has a sting (23.18); but Aelred also saw the bee as 'an utterly chaste creature' (22.24) which

> wings its way . . . through the field of the Scriptures by assiduous meditation. There it gathers from the sayings and examples of the saints spiritual flowers and from these there is produced in its heart wondrous joy and a great sweetness, one of heavenly savor. Thus it experiences that the Spirit of the Lord is sweeter than honey. (22.24)

As Aelred shares with his listeners the fruit of his circular contemplation, his thought usually progresses through the sermon not logically but by means of the association of ideas and even of words. These associations find him reaching out into all parts of Scripture, giving witness to a remarkable familiarity with the Sacred Text. Not that Aelred was incapable of pursuing an idea logically and with great order. Some of his developments are intricately worked out. In the third sermon for the Feast of All Saints, Sermon Twenty-Seven, he relates the eight beatitudes recorded in Matthew[41] to the seven gifts of Holy Spirit enumerated in the eleventh chapter of Isaiah[42] and to the six days of creation in Genesis.[43] More often, however, it was simple biblical allusions or the association of ideas that sent the preacher scurrying in all directions through the sacred text. Thus in the same All Saints' Day sermon, the Lord going up the mountain reminded him of Zacchæus shinnying up the sycamore tree (27.3). In Sermon Thirteen, the Ascension theme readily enough drew reminiscences of Elijah going up

41. Mt 5:3–7.
42. Is 11:2.
43. Gen 1:4–31.

to heaven in a fiery chariot (13.11–16), but for Aelred it also evoked Moses praying with arms uplifted, bringing Israel victory over the Amalekites, because Jesus, before he ascended, raised his hands in blessing (13.27–31). The Advent theme of Sermon One naturally evoked desire, which in turn reminded him of our Lord's statement, *many kings and just have longed to see what you now see*,[44] which in its turn calls forth Kings Solomon and David and the lessons they have to teach (1.15ff). Rachel, whose name means 'sheep',[45] prefigures Mary, the mother of the Lamb who was led to slaughter (9.17).[46] Sometimes the association may strike us rather farfetched. In Sermon Fourteen for the Feast of Saint John the Baptist, for example, Jesus' possession of the seven gifts of the Holy Spirit make him the man on whom the seven women of Isaiah 4:1 laid hold (14.6ff).

Aelred's familiarity with some of the Fathers of the Church is also evident. Augustine, not unexpectedly, was his favorite. He is mentioned by name a number of times,[47] but his influence is far more pervasive than is immediately apparent. Gregory the Great, who was greatly favored by Aelred's mentor, Bernard of Clairvaux, and indeed the whole monastic tradition, is also mentioned by name.[48] Especially fond of Gregory's life of Saint Benedict, Book Two of the *Dialogues*, he is also influenced by Gregory's *Homilies on Ezekiel* and his commentary on Job. Aelred had recourse to Saint Jerome's *Interpretation of Hebrew Names* in more than half the sermons in this collection and sometimes uses it half a dozen or more times in the course of a single sermon. He also shows a familiarity with other works by this Father.[49] Benedict's *Rule for Monasteries* was his primary source for the sermons on Saint Benedict's feast[50] and inspires

---

44. Mt 13:17.
45. Jerome, *Interpretatio Hebraicorum nominum*, 9 et passim.
46. Ac 8:32; Is 53:7.
47. 3.12; 8.3; 15.32; 21.43.
48. 3.36; 7.6, 10; 8.3.
49. See the notes for the many uses of the *Interpretatio* and other references to Jerome.
50. Sermons 6–8.

his monastic teaching throughout the sermons. The influence of his fellow countryman, the Venerable Bede, is discernible, as is that of Ambrose and Origen. How much of all of this came to him through Bernard and other contemporaries and how much from direct contact with the Fathers' works, especially through the readings at the Divine Office, would be impossible to discern. What is certain is that Aelred is very much in the patristic tradition both in what he has to say and how he says it.

Aelred's teaching

Aelred's sermons gave monks what they were familiar with, what they were looking for. They correspond to daily life, to experience. They clarify basic monastic themes, they comfort the struggling, they stimulate and ward off *acedia*. The teaching is rich, not pedestrian; it is elevated but neither abstract nor theoretical.

Christ at the center

Christ is central to the spirituality and teaching of Aelred of Rievaulx. Many of his sermons are directly concerned with Christ, having been preached on the feast days celebrating his mysteries or those of his mother. But Christ is never absent from any of the sermons. Although the sermons for the feast of Saint Benedict have a flavor somewhat different from that of the rest of the sermons, as they draw extensively on Benedict's *Rule for Monasteries*, the christocentrism is not lacking in them. Aelred expresses it in a quotation from the *Rule*: 'Let them prefer absolutely nothing to Christ'[51] as well as by other elements of Saint Benedict's teaching, for he was convinced that Benedict, too, was wholly centered on Christ. Christ is the way, the whole way; and the goal is Christ (7.4).

51. RB 72:11.

Aelred collects a whole litany of biblical images to explore different facets of Christ: he is both cloud and light (9.7), a lamb (9.12, 11.13, 12.26), a bracelet (9.22), the ark (10.7), the keystone (10.21), the sweetest of grapes (11.29), bread (12.12), the head (13.37), the sun—the greater light (19.17, 27.17), the husband of a strong woman (21.15), wisdom (22.16ff), emperor (26.1), a mountain (27.2) and the mediator (28.7). Aelred also refers to various biblical persons as types of Christ: Adam (21.2), Jacob (26.31), Joseph (9.3ff, 15.14), Elijah (13.11), David (20.12), and Solomon (14.18). And he fills this out by collecting phrases from the New Testament, as in his Twenty-Eighth Sermon:

> ... the *Mediator between God and the people*,[52] *our Ruler and our Judge*,[53] *the Lord our lawgiver*[54] was sent to the wretched to be for us not only *high priest of good things to come*[55] but also *King of kings and Lord of lords*.[56] (28.7)

At the same time he borrowed from Scripture, Aelred was capable of setting forth the mystery of Christ with almost scholastic conciseness and clarity:

> In our Lord Jesus there are two natures, the divine and the human. These two natures are so perfect in him that the divine nature was not diminished on account of the human nor the human reduced to nothing on account of the divine. That is why he is at once equal to the Father and less than the Father: equal because of his divinity and less because of his humanity. (20.4)

And he was also able to express his love poetically, as in this passage:

52. 1 Tm 2:5.
53. Jm 4:12.
54. Is 33:22,
55. Heb 9:11.
56. Rv 19:16.

You know his name. What is the sound, the flavor, the fragrance of his name? It is oil. *Your name is oil poured out.*[57] Why oil? Because his name savors of charity, savors of mercy. For what is the meaning of that dear name of Jesus? It speaks of our salvation, for he is my God and my Jesus, that is, my Savior, my well-being and therefore my mercy. (12.16)

Aelred taught his listeners, and teaches us, to build a tabernacle for Christ in our hearts (6.5). In us Christ is to reign; in us Christ is to be a pilgrim. Christ is to be identified with us, hungering in us, thirsting in us (8.4). We are to be united with Christ in his death. We are to be renewed in his resurrection (8.15). And 'when Christ our life appears, we will appear with him in glory'.[58] All of this is to be accomplished in us through the grace of our Redeemer, Jesus Christ, one with the Father and the Spirit (7.15).

MAN OF THE CHURCH

Not only did Aelred speak out of the living Tradition of the Church and have a great and tender love for Christ its Head— 'Let it be our sole anxiety to remain attached to him *with our whole heart, our whole mind, our whole strength,*[59] remembering who is our Head, where our Head is. Let us live as befits the members of that Head . . . (13.38)—but a sense of the Church pervaded his life and found expression in his writings.

Aelred had a very broad sense of the Church:

For God's Church is not only this assembly of the faithful who believe in him after his coming. All the

---

57. Sg 1:2.
58. Col 3:4; 8:19.
59. Mk 12:30.

saints from the just Abel to the last just person who will live in this world belong to the holy Church. (1.47)

For he said, 'Go forth into the whole world, preach the Gospel to every creature',[60] that is, to the whole human race, Jews and Gentiles, wise and unwise,[61] rich and poor, all of whom make up holy Church' (13.12).

Yet even the Church has its limits and 'those without this faith are outside the Church' (2.37).

Again, Aelred drew on scriptural images to bring out facets of the mystery of the Church in all its beauty. 'Jerusalem signifies the holy Church' (2.9, 4.6ff). Christ came to his Church when on Palm Sunday he came into Jerusalem (2.24); the Church welcomed him and by the cries of the people expressed its faith (2.37). A few days later, 'when his side was opened, he united the Church to himself and made it one with himself, so that they might be *two in one flesh*'[62] (2.12), and so the Church is also the Bride of the Song of Songs (2.38).

> ... although holy Church is called and is in fact one city, there are various vocations in it, different cities as it were, in which each declares himself, that is, makes his profession." (3:5) Not all are called to be bishops, abbots, priests; but all can feed Christ's sheep by their good example. (18:12)

Then, too, 'Bethlehem, "the House of Bread",[63] is the holy Church in which the Body of Christ, the true Bread, is administered' (3.39). In general, Aelred does not speak much about the sacraments of the Church. The priest (*sacerdos*) is someone who gives (*do*) holy things (*sacra*): 'The grace of

---

60. Mk 16:15.
61. Rm 1:14.
62. Gen 2:24, Eph 5:31.
63. Jerome, Epistle 108, 10; CSEL 55:316.

baptism and the remedy of penance with the other sacraments are yours to give to the People of God', he tells priests in Sermon 28.13. He assures his monks that ' . . . all uncleannesses are purified by baptism and after baptism by penance—and that on the eighth day: through faith in the resurrection of our Lord Jesus Christ' (5.15; 12.10, 23.1), but most of his consideration is given to the Eucharist about which he speaks frequently.

After speaking of the Church as Bethlehem, Aelred goes on to say:

> What the crib is at Bethlehem the altar is in the Church. There are fed Christ's animals of which is said: *Your animals shall dwell in it.*[64] This is the table of which it is written: *You have spread a table before me.*[65] In this crib is Jesus wrapped in swaddling clothes. The swaddling clothes are the sacramental veils. In this crib under the appearance of bread and wine are the true Body and Blood of Christ. There, faith tells us, is Christ himself, but wrapped in swaddling clothes, that is, visible not to the eye but within the sacrament. There is no greater or more evident sign of Christ's birth than that we daily receive at the holy altar his Body and Blood, daily see immolated for us him who was once born for us of the Virgin. (3.39f)

If there is a true Presence in the Word of God, there is also a true Presence in the Eucharist, and for the same reason:

> When Jesus, our Lord and Saviour, left us corporally, he promised us the presence of his divinity, the presence of his grace: *Behold, I am with you all days until the consummation of the world.*[66] But because it was expedient for us always to be mindful of his benefits which he bestowed on us through his bodily presence and because he

---

64. Ps 67:2.
65. Ps 22:5.
66. Mt 26:20.

knew that our memory is impaired by forgetfulness, our intellect by error, our zeal by cupidity, he kindly provided for us. Not only do the Scriptures recount his benefits to us; these benefits are also re-presented for us by certain spiritual actions. Thus, when he gave his disciples the sacrament of his Body and Blood he told them: *Do this in memory of me.*[67] (9.1)

Comparing the old dispensation with the new, Aelred tells his monks: 'If you compare with the manna which the Jews ate in the desert the spiritual joy which you often experience in devouring Christ . . . you will see indeed that the things which you have received are much greater because they are spiritual' (6.9).

> At that supper the old passover which the Jews were accustomed to celebrate came to an end and there began the new passover which we celebrate. How could he have shown us greater sweetness than by leaving us as a memorial of himself his own body and blood? . . . Today, my brothers, the whole world is nourished with that wine which flowed from him. For what Christian is there who does not drink Christ's blood today? (11.6ff; cf 12.26f)

> You, O chosen race, derive your name of Christians from Christ and you have been found worthy through your faith and communion at the altar to become his body and his members. You, I say, have a much happier cause for rejoicing, an incomparably greater reason for boasting. (28.1)

The 'Queen of the East' (4.8) and the three kings who came to Bethlehem were for Aelred types of the Church precisely as the 'Church of the Pagans' or the 'Church of the Gentiles' which

---

67. Lk 22:19, 1 Cor 11:24.

was born on Epiphany (4.9–10) and is called to be illumined by the light that is the Gospel (4.28).

Elijah's cloak provided another image of the Church, for Christ, like Elijah, left it behind when he went up to heaven, entrusting it to his chosen disciples, the apostles (13.12). The apostles are the pillars of the church, the mountain on which it is founded (15.2, 18.18), 'the fountains which water the Lord's paradise and quench the thirst of the holy Church with a pleasant drink' (15.13). Among them, Peter 'is the prince of all the apostles and the head of holy Church; to his care the Church of Christ has been quite especially committed' (15.3).

The Church established the very feasts on which Aelred was preaching:
> so that by representing now his birth, now his passion, now his resurrection, now his ascension, there may always be fresh in our memory the wonderful love, the wonderful goodness, the wonderful charity that he [Christ] showed towards us through all of these. Our faith, too, should derive the greatest profit from these reminders, when we hear with our ears and, as it were, see under our eyes what Christ suffered for us, what he gives us even in this life, what he promises us after this life. He suffered death for us once, at present he gives us forgiveness of sins, after this life he promises eternal happiness. We must recall to memory, dearest brothers, this liberation of ours, this hope of ours, this happiness of ours when we celebrate a feast of his. (26:3–4)

The Church is to be the earth that has melted,[68] melted by the fire of love (18.7). In this way it will become 'the fellowship of the saints'(25.39).

68. Ps 74:4.

Mary, the Blessed Mother of God.

Aelred readily joined the 'world-wide' chorus that honors all the saints (25.2) and first among them 'the blessed Mother of God, Mary' (25.10). 'Indeed, brothers, we ought always to praise and honor her and with total devotion recall her sweetness' (20.2). For Aelred she was the quintessential human person, the 'virgin purer than all other virgins, holier than all other women, stronger than all men, fairer than the sun, more ardent than fire . . .' (20.20, cf 21.6). Childbirth, giving birth to the Divine, did not deprive her of her unique virginity (19.17). With Christ, she is our advocate (20.36), our mediator:

> Let us seek the help of one whose prayers he will never despise. Let us approach his Bride. Let us approach his Mother. Let us approach his most wonderful Handmaid. The blessed Mary is all of these. (23.3)

Seven sermons for feasts of Mary[69] offered Aelred ample opportunity to explore and praise the wonders of this woman of God. Yet even that was not enough. Her presence is found throughout the sermons. As he did with Jesus, the abbot reached out in all directions to find biblical types and images to help him describe her beauty and her unique role. Mary is Rebecca and Rachel (9.17ff). She is Mary the sister of Moses (22.14), and the virgin Abisag in the bosom of David (20.26). She is a sheep and a fleece (9.12), a cloud and light (9.34). She is a castle, a village (19.15), and the eastern gate into it (19.16). She is the lover of the Song of Songs (20.6ff) and King Solomon's strong woman (21.6ff), 'the woman about whose strength the Lord warned the serpent'[70] (21.2). She is the seed of Abraham from which arose the Sun of Justice (24.3). She is the Star of the Sea (24.20).

69. Sermons 5.19–24.
70. Gen 3:15.

Aelred did not display the lyricism of his mentor, Bernard of Clairvaux. Even though the Star of the Sea did not call forth anything comparable to that unforgettable paean of love which is found in Bernard's Second Homily on the *Missus est*,[71] Aelred was capable of passages of great beauty:

> She who was full of God, greater than the world, higher than heaven, more fertile than Paradise, the luster of virgins, the glory of women, the praise of men, the joy of angels, she whom the Son of God chose to be his mother, called herself a handmaiden. She whom the angel greeted subjected herself in all obedience to a workman. She who was queen of heaven, mistress of the angels, she who bore God in her womb, humbly greeted her relative because that relative was older than herself. How right it is then that it is said to the blessed Mary: *You are beautiful and fair, most chaste in the midst of delights.*[72] (9.25)

THE SAINTS

'Because we are unworthy and not such as he should listen to, he sets before us his friends, in order that we may entreat them and through them approach him and with him be reconciled' (23.1). For Aelred, the friends of God, the saints and foremost Saint Mary, are intercessors. They are also exemplars, sources of encouragement and inspiration.

Unlike Bernard,[73] Aelred devoted no passage to extolling the husband of the Virgin. In the course of speaking of the Lord's genealogy, he simply gives the meaning of Joseph's name (24.17).

---

71. Miss 2.17, english translation by Marie-Bernard Saïd OSB in Bernard of Clairvaux and Amadeus of Lausanne, *Magnificat. Homilies in Praise of the Blessed Virgin Mary*, CF 18 (Kalamazoo, MI: Cistercian Publications, 1979) 30–31 = *Bernard of Clairvaux: Homilies in Praise of the Blessed Virgin Mary*, CF 18A (1993) 30–31.
72. Sg 7:6.
73. Miss 2.16, CF 18 [CF 18A]:28–29.

On the other hand, the liturgical feast gave him opportunity to explore and give expression to the grandeur, mission, and meaning of the Lord's cousin, Saint John the Baptist, 'someone who was praised by angelic authority before he was born and who in the womb, into which he came by the way that is infected with sin, was by an ineffable grace made a competely worthy dwelling place of Holy Spirit[74] . . . a priest was chosen to be his father, the temple was chosen to be the place where his birth was foretold, the name to be given him was determined beforehand and it was imposed by an angel'[75] (14.3).

But it is those 'pillars' of the Church, Saints Peter and Paul, who receive the most attention. More sermons in this series are devoted to their feast than to any other.[76] Yet this is a bit of an illusion, for one of the sermons is cut short[77] and another hardly mentions them.[78] Even so, there is not a single sermon in this series that does not evoke 'the Apostle', Saint Paul. And Aelred not only uses his texts but often cites Paul as an example of the teaching he is seeking to set forth. Since we have only two letters from Saint Peter, it is not surprising that he is cited much less frequently even though his presence as an exemplar is more apparent. The abbot did not hesitate to point out the weakness of both of these 'pillars who uphold the holy Church by their teaching, by their prayers and by the example of their patience', who were made firm by the Lord (18.8ff). But it is the ever-bungling Peter with whom Aelred closely identified.

MORAL TEACHING

As is usual with the Cistercian Fathers, Aelred concerned himself with the moral life. The whole aim of these sermons

74. Lk 1:15ff.
75. Lk 1:5ff.
76. Sermons 15–18.
77. Sermon 16 is cut off after paragraph five.
78. Sermon 17 devotes but a paragraph to the Apostles as exemplars while setting forth a rich monastic teaching.

was to edify and instruct his monks in the way of the Spirit. His descriptions of human endeavor and human weakness are graphic and true to life:

> How often the scourges of his own heart drove him to resolve and say: 'I will never do that again. Never again will I get bogged down in that vice'. And nevertheless the servants of Pharaoh, the unclean spirits, pressed upon us, as it were, against our own wills, to make mud bricks, that is, to do sordid and foul things. And so we built the city of Pharaoh, the devil, in our hearts. Each one [of us] can recall the violence which he suffered from his own evil habits and see how, by the grace of God and the doctrine of Saint Benedict, he is now free. (6.8)

Aelred offered his own insights into our fallen nature, which is ruled by passion, and on the effects of this rule on our life and relations with others. Perhaps in this Aelred was drawing on his own experience at the court of Scotland.[79] If we think he presents too negative a view of life when he calls it: '. . . not that of the living but of the dying. All the things which I have mentioned—death, prison, and misery—are found in this life. Indeed, all these things are this present life' (7.3), we have to admit it is wholly and solidly based on revelation. It is christian realism. Aelred accepted with full human sympathy the fact that beginnings are difficult when fallen human nature tries to rise to its transcendent dignity in Christ. But he holds out the encouraging promise that life, even here, can be one of 'untold sweetness and delights' (7:6).

The ultimate goal he never lost sight of. We are already there where the saints have gone (7.2, 4) because we have placed our hearts upon it (7.2), *for where your treasure is, there will be your*

---

79. Walter Daniel, *Life* 2, suggests that the court was the site of 'elaborate confections', vengeance, effeminacy, and self indulgence (CF 57:91–92).

heart also.[80] The whole purpose of following the monastic way, the christian way, is to attain to the vision of love (7.8). *Lectio*, meditation, and prayer are for us sinners 'cities of refuge'[81] within the very Land of Promise (8.12). There we will at length find 'a twofold rest, a twofold perfection: immortality for the body, beatitude for the soul' (8.6).

MONASTIC ASCESIS

The monk's first step along the way that is Christ is to withdraw from the world, not only in body but also in mind and heart (6.10). This is monastic conversion. It is an intensely personal thing. By his own good will, his desires, the good thoughts sown in him by the grace of God, the monk turns from his sinful ways (6.7). He is open to all sorts of rationalizations (6.8) but by God's grace he goes out into the desert, into solitude.

> And what does it mean to go into solitude? It means to consider this whole world as a desert, to desire the Fatherland, to have only as much of this world as is necessary to accomplish the journey. (6.34)

Having entered the desert, the monk must follow the steps of humility and the exercises—the disciplines—of monastic life (6.12ff, 8.12) Fear of the Lord, the beginning of humility as it is of wisdom, led the monk to give up the things that this world values. He must now seek to mortify the desires of the flesh that have come with him into the desert. For this Aelred prescribed what he considered the three basic corporal exercises of the monastic life: work, watching, and fasting. Only when these disciplines effectively achieve their purpose will the monk become a spiritual man and be able to enjoy the spiritual exercises—*lectio*, prayer, and meditation— which were for Aelred 'cities of refuge' in the Promised Land

---

80. Mt 6:21.
81. Nb 35:11–15.

itself (3.13f). All these exercises are means to creating a deep sense of compunction, true poverty, and profound humility, the dispositions which will render the monk wholly open to the divine goodness and mercy.

But the fullness of this transformation is not yet achieved. The monk must take a further step on the way of humility; he must subject himself, obey, give up his own likings, his self-will, the *voluntas propria*. Only then will he be totally open to the divine movement and ready to follow it into the fullness of divine love. There is here the negative element of self-sacrifice, of leaving oneself totally (*ex toto relinquit seipsum*; 6.27). He must go out of himself—in love. In all this the positive element is total donation of self to God: 'for love of God he subjects himself'.[82] The concern of Aelred here, as with Saint Benedict, was not primarily hierarchical obedience but the gift of oneself to others to the point of accepting 'with a quiet mind' even hard things and even injuries.[83] This is simple gospel teaching: *When they are struck on one cheek they offer the other. When they are forced to go one mile they go two. They sustain false brethren and persecution.*[84]

THE WAY

Throughout his sermons Aelred traced steps along the path to God. These may be seen as different stages. At first we are driven before the Lord by fear; then we come to follow him in love (1.39f). Again, using an image that would be employed later more fully by Saint Teresa of Jesus, the mystic of Avila, Aelred described a castle with its moat, wall and tower—humility, chastity, charity—which leads to divine union (19.6ff). In most instances, Aelred offers only a portion, an aspect of the way or a quick general overview. But in two sermons he traces the spiritual journey more thoroughly.

82. RB 7:34.
83. RB 7:35.
84. Mt 5:39ff.

The genealogy of the Lord which is read at Mass on the Feast of the Nativity of Saint Mary[85] invites the abbot to develop an extensive teaching that is filled with biblical typology. For 'from these fathers through whom Christ descended to us we ought to discern some spiritual meaning and to discover certain steps by which we are to ascend to him' (24.5). The three groups of fourteen forebears are interpreted as stages and each of the fathers as a step. Abraham, the Father, is the goal. We begin from Joseph, whose name—Jerome tells us— means 'increase',[86] but it is an increase that is brought about by decreasing: 'None of you can be my disciple who does not renounce all his possessions'[87] (24.23). Mary, the 'Star of the Sea',[88] is our enabler: she 'leads us that she may enlighten us, that she may show us these steps so we shall know them, that she may help us to be able to ascend' (24.20). Yet, because 'it would take a long time if we wished to work through all these names and look for the steps in each of them' (24.22):

> ... we may pass on to the second stage. Beginning there to purify ourselves, let us ascend from step to step until we come to Solomon, whose name means *peacemaker*,[89] so that, purified from evil passions, we may come to possess a certain peace and tranquillity. And thus we enter upon the third stage, which begins with David, whose name means *desirable*,[90] so that we too may desire and burn to see that object of desire, the face of our Creator. In this desire of ours we come to Abraham, to the Father on high, that we may see *the God of gods in Sion*.[91] (24.21)

The Gospel for the Feast of All Saints, the proclamation of Saint Matthew's summary of Christ's teaching in the eight

---

85. Mt 1:1–16.
86. Jerome, *Interpretatio Hebraicorum nominum* 7 et passim.
87. Lk 14:33.
88. Jerome, *Interpretatio Hebraicorum nominum* 14.
89. Jerome, *Interpretatio Hebraicorum nominum* 63.
90. Jerome, *Interpretatio Hebraicorum nominum* 74 et passim..
91. Ps 83:8.

beatitudes,[92] enables Aelred, like other Cistercian Fathers,[93] to trace out most fully the way to divine likeness and union (27.9ff). In true patristic fashion Aelred, using the Old Testament to disclose the meaning of the New, explores the eight beatitudes through the use of the seven days of creation and the seven qualities of the Messianic King enumerated by Isaiah,[94] which Catholic theology commonly speaks of as the seven gifts of the Holy Spirit. Aelred provides further details of his path by indicating qualities of each day's evening and morning; in this he follows the jewish and liturgical practice of beginning the day at sundown the previous evening. This very intricate sermon presents the path from its humble beginnings in servile fear right up to the peace of the eternal sabbath enjoyed by the child of God in filial fear.

BEATITUDE	GIFT	DAY OF CREATION	EVE	MORNING
Poor in spirit	servile fear	light–humility	weakness	restoration
Meek–quick to listen	piety	firmament– Scriptures	our ignorance	light of grace
Mourn–tears	knowledge	waters separated	mourning	contemplation
Hunger–thirst for justice	fortitude	lights great–Christ lesser–Saints	temptation	fulfillments
Merciful	counsel	living creatures	own deeds	divine mercy
Clean of heart	understanding	man–woman created	in a mirror riddle	sight
Peacemaker	filial fear	Sabbath	Persecuted	fidelity to the Way

92. Mt 5:1ff..
93. See M. B. Pennington, 'A Way to Holiness, the Beatitudes in the Sermons of the Cistercian Fathers' in *The Last of the Fathers* (Still River, MA: St Bede's Publications, 1983) 35–47.
94. Is 11:3.

Community

One of the valuable contributions a study of Aelred makes to our present-day concerns is his teaching on the full christian dimension of community. The person who seeks his own advantage quickly becomes envious of others, and this leads to suspicions. In the sweet oil of the communal love which gives true sweetness to community life, these are the flies which destroy all its beauty (6.12). Aelred did not regard community as merely living together, as shallow communication, but as, above all, a deep sharing of life, of the Christ-life. Living in community means being members of Christ and, therefore, members of one another. In this true oneness each person realizes that whatever one member has received, he has received not for himself alone but for all his fellow members. His total sharing of life and all its joys and sorrows does not deny in any way the uniqueness of each individual. 'Each has his proper gift from God.'[95] (3.9) Each brings his particular gift, his talent, to the community. There is a deep appreciation of the unique contribution each makes and at the same time a very valuable sense of need, a realization that we do need our sister and brother in order to realize fully our own potential in Christ. This, of course, is simply Saint Paul's doctrine of the mystical body,[96] very beautifully and very humanly expressed by Aelred.

A corollary of this appreciation of showing full respect for both total sharing and the particular functioning of the different members of the one body is the affirmation that each person in the community will observe a different measure in the practice of the various exercises of the christian life. To those accustomed to thinking of early Cîteaux as imposing absolutely uniform monastic observance on all its houses, it will come as a surprise to hear this early Cistercian Father telling his

---

95. I Co 7:7.
96. Rm 14:4; I Cor 12:12ff; Eph 4–16.

community that, 'it must be realized that no one has the same grace in all these exercises' —work, watching, fasting, *lectio*, meditation, prayer— '. . . each should take refuge in that practice which he finds of greater help' (8.17).

INTERIORITY

Another note in these sermons that rings true to modern concerns is Aelred's great insistence on interiority. Deeds are certainly important. It is not enough for a monk to withdraw from the world in spirit only. He has actually to withdraw from the world, leaving behind riches and honors. Yet what he does once in an exterior way, he has to do daily from the depths of his heart. With Benedict, Aelred taught that it is not enough to give up one's own likings, to be obedient, to suffer injuries and contradiction. To reap the fruit of all these actions, one must be able to do it all with 'a quiet mind'.[97] Only then has one truly embraced the way. When outer actions reflect deep inner convictions of mind and heart, then the Christian will truly have gone forth from Egypt, from the world of frivolity and sin, and be ready to offer sacrifice pleasing to the Lord. When he loves to be what he is for Christ's sake, the true follower will 'come to the pastures of eternal happiness, to the inheritance of the servants of God, to the joy of the disciples of Christ' (6.35).

This brief overview gives only a hint of the richness Aelred has to offer us in these sermons for the feasts of the liturgical year. In this translation the Scripture passages have been translated from the Latin to fit the context. While the references follow the New Revised Standard Version, it must be remembered that Aelred was familiar with the latin Bible which differs in places from modern english translations. We have italicized the

97. RB 7:35.

Scripture texts whenever Aelred quotes directly, hoping this will make evident how the abbot wove his sermon on the warp of the biblical text.

M. Basil Pennington OCSO

Our Lady of Joy Monastery
Lantau, China

CONCORDANCE

The Sermons in this translation follow the order and number of the critical edition of Gaetano Raciti, OCSO. The following table provides the number given to these sermons in the Tissier-Migne edition (*Patrologia Latina* 195).

Raciti		Tissier - Migne
I	SERMON ONE *For the Coming of the Lord*	1
II	SERMON TWO *For the Coming of the Lord*	10
III	SERMON THREE *For the Nativity of the Lord*	2
IV	SERMON FOUR *For the Epiphany of the Lord*	3
V	SERMON FIVE *For the Purification of Saint Mary*	4
VI	SERMON SIX *For the Feast of Saint Benedict*	5
VII	SERMON SEVEN *For the Feast of Saint Benedict*	6
VIII	SERMON EIGHT *For the Feast of Saint Benedict*	7
IX	SERMON NINE *For the Annunciation of the Lord*	8
X	SERMON TEN *For Palm Sunday*	9
XI	SERMON ELEVEN *For the Feast of Easter*	11
XII	SERMON TWELVE *For the Feast of Easter*	12
XIII	SERMON THIRTEEN *For the Ascension of the Lord*	13
XIV	SERMON FOURTEEN *For the Nativity of Saint John Baptist*	14
XV	SERMON FIFTEEN *For the Feast of the Holy Apostles Peter and Paul*	—
XVI	SERMON SIXTEEN *For the Feast of the Holy Apostles Peter and Paul*	—
XVII	SERMON SEVENTEEN *For the Feast of the Holy Apostles Peter and Paul*	15
XVIII	SERMON EIGHTEEN *For the Feast of the Holy Apostles Peter and Paul*	16

XIX	SERMON NINETEEN *For the Assumption of Saint Mary*	17
XX	SERMON TWENTY *For the Assumption of Saint Mary*	18
XXI	SERMON TWENTY-ONE *For the Assumption of Saint Mary*	25
XXII	SERMON TWENTY-TWO *For the Nativity of Holy Mary*	19
XXIII	SERMON TWENTY-THREE *For the Nativity of Holy Mary*	20
XXIV	SERMON TWENTY-FOUR *For the Nativity of Saint Mary*	21
XXV	SERMON TWENTY-FIVE *For the Feast of All Saints*	22
XXVI	SERMON TWENTY-SIX *For the Feast of All Saints*	23
XXVII	SERMON TWENTY-SEVEN *For the Feast of All Saints*	24
XXVIII	SERMON TWENTY-EIGHT *To the Clerics at the Synod*	—

A Note on the Translation
by the editor

One of the glories of twelfth-century cistercian literature is the monks' command of latin rhetoric. Having given up the world and its vanities—as Aelred several times points out to his monks in these very sermons—many of the monks brought with them into the cloister their love of language. As the eminent medievalist Étienne Gilson aptly observed, they 'renounced everything save the art of good writing'. In this, as in much else, Bernard of Clairvaux was preeminent. Yet Aelred of Rievaulx, who protested that he had been brought up in the scullery and not in the schools,[1.] wrote, and presumably spoke, with a skill and beauty that makes his works memorable—even, we hope, in translation.

To these twelfth-century humanists a word is a verbal symbol of an inexpressible reality. No single word can fully express that reality, so they considered it necessary to draw into service a number of near synonyms to open ever wider their readers' and their auditors' comprehension of divine reality. Deftly but unobtrusively—and often to us who are less sensitive to words, invisibly—applying the rules of medieval rhetoric, they created a prose unmatched in its power and its simplicity.

In this translation, we have tried whenever it was possible to reproduce something of this style by not paraphrasing Aelred's constructions except when recasting was unavoidable. Where it has been necessary to insert words to achieve a coherent English sense, the extraeous words have been placed in square brackets [ ]. Words which have been inserted by the editor of the

---

1. *The Mirror of Charity,* Prologue 2 (CF 17:73–74)

critical Latin edition and translated have been placed in pointed brackets < >.

We have tried to use only a single english word to represent a single latin word. The polyvalent and nuanced meanings of words in both languages has in some passages forced us to abandon this attempt in the hope of avoiding incomprehensible sentences or precious artificiality. The specifically theological meanings that certain words have taken on over the centuries has meant that the most variation occurs with terms which have both a general and a specific meaning. The following list, by no means exhaustive, indicates the words used to translated key terms in Aelred's Sermons.

affectus	attachment; feeling, emotion
cognitio	knowledge, thoughts
cognosco	to know, recognize
cogito	think, conceive
concupiscentia	unruly appetites, cravings, obsession, concupiscence
concupisco	to crave
congregare	to gather
congregatio	gathering
considerare	reflect
curiositas	idle speculation
dulcedo	charm, delight, sweetness
dulcis	sweet, fragrant, pleasing, pleasant, attractive
impius	wicked, godless
Ineffabilis	inexpressible
instituta	provisions
intellectus	intellect, understanding
Intelligo	understand
justificatio	righteousness
justus	righteous
mansuetudo	meekness

memoria	remembrace
mens	mind
mundus	untainted
munditia	untainted state
ordo	rank, position
ordines	ways of life / vocations
pietas	fondness, loving kindness, piety
pietatis viscera	depth of fondness
pius	caring, kind
pusillanimitas	indecisiveness
sermo	comment
verba	words
verecundia	bashfulness
verecundus	abashed
virtus	might, potency, power, virtue
vis / vim	impulse
vitium	fault, evil deed, vice
voluntaria	self-willed
vox	utterance / comment / cry, voice

Sermon One
FOR THE COMING OF THE LORD

YOU SHOULD KNOW, dearest brothers, that this blessed season which we call *Adventum Domini*—the Advent or the Coming of the Lord—represents two things to us. Therefore we should rejoice in both for both should bring us benefit.

2. This season makes present to us both comings of our Lord. First of all, that utterly gentle coming when the Son of God, *the fairest of the sons of the human family,*† *the Longed-for of all nations,*‡ gave to this world his visible presence in the flesh which had been long awaited and ardently desired by all the Fathers. At that time *he came into this world to save sinners.*† And secondly, that coming which we must await with firm hope and indeed often call to mind with tears, when this same Lord of ours, who first came hidden in the flesh, will come manifested in all his glory. As we sing in the psalm: *God shall come manifestly,*† and so on— that is, on the Day of Judgement when he comes manifestly to judge. 3. His first coming was made known to only a few just persons. In his second coming he will appear manifestly to the just and to sinners alike, as the Prophet clearly implies

†Ps 44:3*
‡Hg 2:8

†1 Tm 1:15

†Ps 49 [50]:3

---

*Ps 44:3 in the Vulgate-Septuagint enumeration which Aelred knew. In the Hebrew enumeration, it is Psalm 45:2. Hereafter psalms will be cited as Ps 44:3 [45:2], i.e. Vulgate [Hebrew].

when he says: *All flesh shall see the salvation of God.*† Just as the day which we shall in a short time celebrate in memory of his birth presents him to us as having been born—that is to say, it more expressly signals that very day and hour when he came into this world—so this season we are observing in preparation for that day makes him present as longed for, that is, as the longing maintained by the holy Fathers, those who lived before his coming.

†Is 52:10; Lk 3:6

4. Beautifully then is it provided in the Church that during this season we read the words of those who lived before the Lord's first coming and their longings are recalled. Nor do we celebrate their longing for only one day, but for quite a long time. This is because whenever we are kept waiting a while for something we greatly long for, when what we love does come it seems sweeter to us. It is up to us, then, dearest brothers, to follow the example of the holy Fathers and to recall their longings and so to set our minds on fire with love of and desire for Christ.

5. You should know that it was for this reason that the observance of this season was enjoined on us: that we should consider the longing which the holy Fathers had for the first coming of the Lord. By their example let us learn to have a great longing for his second coming. We should reflect on what good things our Lord did for us by his first coming and what yet greater he will do for us by his second. And by considering this, we should love that first coming of his very much and very much long for the second.

6. And if we do not have a good enough conscience to dare to long for his coming, we should at least fear his coming and by that fear correct our faults. Then, even though we may not be able not to fear him now, we shall at least not fear him when he comes, but may be confident. It is indeed true, brothers, that those who pay careful attention to themselves now and fear the day of judgement before it comes will undoubtedly have no fear then when it does come.

7. And who is so hardened as to be unable to fear that day on which our Lord will come *in his majesty*[†], when heaven and earth will go up in flames, when all the evil that human beings have done in this life will lie open before God and his angels, before the devil and his angels, before the whole human race from Adam to the very last person to exist in the world? Without doubt every fault and every sin which confession has not covered over in this life will there be made public. Who cannot fear that day on which every person is obliged to receive what he will possess for all eternity? 8. It is extremely good to think often about these things, brothers, especially when temptations arise. Then every person who chooses a life more perfect than that of those who are in the world should try, by the goodness of his upright way of life, to attain such a conscience[†] that, rather than fearing punishment on that day, he will long for the glory and the joy which the just will have on that day. Just as the holy Fathers longed for that day on which they were to be redeemed, so he should long for that day on which all the saints are to be glorified.

†Cf. Mt 25:31, Lk 9:26

†Aelred here relates *conversatio* and *conscientia*.

9. The Lord came the first time to free us from our sins, but at his second coming he will heal *all our infirmities*. So it is that the person who bids his soul bless the Lord also gives his reason: *Who forgives all your iniquities,* he says, *who heals all your infirmities.*† The one refers to the Lord's first coming; the other to his second. For by his first coming he eradicated our sins, but we still suffer great infirmities in punishment for those sins. 10. Who can count all the infirmities of this life: hunger, thirst, toil, pain, disease, lethargy, weariness? Yet these apply to the body. How many infirmities of the soul there are! How much concupiscence, how many temptations! All these infirmities—and all the others which we cannot pause to mention—the Lord will heal by his second coming. Then will be fulfilled the apostle's words: *This perishable body must be clothed in incorruptibility,*† and so on.

†Ps 102 [103]:3

†1 Co 15:50–53

11. By his first coming our Lord raised us up only in soul; by his second coming he will raise us up in body, too. As we now serve God with both—the body and the soul—so then in both shall we enjoy perfect happiness with God. At his first coming he gave us the faith that enables us to believe in him. At his second coming he will endow us with the capacity to see him, not as the wicked will see him on the day of judgment—for on that day of judgment the good and the bad alike will all see him in the likeness in which he bore his sufferings for us and in which he rose and ascended into heaven—but we shall see him as those who are pure of heart will be able to see him. 12. For the Lord says: *Blessed are the pure of heart for they shall see God.*† That is to say, we shall see his godhead too, that excellence and that beauty which now

†Mt 5:8

the angels see. For we shall be *like the angels of God in heaven.*† Yet if we love him now and long for him and scorn all worldly pleasures and honors, then surely we shall see him confidently in the likeness in which he will judge *the living and the dead.*† And we shall have the happiness of seeing him in that likeness in which he will show himself only to the good whom he will take with himself from judgement into the kingdom.

†Mt 22:30

†Cf 1 P 4:5

13. Let us think a moment, so far as we can, about how much joy we shall have and how much happiness if—on that day when heaven and earth are in flames, when the Lord comes with such power and might—we can be confident and not only not fear him when he comes but love him very much and look to him with confidence. And therefore, brothers, if we want to enjoy that gladness and confidence then, let us strive to love our Lord greatly. Whom should we love so much as our Creator and our Lord, and above all our Redeemer? 14. There is this further point, that we can love nothing else with as much confidence, for whatever else we love we shall surely have to lose. If we take delight in things we must lose, then, when the time comes for us to lose them, we shall feel distress equal to our former delight. Let us, therefore, love confidently him who is eternal and who is eternally good in the same way and always delightful in the same way. Let us love him so much now, brothers, that when we see him coming *from heaven with his angels*† we may have no fear of his coming but may immediately, with great longing, run to him as to a cherished friend.

†Cf Mt 16:27; 2 Th 1:7

15. Let us see how all the saints who lived before his first coming longed for him and let us follow

their example, not the example of those who love the world. For Scripture says: *The world will perish and so will its unruly appetites.*[†Cf 1 Jn 2:17] So those who love the world will perish together with the world when it perishes. To know how much the Fathers longed to see our Lord, let us listen to what the Lord himself says in the Gospel: *Amen I say to you, many kings and just persons have longed to see what you now see and did not see it,*[†Mt 13:17; Lk 10:24] and so on.

16. This is what Scripture signifies when it says of Solomon: *All the kings of the earth longed to see the face of Solomon and hear his wisdom.*[†2 Ch 9:23; 1 K 10:24; Lk 11:31] Now surely only those who long *to see Solomon's face and hear his wisdom* are called to be kings. They are the ones who govern themselves well and keep their members free from the stain of sin. Those who possess extensive territories and have many people under them are not really kings, but are themselves slaves of sin; as our Lord says: *Everyone who commits sin is the slave of sin.*[†Jn 8:34] Surely no one should be called a king who is a slave and so vile a slave as to be dominated by sin. 17. For that reason, brothers, let us work hard at governing ourselves well and keeping guard over our members. Then we too shall be kings and we shall begin to long *to see the face of* the true *Solomon,*[†2 Ch 9:23] our Lord Jesus Christ. There is no need, brothers, to tell you the reason why our Lord is called Solomon. You have often heard that 'Solomon' in our language means 'Peacemaker'[†Jerome, *Interpretatio* 63 (CCSL 72:138, 5) *et passim.*] and our Lord is himself truly the peacemaker who has made peace between us and God and has reconciled us with his Father by his own blood.

18. Holy David himself was indeed one of those kings who *longed to see the face of the* true *Solomon.*

This he made plain on one occasion when he longed for some water from the fountain which was in Bethlehem. Scripture tells how the king *longed for it and said: Oh that someone would give me water from the cistern at the gate of Bethlehem.*† Some of the men present thought that what he wanted was visible water from that cistern, and at great risk they passed through the enemy camp, drew some of the water, and brought it to the king. But, because he wanted to show that he had said this through the spirit of prophecy and not to obtain that physical and worthless water, he immediately poured it out on the ground.† 19. What he longed for was not water from that physical cistern but water from that Fountain which was *born in Bethlehem.*† This is why he says elsewhere: *My soul thirsts for God, the fount of living water,*† and so on. This is the true fount, our Lord Jesus Christ, *who was born in Bethlehem in Judah;* he who says: *If anyone is thirsty, let him come and drink, and streams of living water shall flow from within him.*† This is the water holy David longed for. This is the fountain to which he ran with great longing, as he immediately goes on to say in that verse. For afterwards he said: *As the hind longs [for flowing streams, so longs my soul for you, O God],* immediately adding: *When shall I come and appear before the face of God?*†

†2 S 23:15

†2 S 23:15–17

†Mt 2:1

†Ps 41:3 [42:2]

†Jn 7:37–38

†Ps 41:2–3 [42:1–2]

20. Let us see, brothers, just how great his longing was. That Fount was *born in Bethlehem* and from it waters flow throughout the world. Surely this is the kind of water used for washing by those who are soiled, for drinking by those who are thirsty, for cooking raw food by those who are hungry. The water which flows from this fount, brothers, is Christ's teaching, which he proclaims

in the Gospel. 21. In it, all who are soiled and shackled by their sins wash themselves, as did those to whom the Lord said: *Now you are clean on account of the message I have spoken to you.*[†Jn 15:3] Notice, they were cleansed by Christ's teaching. This is the water, too, which those who thirst to know our Lord drink and which inebriates them, for in Christ's teaching we can know him. If our heart is not occupied by physical thoughts, if we listen gladly to God's word and understand it, there will be kindled in us a fire that will not allow us to think of anything except what concerns the love of our Lord.

22. If holy David, like a hart,[†Ps 41:2–3 [42:1–2]] felt so great a longing for that water before the Fount was born, we, who see this Fount born and have had some taste of the water that flows from the Fount, should be much ashamed not to experience great longing and love. We see that now there is fulfilled what Isaiah the prophet greatly desired when he said: *Would that you would burst the heavens, Lord, and come down. The mountains would dissolve before your face.*[†Is 64:1]

23. What do we think the holy prophet was longing for by these words? Christ's first coming, surely, and with great longing. And immediately he states the reason for longing so ardently for him: *The mountains would dissolve before your face.*[†Is 64:1] For that holy man saw how the devil, who fell from heaven through his own pride,[†Cf. Is 14:12, Lk 10:18] held the whole human race in his possession. He saw how the devil swelled [with pride] and strutted because the kings and princes of this world adored him and because nearly every human person in the world was imitating his pride. 24. This the prophet saw

and it caused him great sorrow. In my opinion he was scarcely able to endure that sorrow, especially because the Lord, who should destroy all that pride, so long delayed. That is why he said with great longing: *Would that you would burst the heavens, Lord, and come down,*† and so forth. The prophet knew that Providence had determined the time of his coming, but he found it very difficult to endure such delay. And therefore he longed for God, if it were possible, to anticipate the hour he had fixed. This is the meaning of the words: *Would that you would burst the heavens Lord, and come down,*† and so on.

†Is 64:1

†Is 64:1

25. It is as if he had said: I know, O Lord, that you are waiting for the time which you foresaw from the beginning. You are waiting until everything has been fulfilled which the holy ones have said must be fulfilled before your coming. But *would that you would burst the heavens, Lord*—that is, if only you would, if it were possible, break through that plan of yours which you have revealed to the heavens—that is, to your saints—and come. I see this devil's pride. He has lured the whole human race into his power and now he is laying his hands on that people whom you have chosen as your own. Among the Jews, who used to be your people, pride, wantonness and every kind of vice now prevail. 26. Why do you still linger? Why do you delay yet longer? We threaten them, telling them, 'Our Lord will come. Christ will come, who will judge the wicked and honor the good.' But they snigger at us and sneer: '*One injunction after another.*† Look how many years have passed since you first promised us that he would come and still he does not come. It would seem that you are only deceiving us.' So said the wretches and,

†Is 28:10

as if they had not a care in the world, they gave themselves up to the service of idols and to every form of pride and wantonness. This is how they behaved, but the holy prophets lamented; they grieved and wept and longed for his coming with a marvelous longing.

27. Hence this plea of Isaiah: *Would that you would burst the heavens, Lord, and come down.*† But what did Christ do in his compassion? Indeed, he did not let his holy prophet suffer such grief for long without great consolation. Listen to what the same prophet says a little further on: *You came down and the mountains dissolved before your face.*† You can hear something amazing in this. First he said: *Would that you would come down, Lord,*† and so on; and now he says: *You came down and the mountains dissolved before your face,*† as though what he had been so longing for had already happened. 28. Why is this? In my opinion, when holy Isaiah was in that distress over the devil's pride and human wickedness, our Lord, to console him, *showed him in spirit*† what we now see, namely, that the whole world would believe in him and kings and princes adore him, that all idols should be destroyed and those who were proud be made humble by the Lord's coming. Surely this is what the prophet saw in spirit when he exalted and rejoiced. And in an excess of gladness, as if he were already seeing fulfilled what he truly saw must come about, he said: *You came down and the mountains dissolved before your face.*†

29. Oh dearest brothers, if only we, now that we see this fulfilled, could feel as much joy as he felt when he saw that it still having to be fulfilled. We now see it. We can turn to our Lord and

say with great joy: Lord, *you came down and the mountains dissolved before your face.*† This has now been fulfilled just as David also desired when he said: *Touch the mountains and they will smoke.*† Our Lord came down. By the grace of the Holy Spirit he touched the mountains—that is, the proud of this world. 30. And look how they dissolved, that is, how they were humbled. They begin to weep for their sins. They cannot endure the smoke— that is, the darkness and obscurity of their sins. Do you not see this every day, brothers? Do you not every day see the proud of this world turning to the Lord in great confusion, with great fear humbling themselves and weeping for their sins? Of course, this happens every day, brothers. Even if it does not happen before our eyes every day, it is happening every day in the holy Church.

†Is 64:3

†Ps 143 [144]:5

31. Accordingly, dearest brothers, in a much better and more obvious way than the Jews suppose, we see fulfilled what holy Isaiah says elsewhere. For in a certain place where he is showing what is to happen at the Lord's coming he says: *The wolf shall dwell with the lamb and the leopard shall lie down with the goat; the calf and the lion shall graze together and a little child shall herd them.*† What would be so great if God did with a number of dumb animals what even human beings are accustomed to do by their skill: bring together animals which are naturally hostile to one another. 32. Indeed we must say with Saint Paul: *Does God care about oxen?*† Brothers, if God does not care about oxen to the extent of giving any commandments in their regard in the Law, much less will he be concerned about lions and leopards to the extent of making such striking statements about them through his prophet. Yet

†Is 11:6

†1 Co 9:9

if we would look at this gathering and reflect upon it, we can see that this prophecy has been fulfilled in a far more beautiful and better way than if those animals were together.

33. Reflect on how God has gathered you here—from what diverse parts of the country, from what diverse backgrounds. One of you, when he was in the world—what was he like but a lion in his wealth and pride, despising others and vaunting himself as superior to them ? Another of you—was he not like a wolf, living by plunder, trying to grab the property of others? The leopard is an animal characterized by changeableness: so were some of you in your slyness, your trickery, your deceit.

34. Again there are many in this community who reeked of wantonness. Those like that were like goats, for the goat is an evil-smelling animal. There were some, too, who when they were in the world lived innocently; they can well be compared to lambs. There are yet others who in the simple lives they led were like sheep. Now look, brothers, in what harmony and peace God has gathered all of them together in one fellowship.

35. Here *the wolf* dwells *with the lamb*, eats and drinks with the lamb, doing it no harm but loving it deeply. There can be no doubt that the person who was like a wolf in the world now lives in great harmony with someone who was innocent as a lamb. The person who was proud as a lion now lives in great peace and quiet with someone who was and still is a sheep in his simplicity. Here the lion not only dwells together with the calf

but—what is more surprising—the lion becomes a calf. 36. You know that for a long time under the Old Law calves used to be offered in sacrifice. Someone who offers himself to God in sacrifice, therefore, spiritually becomes a calf. In this way many lions become calves, in that many who were formerly cruel and rapacious now sacrifice themselves to God by work and vigils and other such disciplines. Likewise not only does *the wolf* dwell here *with the lamb* but here the wolf has become a lamb. How beautiful it is to see some of you, who in the world were so wise, so powerful, so proud, and so cunning, become now so simple and guileless as if you knew nothing. Why has all this come about, except because our Lord came down *and the mountains dissolved before his face.*† †Is 64:3

37. Even if we were not able to demonstrate that in this community, would this mean that the Lord's coming had not brought it about? Think how Paul raged like a wolf, how he seized Christians, Christ's sheep, stripped them, stoned them. Reflect on how suddenly he was changed and became a sheep; how pleasantly, how gently, how kindly he lived afterwards with Christ's other sheep. Not only did he abstain from attacking them but he gave himself up to death for Christ's sheep. Surely, brothers, if we reflect on this change [we must admit that] the Lord worked a greater miracle in this than if he had made those animals, the wolf and the sheep, live together.

38. *And a little child shall herd them.*† Who is this *little child* if not he of whom Isaiah says: *For us a child is born and a little one is given to us?*† It was he, surely, who herded Paul and made him go to Ananias.† It was also he who herded the wolves

†Is 11:6

†Is 9:6

†Ac 9:10ff.

and the lions who have come into this fellowship from the world and he still herds them along in front of himself towards all the things we do. He has to herd us ahead of himself, brothers, until we are in the condition of being able to follow him.

39. These are two stages we must consider in our life, brothers: the one relates to herding as he herds us ahead of himself; and the other to following as we follow after him. Now an earthly shepherd herds ahead of himself the animals who cannot or will not follow him. Yet we see some so tame that they know enough to follow their shepherd. 40. Let everyone now reflect on whether he follows this shepherd of ours or is still being herded ahead of him. In the case of Saint Paul, surely [Christ] herded him at first when he threw him to the ground and, as it were, forced him to go to Ananias to be baptized. But afterwards Paul followed him with the utmost readiness, when he said: *I long to be dissolved and be with Christ,*† and the rest of it. Herding, brothers, is a matter of fear; following a matter of love.

†Ph 1:23

41. He herded us ahead of himself when he caused us to reflect on our sins, on our wicked way of life, when he made us fear the pains of hell and by means of this fear made us leave the world and come here. And even now, brothers, our Shepherd is still herding ahead of himself anyone who is here and is obedient and humble and does what he is supposed to do out of fear—to avoid being damned—because he knows that someone who abandons what he has begun cannot be saved; [He is herding] anyone who does what he is told and carries out those [duties] relating to his state of life while reflecting on this. 42. Yet

someone who has already often tasted *how sweet our Lord is*,† who has begun to love him, who has so found his own heart that, even though no other punishment would follow save an affront to his Lord or a slight diminishment in the love of the Lord who does not abandon what he has begun—that person is now following [Christ]. His shepherd has no need to herd him but has only to go before him and show him the way by which he wants him to follow. This person can say: *I have run the way of your commandments now that you have enlarged my heart.*† It is not as when he had to cry out: *Pierce my flesh with your fear.*† Until this happens he had not yet accepted that *broad commandment*† by which his heart was enlarged while he was running.

†1 P 2:3

†Ps 118 [119]:32
†Ps 118 [119]:120

†Cf, Ps 118 [119]:96.

43. Brothers, the Lord did indeed herd those who lived before his coming, because they were, as it were, ahead of him. Therefore he gave them the Law, which signified fear. To it, without doubt, are still subject all whom he herds, for as long as they do good out of fear they are subject to law. But because this is our beginning-point, we ought to aim at passing beyond this stage and reaching one at which we follow him with joy. For we are subject to charity, which is especially appropriate to us who live after the Lord's coming and look to where he has ascended before us. 44. And whom should we follow so readily as this child who is a child for our sake? Surely, brothers, we should not only follow, but run, after him. For even if his charm did not attract us and, as it were, compel us to follow him, eagerness for the happiness, for the joy, which exists in the place to which he has gone before us should make us only too glad to run after him. For it is not to transitory and fleeting

joys that we follow him but to *what eye has not seen, nor ear heard nor the human heart conceived,*[†1 Co 2:9] that is, to that blessed homeland of which the prophet says: *My portion, O Lord, is in the land of the living.*[†Ps 141:6 [142:5]]

45. Therefore, dearest brothers, if we want to arrive at that happiness, it behooves us not only to follow our Lord in the way we have just described, but also both follow him and go ahead of him in the same way as those who escorted him into Jerusalem, those of whom today's Gospel tells us,[†In Aelred's time the Gospel read at the Eucharistic liturgy on the First Sunday of Advent was Saint Matthew's description of our Lord's triumphal entry into Jerusalem.] went ahead of and followed him. For when the Lord came to Jerusalem, the Gospel says: *A large crowd spread their clothes over the road. Yet others cut branches from trees and cried: Hosanna to the Son of David, blessed is he who comes in the name of the Lord.*[†Mt 21:1, 8–9]

46. You have often heard about the coming of the Lord, dearest brothers, how and in what manner he came to Jerusalem—that is, to his Church. There is no need to tell you, therefore, of the manner in which he came, especially since the day is short and—because it is Sunday and we receive Holy Communion and have two meals—very busy. Yet, on account of the Gospel which is read today in our holy Church, I would like to speak briefly about the way the Church itself welcomed his coming. Certainly some in the Church went before his coming and others follow it. 47. God's Church is not only this gathering of the faithful who believed in him after his coming. No, all the saints from Abel the Just to the last just person to live in this world belong to the holy Church. All of them make up that one Church to which is said: *My dove is one.*[†Sg 6:8] But one part went before

his coming: Abel, Noah, Abraham, David and still other holy persons. After his coming there were apostles, martyrs, confessors and all the faithful, among whom. by his mercy. we are numbered.

48. But among them were some who laid their *garments* down at Jesus' feet and *others* the *branches* of trees.† Those who reject all the glory of the world for Christ's sake are laying down branches. For what are the riches and glory of this world but leaves and branches of trees which turn green in summer and wither in winter? For surely all the glory of the world flourishes, so to speak, in prosperity but in adversity, especially at a person's death, when winter weather—that is, the final condemnation—comes, it becomes worthless and squalid. 49. But blessed is the person who lays such things down at Jesus' feet by giving them to the poor who are, as it were, his feet—that is, his weak members. More blessed still is the person who for Christ can despise his own garment and lay it down at his feet. For what is our garment but our own body by which our soul is somehow clothed or covered? Blessed is the person who can despise his very members, his own body, for Christ and consign all the actions of his body to God's service.

†Cf Mt 21:8–9

50. Those who went before the Lord's coming, no less than those who followed it, did both. The holy Fathers in the Old Testament counted as nought the world's riches and glory on account of the faith they had in Christ's coming. Many even subjected their bodies to martyrdom, like Abel, the first martyr, like Isaiah, like the Maccabean martyrs, whose extraordinary passion you heard about a few days ago.† 51. Nor is it a matter of

†The Books of the Maccabees are read in the liturgy during the month of November, just before the beginning of Advent.

only one person here or there. Who can number the thousands of persons who did all this after his coming? You, too, belong among their number. For you have thrown down tree branches—that is, all the world's pomp—to worship and honor Christ. What is more, for him you have despised your very bodies. Your very soul you have spent in Christ's honor, which is going further still, for you have given up your own will, the will of your soul.

52. Now all *who went before and all who followed cried out: Hosanna to the Son of David, blessed is he who comes in the name of the Lord.*[†] This is great faith, a great proclamation, great praise. *Hosanna* is a cry which asks for salvation, which says, as it were: *Make safe.*[†] Surely the one from whom they ask salvation they proclaim the Saviour. This is properly an attribute of God. They call him Son of David and proclaim him true man. They bless him because he *comes in the name of the Lord,*[†] By this they show clearly that he is the one who, through the prophets, God the Father promised would come. 53. In this faith holy Church receives the coming of the Son of God. It believes that he is true God, true man, true Saviour of the world, promised by God the Father, foretold by the holy prophets. In this faith both those who lived before his coming and those who come after it agree and come together in and are one Church. In this faith both are saved. Those who are without this faith are outside the Church. Christ did not come to them and therefore they are not saved in Christ. Enough said about the first coming.

54. We should, however, know, brothers, that in the same form in which he came the first time to redeem his Church, he will come a second

[†]Mt 21:9; Mk 11:9
[†]*Salvifica:* alternatively, 'save me'. Jerome, *Interpretatio Hebraicorum nominum,* 62 et passim.

[†]Mt 21:9

time to glorify it. That is what the angels told the Apostles after the Lord's ascension: *He will come just as you have seen him going into heaven.*† This will crown the doom of the wicked, brother. With utter dismay and sorrow they will see in glory and power him whom they despised in human weakness.

†Ac 1:11

55. The account which the other evangelists also give [of the entry into Jerusalem] is quite appropriate to this second coming of the Lord. For when Jesus came to Jerusalem *the children of the Hebrews* took *branches of olive* and palm and came *to meet him.*† So it will be at the Lord's second coming. When he comes, in the form in which he redeemed the Church, to glorify it and to *present it to himself without spot or wrinkle or anything of the sort,*† then indeed the *children of the Hebrews* will come *to meet him* with palms and *olive branches.* 56. And who are these children if not those of whom the prophet says: *Children, praise the Lord.*† And elsewhere: *The Lord keeps watch over little ones.*† For he keeps watch, not over the great and the exalted and the proud, but over the *little ones*—that is, the humble. They it is who praise the Lord, provided they are Hebrews— that is, *those who leap.*† If now they are humble, if now they forego the deeds and the vices of the flesh, if now they know how to take spiritual leaps through contemplation and through good thoughts, then on the day of judgement, when Jesus comes in his power, they will, without doubt, come *to meet him* with palms—that is, with the insignia of the victories which they have won here over the devil. For palms signify victory. 57. Then they can, as if with palms, glory and say: *Where, death, is your victory? Death, where is your sting?*†

†Jn 12:12–13;cf. Hesbert 3:4415

†Eph 5:27

†Ps 112 [113]:1
†Ps 114 [116]:6

†Jerome, *Interpretatio* 35 (CCSL 72:103, 16) *et passim.*

†1 Co 15:55

Then they will come with olive branches, which symbolize peace. At present they do not have peace, not as long as they fight with the devil, as long as they fight against their vices, against their own flesh. But then there will be perfect peace, perfect tranquility, because the flesh will not be able to resist the spirit or the spirit [resist] God, nor will the devil be able to attack, nor will death or any weakness burden them.

58. If we want to have this peace at the Lord's second coming, let us make it our aim to receive his first coming *with faith and love*,[†] persevering in those tasks which he showed us and taught us by his first coming. Let us cultivate a true love for him and through love longing, so that when he, *the Desired of all the nations*,[†] comes, we may be able to look *with complete confidence*, upon him

[†] 1 Tm 1:14.

[†] Hg 2:8; Acts 4:29. 28:31.

who lives and reigns
with the Father and Holy Spirit
through all ages of ages.
Amen.

Sermon Two
FOR THE COMING OF THE LORD

YOU HAVE HEARD in the Gospel reading, my dearest brothers, how our Lord, *when he drew near to Jerusalem*, had an ass and a colt brought to him.† You have also heard of the devotion of the Israelite people, how *they went out to meet him*‡ with palm branches, and *they went before him and followed after him, crying out: Hosanna to the Son of David.*† But someone may say: It is true, indeed, we have heard this. And we have heard it with great rejoicing. But what has this to do with this day on which we commemorate, not the passion of the Lord, but his coming? It is true, brothers, that this took place without doubt a few days before his passion—as the other evangelists clearly show. For it was on account of this glory that the pharisees and high priests were tormented by the greatest envy and, gathering together the council, planned his death. Nonetheless I think it is not without reason that this account is read today in every church and that this [custom] was established by the holy Fathers.

2. You know that the wheel Ezekiel saw had four faces.† That wheel signifies holy Scripture.‡ So it is that the Psalmist says: *Your voice resounds in a wheel.*† This wheel has four faces, and sometimes we consider only one of its faces, sometimes

†Mt 21:9
‡Jn 12:13
†Mt 21:9

†Ez 1:15
‡Gregory the Great, *On Ezechiel*, I, Homily 6.2; CCSL 142:67, 17–18
†Ps 76:19 [77:18]

two, sometimes three, and sometimes even all four. Its first face is history,[†] the second morality, the third allegory, the fourth anagogy—that is, a sense of what is above. 3. To those who cannot grasp the deeper [meanings], Scripture shows its first face—that is, mere simple history. And they delight in the beauty of this face. It happens, too, that some see only this face of Scripture, which in some parts is not so beautiful—as when the patriarch Judah slept with his daughter-in-law or when David, having killed Uriah, took the man's wife. When they could not see another face of Scripture which is beautiful—because of this one face which they did see, they have despised it. 4. Therefore, brothers, we have heard this Gospel and have considered its one face, the simple story, and it appears beautiful enough to us. For what Scripture is more beautiful than what tells of the glory of our dearest Lord and the devotion of a faithful people? Yet by means of this face it does not show us how this reading pertains to this season. Let us therefore reflect on another face of the text and see whether that reveals to us something of the mystery of this season. But first we should indicate briefly what hidden meaning[†] this season contains in itself.

[†]*Historia*, here translated as both history and story.

[†]*Sacramentum*

5. This season has been established, brothers, that we might call to mind the coming of our Lord Jesus Christ: how he, whom the holy Fathers of the Old Testament had long expected and greatly desired, humbly came to redeem us. It has been established, too, that we not forget his second coming, in which he, whom all the saints expect and desire, will come *with great power and glory*[†] to judge the whole world and to render *to each person according to that person's works.*[†] 6. It is

[†]Lk 21:27

[†]Mt 16:27, Ps 61:13

principally because of these two—the memory of his two comings, that is—that this celebration has been established. And this is necessary. For it is remarkably good that we always have these two things in mind: the first coming of the Lord and the second. For the first begets love in our hearts and the second fear. Therefore let us reflect on the Gospel which has now been read and see what hidden meanings are contained in it.

7. *When the Lord Jesus drew near to Jerusalem.*[†] You know, brothers, that—literally—Jerusalem is that city which Holy David acquired and built and in which Solomon constructed that wondrous temple of which you have often heard. According to this face—that is, according to history—nothing that pertains to this celebration is being shown to us. Therefore it is necessary that we turn our attention to another face of this Scripture.

[†]Mt 21:1

8. Jerusalem, as you have been accustomed to hear, is interpreted as the *vision of peace*.[†] This name belongs first of all to those who abide in the perfect vision of God, who is true peace and true tranquility of mind, and thereby they sense true peace and tranquility within themselves. This is that blessed company of angels which is indeed called Jerusalem. And rightly so according to what the apostle Paul says: *The Jerusalem which is above is free; it is our mother.*[†] But how is Jesus said to draw near this city when he was always in it and that city never departed from him? This is that other face of Scripture, anagogy, the sense of what is above.

[†]*Interpretatio*, 50 (CCSL 72:121, 9–10) *et passim*.

[†]Gal 4:26

9. Let us look now at that face which we call allegory. According to this sense Jerusalem signifies the holy Church as it exists among men and

women to whom Isaiah says: *Arise, be illumined, Jerusalem, because your light has come.*† The Church is called Jerusalem, not because it sees perfectly that peace which angels see, but because it is directed toward it by believing rightly, acting well, and loving fervently him who *is our peace*, our Lord Jesus Christ.† But how does God, who is everywhere present and absent from nothing, draw near this Jerusalem? And yet he has said through the prophet: *Draw near to me and I will draw near to you.*† 10. And how do we draw close to him, *in whom we live, move and are?*† Nevertheless the Prophet says: *Draw near to him and be enlightened.*† And the Lord condemned some saying: *Woe to those who have withdrawn from me.*† What is this drawing-near and withdrawal? Not from place to place, but from one attachment to another.† If you love the world, you withdraw from God.† If you withdraw from love of the world and begin to love God, you then draw near to God. So we draw near God when we grow in his love. He draws near us when he deigns to have mercy on us.

11. In this way Adam withdrew from God, by loving him less and the world more. For he loved his own private excellence which related not to God but to the world. In this way the whole human race withdrew from God; and thus what is now the Church of God withdrew from God in the same way. And so far from him that on its own it can in no way draw near God or approach him. Therefore it was necessary, because [humankind] could not approach God its salvation, that God its salvation should approach it. But first he drew near. 12. He approached it indeed when he showed that wondrous mercy by which, when

†Is 60:1

†Eph 2:14

†Js 4:8
†Ac 17:28

†Ps 33:6 [34:5]

†Hos 7:13

†*De affectu in affectum.* *Affectus* is usually translated 'attachment'.
†1 Jn 2:15

he was hanging on the cross, he poured out his blood for it. And, when his side was opened, he united the Church to himself and made it one with him, so that they might be *two in one flesh*.† If indeed then he approached the Church, he drew near it when he promised his mercy to it, preached that mercy and began to show it. Jesus, the salvation of the Church, the salvation for the world, the salvation of miserable humans expelled from paradise, drew near Jerusalem when he foretold that he would become man and when he promised Abraham that mercy which he later fulfilled: *In your seed all the peoples will be blessed.*† 13. From the seed of Abraham, Christ would be born. Through him would be abolished the curse which had been laid on Adam.† Through him would be given that blessing which Isaiah foretold, saying: *And you will call your servants by another name.*† At first his servants were called Jews but now they are called Christians. *And you will call your servants by another name, in which he who is blessed upon the earth will be blessed in the Lord.*† Because without doubt no one can escape damnation or be blessed who does not bear this name.

†Gen 2:24, Eph 5:31

†Gen 22:18, 26:4; Gal 3:8

†Gen 3:17

†Is 65:15

†Is 65:15

14. Therefore, Jesus drew near Jerusalem—that is, the Church—when, through holy Abraham, he promised the Church that he would come. He clearly meant the holy Church when he spoke of *all nations*† because the holy Church is made up of peoples from all nations. Then, therefore, he began to draw near, but he had not yet come to Bethphage. Bethphage is understood to mean the *house of the cheek* or the *house of the mouth*.† He came perhaps to Bethany, yet not to Bethphage. For as the other evangelists clearly show, he first

†Gen 22:18

†*Interpretatio* 60 (CCSL 72:135, 24–25)

came to Bethany and then, *when he drew near Jerusalem, he came to Bethphage, to the Mount of Olives.*† 15. Bethany is understood to mean *house of obedience.*† And what was that holy soul of Abraham if not a *house of obedience*. To preserve *the good of obedience*† he did not believe his own son—and such a son—should be spared.† Jesus first came here because the promise of the coming of our Lord Jesus was first made to Abraham. Only he and his sons—and if there were any others they were few—knew of this promise, this future mercy of the Lord. But they did not make it known to others. hey did not make it known by word of mouth but only through some hidden and wondrous signs. Therefore the Lord had not yet come to Bethphage—that is, to the *house of the mouth.*†

†Mt 21:1
†*Interpretatio* 60 (above, n. 27)
†RB 71.1
†See Gen 22

†*Interpretatio* 60 (CCSL 72:135, 24–25)

16. Now, without doubt holy Abraham through a certain hidden sign showed the incarnation of the Lord when, sending a servant to find a wife for his son, he said: *Place your hand under my thigh and swear by the God of heaven.*† What is this? The God of heaven was in Abraham's thigh? He certainly shows in a beautiful, but hidden, way why he wanted his son to take a wife: not indeed to satisfy his lusts but to bring forth the seed from which the God of heaven was to be born. 17. Therefore, he ordered him to place his hand under his thigh to swear by the God of heaven, because without any doubt from his thigh—that is, from his progeny—the God of heaven was to be born. To use the word 'thigh' for progeny is common enough in Scripture, as for example: *All the souls who came forth from the thigh of Abraham were seventy.*† Or, *The scepter will not be taken away from Judah and a leader from his thigh.*† But this sign

†Gen 24:2ff

†Gen 46:26f
†Gen 49:10

of the Lord's coming was hidden because Jesus had not yet come to the *house of the mouth*[†]— that is, his incarnation had not yet been preached openly to any house—that is, to the people.

[†]*Interpretatio* (above, n 27)

18. But once the sons of Israel had been led out of Egypt, once they had accepted the Law, once they had celebrated sacrifices and constructed the tabernacle, then Jesus began to come to the *house of the mouth*[†] because he began to reveal his coming openly to all the people. Openly before all the people Moses said of him: *A prophet like me will be raised up from among your brethren; listen to him. Every soul who does not listen to that prophet will be wiped out from among his people.*[†] The apostles have shown that this was a prophecy of the Lord Jesus. They often used this testimony against the Jews.[†] 19. The Lord came to Bethphage when Isaiah the Prophet foretold the coming of the Lord and the virgin birth, saying: *Behold a virgin shall conceive in her womb*, and so forth.[†] When did he come to the Mount of Olives? *Oleos* [olives] in Greek means mercy <in Latin>. The Mount of Olives therefore signifies the excellence and, if I may say so, the culmination of his mercy of which we are speaking. He came to the Mount of Olives when the time was already at hand when he willed to show that wondrous and excellent mercy which he had first promised to the obedient Abraham and afterwards through his prophets to all the people.

[†]*Interpretatio* 60 (above, n 27)

[†]Ac 3:22f; Dt 18:15ff

[†]See Acts 3:22, 7:37

[†]Is 7:14; Mt 1:23

20. *Therefore as Jesus drew near Jerusalem and came to Bethphage on the Mount of Olives, he sent two of his disciples, saying to them: Go to the village which is opposite you and you will find a <tethered> ass and a colt with her. Loose them and bring them to me.*[†]

[†]Mt 21:1f

These two disciples whom the Lord sent—what do they signify? They are the ones who go before his face into every place and village to which he is to come. For so you have in the Gospel of Luke: *Jesus appointed another seventy-two disciples and sent them two by two before his face into every city and place in which he was to come.*†

†Lk 10:1

21. Perhaps therefore these two signify those two things which everywhere go before his face, of which the Psalmist speaks: *Mercy and truth go before his face.*† His face signifies his presence, the presence of his mercy, the presence of our salvation through his coming. This face of his, this coming of his, mercy and truth go before in order to bring an ass and a colt to him. I think that the ass and colt we can, not inappropriately, take to mean the whole of human nature, body and soul: the body the ass because of slowness and heaviness, the soul the colt because of lightness and mobility.

†Ps 88:15 [89:14]

22. *Mercy and truth* lead *the ass and the colt* to the Son of God because, in order that *the Word might be made flesh and dwell among us,*† *mercy and truth went out to meet him.*† Mercy and truth bring the ass and the colt to the Son of God, for without doubt mercy and truth caused the Son of God to assume an integral humanity, both body and soul. Mercy did not do it alone, for without truth it could not do it. Nor did truth do it alone, for without mercy it would not do it. 23. Again, it was both mercy and truth that caused the Son of God to have both the ass and the colt, both body and soul: truth, because he promised [it] to the Jews; mercy, for this is what he wanted to show the pagans. Therefore, very fittingly he

†Jn 1:14
†Ps 84:11 [85:10]

sent these two in advance, because before his coming, he had promised them to the Jews by an oath, as it were in truth, and this mercy he intended to show to the nations. The Apostle brings this out clearly: *For I declare that Jesus Christ was the minister of the circumcision because of the truth of God, confirming the promises to the Fathers; the nations however honor God because of his mercy.*† †Rm 15:8–9

24. Therefore *mercy and truth went out to meet him.*† And *Truth rose up out of the earth,*† and, †Ps 84:11 [84:10] assuming an ass and a colt, a body and a soul, came to Jerusalem. He came to visit his Church. He came to save it. This surely he could not have done save in this way—as we have said, seated on an ass and a colt. Nor ought one set aside his words: *Loose them.*† Although the body-and-soul †Mt 21:2 which the Son of God assumed was never bound by sin—for from the moment he was created man he was certainly perfect God—nevertheless, since until that time, human nature in all men and women had been bound by the chains of sin, therefore, in our Lord—in whom it was always free—it is not inappropriately said to be loosed. 25. If, however, we wish to say that mercy and truth freed the most blessed Mary from whom he was born, both in body and in soul from every bond of sin before he was conceived in her, so that this is would be to loose the ass and colt and bring them to Jesus: to cleanse the body and soul of his most blessed mother from all sin and so to impregnate her with the Son of God—either one or the other interpretation I think fits the passage here.

26. We have heard how Jesus came to his Church, namely, in accord with the body and soul which

he assumed. For according to his divinity he could neither come nor go, for he is everywhere present. But what is the signification of the clothes with which the disciples covered the animals on which the Son of God sat? The evangelist says that *they brought an ass and colt to him and covered them with their clothes and made him sit on them.*† 27. How could he sit on both of them? Prescinding from the literal, we are compelled to investigate the spiritual sense. Respecting that other sense based on another [level of] meaning by which the two animals signify two peoples—the Jews and the Gentiles; respecting that interpretation, I say, we say that he came to Jerusalem on both animals because he presented himself to his Church, to his faithful, in a human nature which he had totally assumed—that is, in a rational mind and a body.

†Mt 21:7

28. But what do these clothes signify? Perhaps these are those clothes by which the older and younger sons of Noah covered *the shame of their father* while they averted their own faces. Brothers, this is *a great sacrament.*† But because we have a lot to do today, I will say briefly that these clothes signify the faith and the teaching of the apostles and the prophets through which the humanity of Christ, as it were, a kind of weakness, hides knowledge of the divinity. Those who have believed and preached that Jesus is only a human being and not God have left naked the ass and colt on which Jesus sat. 29. They leave his humanity naked, but the faith and the teaching of the apostles and the prophets do not leave it naked, because by their preaching they have covered his weakness, which the infidels scorned, with the strength of divinity. As Isaiah says: *Behold*

†Eph 5:32

a virgin shall conceive and shall bear a son.† *Behold a man.*† But lest this man be thought weak and little, he immediately adds: *His name will be called Emmanuel, which is interpreted God with us.*† So Paul, although he spoke of his weakness: *He was made obedient unto death,*† added a little later: *The Lord Jesus is in the glory of God the Father.*†

†Is 7:14
†Jn 19:5
†Is 7:14; Mt 1:23
†Phil 2:8
†Phil 2:11

30. *Many from the crowd spread their clothes on the route. Others cut down branches from the trees and cried out: Hosanna to the Son of David.*† First we are told how Jesus came to Jerusalem; now we are told how Jerusalem—that is, the holy Church—responded to his coming. The Church went before and the Church followed after his coming.† 31. For the Church is not only this assembly of the faithful that believes in Christ after his coming, but all the holy—from the just Abel to the last just person to be in this world—belong to the holy Church. From all of them is formed that one Church to which is said: *One is my dove.*† But one part went before his coming: Abel, Noah, Abraham, David and the rest of the holy. Another part followed it: apostles, martyrs, confessors and all the faithful, among whom by his mercy we too are numbered.

†Mt 21:8–9
†The rest of Sermon Two is virtually identical with the concluding part of Sermon One, beginning from paragraph 47.
†Sg 6:8

32. Of all these some laid down their garments at Jesus' feet, others [laid down] the branches of trees. Those who laid down branches reject all the glory of the world for Christ's sake. For what are the riches and glory of this world but the leaves and branches of trees which thrive in summer and wither in winter? Surely all the glory of the world flourishes, so to speak, in prosperity, but in adversity, especially at the person's death, when winter weather comes—that is, the

final condemnation—it becomes worthless and squalid. 33. But blessed is the person who spreads such things at Jesus' feet by giving them to the poor. They are, as it were, his feet—that is, his weak members. More blessed still is the person who can spurn his own garments for Christ and lay them under his feet. For what is our garment if not the body by which our soul is somehow clothed or covered? Blessed is the person who can scorn his very members, his own body, for Christ and dedicate all the actions of his body to God's service.

34. Those who went before the Lord's coming, no less than those who followed it, did both. For the holy Fathers in the Old Testament made nought of the world's riches and glory on account of the faith they had in Christ's coming. Many even subjected their bodies to martyrdom, like the first martyr Abel, like Isaiah, like the Maccabean martyrs. 35. Nor is it only a matter of one here and there. Who can count the thousands of persons who did all this after his coming? You, too, belong to their number. For you have thrown down the branches of trees—that is, all the world's pomp—to worship and honor Christ. What is more, you have scorned your very bodies for him. Going further still, your very soul you have spent in Christ's honor, for you have given up your own will, the will of your soul.

36. Now all *who went before and all who followed cried out: Hosanna to the Son of David, blessed is he who comes in the name of the Lord.*[†Mt 21:9; Mk 11:9] This is great faith, great witness, great praise. *Hosanna* is the utterance of someone asking for salvation, as if to say: *Make safe.*[†Interpretatio 62 (CCSL 72:137, 29) et passim] Without doubt, the One from whom they ask salvation they proclaim the

Saviour. This is uniquely a divine attribute. They call him Son of David and proclaim him true man. They bless him because he *comes in the name of the Lord*,† and thereby they show clearly that he is the one who God the Father promised through the prophets would come. 37. In this faith the Church receives the coming of the Son of God. It believes that he is true God, true man, true Saviour of the world, promised by God the Father, foretold by the holy prophets. In this faith both those who went before his coming and those who follow it agree and are united and are one Church. In this faith both are saved. Anyone without this faith is outside the Church. To them Christ did not come and therefore they are not saved [in Christ]. Enough about the first coming.

†Mt 21:9

38. Yet you ought to know, brothers, that in the same form in which he came the first time to redeem his Church, he will come a second time to glorify his Church That is what the angels told the apostles after the Lord's ascension: *He will come just as you have seen him going into heaven.*† This, brothers, will crown the doom of the wicked. For not without the utmost dismay and sorrow shall they be able to see in such glory and power the One whom they despised in human weakness.

†Ac 1:11

39. The account which the other evangelists also give of the entry into Jerusalem is quite appropriate to this second coming of the Lord. For as Jesus came to Jerusalem *the children of the Hebrews took branches of olive and palm and came to meet him.*† So it will be at the Lord's second coming. For when he comes to glorify his Church and *present it* utterly perfect, *without spot or wrinkle*,† then indeed *the children of the Hebrews will come to meet him* with palms and

†Jn 12:12–13; cf. Hesbert 3:4415

†Eph 5:27

olive branches. 40. These are the children of whom David says: *Children, praise the Lord.*[†Ps 112 [113]:1] And elsewhere: *The Lord keeps watch over little ones.*[†Ps 114 [115]:6] Not over the great and the exalted and the proud does he keeps watch but over the little, that is, the humble. They it is who praise the Lord, provided they are Hebrews, that is, *those who leap.*[†Interpretatio 35 (CCSL 72:103, 16) *et passim*.] If now they are humble, if now they forego the deeds and the vices of the flesh, if now they know how to take leaps through contemplation and good thoughts, then surely on the day of judgement, when Jesus comes in his power, they will come to meet him with palms—that is, with the insignia of the victories which they have won here over the devil. For palms signify victory. 41. Then they can, as it were, with palms, glory and say: *Death, where is your victory? Death, where is your sting?*[†1 Co 15:55] Then they will come with olive branches, which signify peace. At present they do not have peace, fighting as they do with the devil, with the world and vices and with their own flesh. But then there will be perfect peace, true tranquility, when the flesh will not resist the spirit nor the spirit [resist] God, nor will the devil attack, nor will death or any weakness ever weigh them down.

42. If we wish to have this peace at the Lord's second coming, let us welcome his first coming *with faith and love.*[†1 Tim 1:14] Let us persevere in those tasks which he showed us and taught us, nourishing within us his love and the genuine desire by which we may run out to meet him as perfected humans[†Eph 4:13] when he comes to judge the world,
who lives and reigns
with the Father and Holy Spirit,
God throughout all ages.
Amen.

Sermon Three
FOR THE NATIVITY OF THE LORD

DO NOT BE AFRAID; I proclaim good news to you. There is great joy coming to the whole people. Today in the city of David there has been born to you the Saviour of the world—Christ the Lord.† The tidings which the angel announced to the world I should quite rightly lay before you today. Already *an edict has gone forth from our emperor, God*,† *that the whole world should be enregistered*. The whole globe is subject to our emperor—that is, to God. His officials have been dispatched throughout the world that all may be enregistered and a census taken. These officials are the apostles and the holy preachers whose *utterance has gone forth to every land and their words to the ends of the earth*.† 2. Just as that earthly emperor willed and ordered that the whole world be registered, that all might know that they belonged to the metropolitan city of Rome and might pay tribute to him—that is, *the silver coin bearing his image*.† In the same way our Emperor, who has already made the whole world his own, wills that everyone should register in that city *which is above, is free and is the mother of us all*.† That city of which the prophet says: *Glorious things of you are spoken, city of God*.† This city may well be called Rome, for the name means 'raised on high'.†

†Lk 2:10–11

†Lk 2:1

†Ps 18:5 [19:4]; Rm 10:18; Lk 2:1

†Mt 22: 19–20; Mk 12:15–16

†Gal 4:26, cf. Ps 86:7 [87:5], Hesbert 3:4936

†Ps 86 [87]:3

†*Interpretatio*, 79 (CCSL 72:159, 21)

3. Blessed is someone who welcomes this edict of his emperor to be registered in that city. For he participates in the joy which the angel proclaims today. The Lord has given *joy and gladness to his hearing*.† For he shares the company and the inheritance of those who heard this from the very source and origin of all true joy, the *Saviour of the world who was born today:*† *Rejoice, because your names have been written in the heavens.*† 4. But what is the silver coin which our Emperor demands of us? Doubtless it is our soul, which bears within itself his image. For God made us *to his image*† but this [image resides] in the soul. Blessed is someone who pays him this tribute, who gives him this silver coin, who restores his image to him. You see, brothers, throughout the world people racing to the officials of our Emperor to be considered worthy of being registered in that glorious city on high and to give back to him his image—that is, their souls. This they do each in his own city.†

5. We are all making our way to one and the same city, eager to be registered in it. But *as long as we are in the body we are exiles from the Lord*† and on our guard against our enemies; we are not all in one city nor do we all keep watch over ourselves in one place. Although holy Church is called and is in fact one city, there are various ways of life† in it—different cities, as it were—to which each declares [his membership]—that is, makes his profession.† 6. There are many who either cannot or will not observe chastity. In order not to fall a prey to their enemies through wantonness and fornication or impurity, they must be in a city where they may protect themselves. This city of theirs, in which they guard themselves

†Ps 50:10 [51:8]

†Lk 2:11
†Lk 10:2

†Gen 1:26

†Lk 2:3

†2 Co 5:6

†*Ordines*,: orders, vocations, states. See n. 15

†*Profiteor* (to declare), *professionem facere* (to make profession)

from those vices, is marriage. It is a city with many, although frail, inhabitants. Then there are the celibates, who decide to observe chastity. Some of them chose one city, some another. Some chose solitude, others a cloister. Some apply themselves more to fasting, some especially to vigils, while some tame the pride of the flesh by hard work every day and some extinguish their vices by heartfelt contrition and abundant tears.

7. Let us take a look at ourselves and our city. Our way of life[†] is a strongly fortified city surrounded on all sides by sound observances which, like walls and towers, rise up to prevent our enemy from deceiving us and enticing us away from our Emperor's army. What a wall poverty is! How well it defends us against the pride of the world, against harmful and ruinous vanities and superfluities. What a tower silence is! It repels the assaults of contention, quarreling, dissension, and detraction. What about obedience, humility, cheap clothing? What about a restricted diet? They are walls, they are towers against vices, against the attacks of our enemies. 8. In this city we declare ourselves, not Romans, but angelic beings. For these observances demonstrate that we belong to the fellowship of the angels and are not among the slaves of the Romans. When we make profession of this way of life the words of Isaiah are fulfilled: *They shall beat their swords into ploughshares and their spears into sickles.*[†] Then he goes on: *Nation shall not lift sword against nation nor ever again be trained for war.*[†]

[†]*Ordo,* which came to be used as monastic 'order'.

[†]Is 2:4

[†]Ibid.

9. There are two nations which sacred Scripture frequently mentions: one, that of the elect; the other, that of the reprobate. The nation of

reprobates is the kingdom of the devil and *it is a kingdom divided against itself*.† Therefore that nation never enjoys peace within itself. They are always fighting, destroying one another either physically or spiritually. This nation used sometimes to lift its sword against the other nation, when the earthly city of the reprobate persecuted God's Church—killing and massacring the holy martyrs of Christ, that is. 10. This does not happen now. Open persecution of that sort has ceased. Then, out of fear, many did not dare to declare themselves Christians. Now those who belong to that city on high confidently make their way to it and declare themselves on the census as the great Emperor, their God, demands of them. For at the present time *nation does not lift the sword against nation*. You can easily see many *beating their swords into ploughshares and their spears into sickles*.

†Mt 12:25–26; Lk 11:17

11. Everyday this is being fulfilled literally, not in the treacherous nation which neither does nor has nor shall enjoy peace, but in the race of the just which is blessed. Do you not see men, nobles in the world, experiencing conversion [to monastic life], laying down *their spears and swords* and earning their food by manual labor like peasants? But this is better, more obviously and more fully understood as being fulfilled in a spiritual way among every class, poor as well as rich, clerical as well as lay.

12. Let us think about the sword of which the Lord said: *Everyone who takes up the sword will perish by the sword*† and the ploughshares by which the earth of our heart is broken, in accordance with the text: *Rend your hearts and not your garments*.† And we shall see at the present

†Mt 26:52

†Jl 2:13

time countless persons changing *their swords into ploughshares*. The sword is wrongdoing. With this sword a person wounds himself before he does anyone else; as Saint Augustine says: 'Every person who is a wrongdoer harms himself before he harms anyone else because, even before he injures the other person, by making up his mind to injure someone else he injures himself, slaying himself with the sword of wrongdoing.'[†] This is the sword of which the Lord says to Peter: *Everyone who takes up the sword will perish by the sword.*[†]

[†]Source unknown.
[†]Mt 26:52

13. How many there are, brothers, who at the present time are beating this sword of wrongdoing into the ploughshare of compunction! Many who have previously killed their soul with the sword of sin now rend their heart by the compunction of penance. Many today are also changing their spears—that is, the subtlety of their wits by which they used to drag many others down into sin with them—into sickles with which they are reaping a spiritual harvest so that they may come to meet the Lord *bearing in their hands*[†] the sheaves of justice and salvation.

[†]Cf Ps 125 [126]:6

14. With good reason then on this day and in this season we commend to you the tidings which the angel proclaimed. And what are these tidings? *Today in the city of David the Saviour of the world has been born to you.*[†] The herald of the Saviour's birth does well to recommend joy. For the joy of salvation is true joy. And the birth of the Saviour does indeed bring us the joy of salvation. We should then rejoice with great joy at what we are told today by the angel, that today the Saviour has been born to us.

[†]Lk 2:11

15. But, dearest brothers, not everyone relishes[†] these tidings. Neither Herod nor the scribes and pharisees relished them. Instead, when they heard them they were dismayed and many others with them. Not even now does everyone relish them. There are many today who relish more the perishable delicacies of the belly than the imperishable delights of the mind. There are many today who take greater joy in a bottle than in Christ's birth. With their ears they hear these tidings but they fail to understand them. For they lack the interior ears which are called for by him who said: *Let him who has ears to hear, hear.*[†] But to you these tidings are well spoken, for you have both ears to hear and a healthy palate to taste. 16. You stay alert keeping the night watches over your flock. Whereas those who make it their business to drain cup after cup to get drunk and revel in wantonness do not keep alert by night because they are weighed down by the sleep of idleness and the wine of drunkenness. As the Apostle says: *It is at night that sleepers sleep and at night that drunkards get drunk.*[†] The night is their day because they do the *works of darkness. Their foolish heart is plunged in darkness.*[†] The brightness of God has shone around you, however, as native sons of the city of daylight who imitate the blessed shepherds of which the Gospel speaks.

17. As I said, you stay alert, keeping the night watches over your flock. You are always on your guard and endeavor to make all your actions pleasing to God. And so indeed it should be. Night time is when that *roaring lion prowls around* Christ's sheepfolds, *looking for someone to devour.*[†] If he finds the shepherds asleep he seizes his prey from their flocks and what he seizes he drags off to

[†] *Sapere*, translated below as 'cherish'.

[†] Mt 2:15. et passim.

[†] 1 Th 5:7

[†] Rm 1:21

[†] 1 P 5:8

death. Therefore let us stay alert and keep watch over our flock.

18. Our flock is our good attachments† and our good thoughts. These are the flocks over which we must keep watch to keep the enemy from having his way with them and robbing us of them, scattering and routing them. To watch over one's flock is to keep a solicitous guard over all one's thoughts, words, and deeds so that they will not incur any fault in any way whatever. It is likewise to keep guard over the senses—that is, sight, hearing, taste, smell, and touch—so that that wicked thief will not steal them or drag them off. 19. He steals sight when through inattention we sin by heedless looking; he drags it off when by force of pleasure he compels us to sin. Similarly he steals the hearing when he entices us, almost without our knowing it, to listen to vanities and idle words; he drags it off when by force of pleasure he impels it to useless trifles. He steals the taste when, all unawares, we let him deceive us through ill-ordered desires of the palate; he drags it off when we surrender to the cravings of our gullet in full awareness. It is the same with the other senses.

†Attachments translates *affectus*. Cf. Bernard, *Sermo de diversis* 17.8 (SBOp 6:156, 7–8)

20. These are the flocks about which the Bridegroom—that is, Christ—says to the Bride—that is, the Church or a holy soul—in the song of Songs: *Your hair is like a flock of goats*.† The hairs of our soul are the subtle thoughts issuing from the rational mind, which is, as it were, the head of the soul.† Hairs grow on our head and fall out without our being aware of them. In the same way, surely, thoughts often come and go without our being aware of them. When our hair

†Sg 6:4

†Cf. Bede, *On the Song of Songs* 4.6.4–5 (CCSL 119B:304, 202–207)

is cut we feel no pain. In the same way when we reject superfluous thoughts we feel joy rather than sorrow. 21. In holy souls these thoughts are compared to a flock of goats which feeds on the mountains with head erect, because the thoughts of the holy always feed on heavenly things and raise themselves towards heaven, carrying out the Apostle's bidding: *Seek the things that are above*[†Col 3:1] and so on. That goats are to be understood as our bodily senses is indicated by the same Song of Songs in the words: *If you do not know yourself, most beautiful of women, go forth and follow in the footsteps of your flock and feed your goats.*[†Sg 1:7] Because it is undoubtedly true that to take one's eyes off oneself, refusing to consider oneself—that is, one's own infirmity—but trying instead to watch and judge the lives of others, is indeed to leave the fellowship of Christ's sheep and feed one's bodily senses with the evil pleasures of sin.

22. But because you follow the example of those shepherds and stay alert to keep watch over your flock, you are still told today what they were told by the angel then and what we said to you at the beginning of this sermon. Listen to it therefore and heed it with spiritual joy: *Be not afraid.*[†Lk 2:10] You are rightly told: *Be not afraid*. But why? Because you are to love. For you have just and manifest reason why you should love rather than fear. 23. Before this day we had to fear. Before this day we had a Creator who was Lord, a Judge who was God. It was only right to fear him, our Creator, because we, his creatures, so greatly wronged him. In the person of the first man we scorned him, not wanting to be subject to him but, following the devil's advice, we tried to become his equals. *You will be like gods*, he said, *knowing good and evil.*[†Gen 3:5] We

had good reason to fear our Lord whom we had offended as wicked servants. We had good reason to fear God's judgment since we had no adequate means of expiating so great a sin.

24. Before this day the human person had no secure grounds for rejoicing except insofar as he realized or believed this day would come. But today you are told: *Be not afraid,* but love. Be not sad, but rejoice. Look, here is an angel from heaven, proclaiming a great joy to you. Rejoice then for yourself and rejoice also for others, because this joy is not only for you but for *all people.* Behold, he says, *I announce to you a great joy which will be for all people.*† O what a joy, how great, how sweet, how desirable! 25. Until now you were sad because you were dead, but now rejoice because life has come to you that you may live. You were sad because blindness had plunged you into darkness, but now rejoice, because today *a light has arisen in the darkness for the upright of heart.*† You were sad because you were wretched but now there has been born One who is *compassionate and merciful,*† enabling you to enter into blessedness. You were sad because you were weighed down by the accumulation of your sins but now rejoice because *today the Saviour has been born who will save his people from their sins.*† This is the joy which the angel proclaims. The Saviour has been born today.

†Lk 2:10

†Ps 111 112]:4; cf. Ps 96 [97]:11

†Lk 2:2; Ps 3:4

†Lk 2:2; Mt 1:21

26. Until now you have feared the One who created you; now love the One who will heal you. Until now you have feared your Judge; now love your Saviour. *A Saviour,* he says, *has been born to you today.*† Who is this, what is he like? Listen: *Who is Christ the Lord.* The greek word *'chrisma'*

†Lk 2:2

means 'anointing' and from it is derived 'Christ' which means 'Anointed'.† This is how our Saviour comes; he comes as Christ, as the Anointed. For he is like *a bridegroom coming forth from his nuptial chamber*† and he has come forth anointed the better to please his bride. But with what is he anointed? Listen: *God, your God, has anointed you with the oil of gladness more than your companions. Your robes are all fragrant with myrrh and aloes and cassia.*†

†*Interpretatio* 66 (CCSL 72:142, 170

†Ps 18:6 [19:5]

†Ps 44:8–9 [45:7–8]; cf. Heb 1:9

27. Behold the stone which holy Jacob anointed with oil. This *stone*, today *hewn from the mountain without human hands*†—that is, born of the Virgin without man's intervention—came forth anointed with the oil of exultation. And it is truly the oil of exultation because he *has exulted like a giant to run his course.*† He exulted and he ran it. He showed us first of all in himself what he commands us to do through his Apostle. The Apostle says: *There should be no reluctance, no sense of compulsion because the Lord loves a cheerful giver.*† So he himself, the first anointed with the oil of exultation, entered upon the way by which he saved us not reluctantly or under compulsion, but out of his own generous will and with great exultation. 28. Rightly then [is he called] Christ, because *he is anointed with the oil of gladness more than his companions*. By his companions are meant all the saints who share his name, called Christians because he is called Christ. This is true also of the saints of the Old Testament; although they did not really bear the name Christian they are not deprived of the reality which the name signifies. They were all anointed with the oil of gladness to which the Apostle refers when he says: *Rejoicing in hope*.† Yet since everyone finds in himself some

†Dan 2:34–45

†Ps 18:8 [19:5]

†2 Co 9:7

†Rm 12:12

element of sin to give grounds for sadness, he who was entirely free from sin is rightly said to be *anointed with the oil of gladness more than his companions.*

29. *Your robes*, he says, *are all fragrant with myrrh and aloes and cassia.*† O Christ, O Anointed, O how fragrant these garments of yours are! His garments are the members of the body he assumed for us. *The Word was made flesh.*† There is myrrh, there is aloes, there is cassia. Oh how fragrant are the ointments of our Anointed. He who in himself was life immortal for our sake has become mortal. Hence myrrh. He who by the presence of his divinity fills all things for our sake *emptied himself taking on the form of a slave.*† Hence aloes. He before whom the angels tremble *humbled himself, becoming obedient unto death— even death on a cross.*† Hence cassia. 30. Myrrh, which is used to anoint dead bodies, signifies mortality. Aloes, which is collected in small drops, signifies the emptying-out which made him for our sake *a little less than the angels.*† Cassia, a humble plant or tree but fragrant, signifies his humility; its fragrance has spread throughout the world. Rightly therefore [are you called] Christ, rightly the Anointed, rightly *oil poured out. That is why the maidens have come to love you*† whom previously they feared. They have caught the scent of this fragrance of your ointments.

†Ps 44:9 [45:8]

†Jn 1:14

†Ph 2:7

†Ph 2:8

†Ps 8:6[5]; Heb 2:9

†Sg 1:2–3

31. Come then, brothers, let us rub these ointments on our heart by assiduous meditation. Let us ponder how sweet the myrrh of his mortality should be to us—by it he has set us free from all mortality; how sweet his abasement— it raises us up to the heavens; how sweet his

humility—by it are we exalted. Let us reflect on how Christ stooped down for our sake. Look at these wonders: at the approach of death Christ is sad, while Paul is happy;† Christ weeps at the death of his friend Lazarus† while that mother of the Maccabees does not weep at the grisly death of her seven sons;† *John the Baptist came neither eating nor drinking, Christ came eating and drinking and* was called *a glutton and a wine-bibber.*†

†Mt 26:37–38; 2 Tim 4:6–8 et passim.

†Jn 11:35

†2 Mc 7:20
†Mt 11:18–19; cf. Lk 7:33–34

†Non sapiunt

32. You do not cherish† these things, whether you are Jew or pagan; you do not cherish them. You do not notice any fragrance. Indeed, these are the grounds on which the pagan accuses us of folly and the Jew takes scandal.† Why is it that you fail to cherish these things, why do you not notice the fragrance? It is not because they lack fragrance and the odor of sweetness but because you yourself are insensitive, because you yourself are foul-smelling. For me certainly your sadness, Lord Jesus, is more to be cherished than all the world's gladness. To me the tears that you shed at the death of your friend are sweeter than the stoic endurance of the philosophers who would have the sage left unmoved by any emotion. More agreeable to me indeed is the smell of your food and drink in the midst of sinners and tax-gatherers than the rigid abstinence of the pharisees. Certainly the *fragrance of your ointments surpasses all scents.*†

†1 Co 1:23

†Sg 4:10

33. How I cherish seeing the Lord of majesty showing himself—so far as bodily exertion and human emotion are concerned—not like the strong but like the weak. What a comfort it is to me in my weakness! Indeed, this weakness of my Lord certainly brings me strength and

steadfastness in my weakness. For this reason you who are strong in religious observance and very quick to embrace all sorts of austerities should be warned not to judge rashly those whom you see tempering their rigor somewhat to the infirmities of the weak.

34. I am entrusted with the care of my brother's body and soul—for I do not love the whole man if I neglect anything belonging to either. If I see him suffering some distress, whether on account of the austerity of the food or of the work or of the vigils—if, I say, I see that he is tormented in body and tempted at heart—for it is extremely difficult for the mind not to be tempted when the flesh suffers grievously—if I see him in such affliction and, *although provided with the goods of this world, I shut up my heart against him, how can it be said that God's love dwells in me?*† 35. Surely, if I always conduct myself according to the rigor of the strong and do not on occasion accommodate myself to the infirmities of the weak, I am running not *in the fragrance of Christ's ointments* but in the harshness of the pharisees. They vaunted themselves on their rigorous abstinence and condemned the disciples of the Lord, indeed the Lord himself, calling him a glutton and a wine-bibber. What must certainly be guarded against is fostering self-indulgent relaxation under the guise of accommodation. Blessed Gregory's maxim must be observed: *observance without rigidity and compassion without relaxation.*†

†1 Jn 3:17

†Gregory the Great, *The Pastoral Rule*, ch. 6; PL 77:38A

36. Let us run, then, brothers, let us run *in the fragrance of* these *ointments* with which Christ is anointed. Let us run with the shepherds to our

Anointed, for what was said to them is said to us as well: *The Saviour of the world has been born for us today, who is Christ the Lord.*† With good reason 'the Lord' is added. If there is someone who because of the stench of his carnal vices cannot perceive this fragrance and therefore cannot love the Anointed—that is, Christ—let him at least fear the Lord. *For there is born to us today the Saviour of the world who is Christ the Lord, in the city of David.*† That is Bethlehem, to which we should run as did the shepherds when they heard these tidings. As you are accustomed to sing: *They sang glory to God and ran to Bethlehem.*†

†Lk 2:2

†Ibid.

†From the hymn *Mysterium Ecclesiae*, verse 6 (PL 17:1202)

37. *Now this*, they were told, *is a sign to you: you will find a baby wrapped in swaddling clothes and lying in a manger.*† Notice what I have said: that you ought to love. You fear the Lord of the angels, but love the little Child. You fear the Lord of majesty, but love the babe wrapped in swaddling clothes. You fear Him reigning in heaven, but love Him lying in the manger. But what sign did the shepherds receive? *You will find a baby wrapped in swaddling clothes and lying in a manger.*† This sign meant that he is the Saviour, that he is the Christ, that he is the Lord. 38. But is there anything great about being wrapped in swaddling clothes and lying in a stable? Are other children not wrapped in swaddling clothes? What does this sign mean then? It means a great deal if only we understand it. We do understand it if we do not merely hear these tidings but also have in our hearts the light which appeared with the angels. He appeared with light when these tidings were first proclaimed to make us realize that it is only those who have the spiritual light in their minds who truly hear.

†Lk 2:12

†Ibid.

39. Many things can be said about this sign, but since our time is short I will say only a little and that briefly. Bethlehem, *the House of Bread*,[†] is the holy Church in which the Body of Christ, the true Bread, is administered. What the manger is at Bethlehem the altar is in the Church. There are fed Christ's animals, of whom it is said: *Your animals shall dwell in it.*[†] This is the table of which it is written: *You have spread a table in my sight.*[†] In this manger Jesus is wrapped in swaddling clothes. The swaddling clothes are the sacramental veils. 40. In this manger, under the appearance of bread and wine, is the true Body and Blood of Christ. Christ is believed to be there, but wrapped in swaddling clothes—that is, not visible yet within the sacrament. There is no greater or more evident sign of Christ's birth than that we daily receive his Body and Blood at the holy altar, daily see immolated for us him who was once born for us of the Virgin.

[†] Jerome, Letter 108.10 (CSEL 55:316)

[†] Ps 67:11 [68:10]
[†] Ps 22 [23]:5

41. Therefore, brothers, let us hasten to the Lord's manger-crib, but as far as we can let us first by his grace prepare ourselves to approach it. Then in the company of the angels, *with a pure heart, a good conscience and an unfeigned faith*,[†] let us sing to the Lord in the whole of our life and our [monastic] conversion : *Glory to God on high and on earth peace to men of good will.*[†] Through the same Our Lord *Jesus Christ,*
        to whom be honor and glory
      through all the ages of ages.
            Amen.[†]

[†] 1 Tim 1:5

[†] Lk 2:14

[†] Rm 16:27

Sermon Four
For the Epiphany of the Lord

†Ps 111 [112]:4

†Ps 44:8 [45:7]; Heb 1:9

A FEW DAYS AGO, brothers, we informed you that *a light has arisen in the dark for the upright of heart,*† he who arose and was anointed by God the Father *with the oil of exultation more than his companions.*† But our comment was incapable of expressing the sweetness and the might of that anointing. Christ's might is such that no tongue can fully express it, no heart conceive of it as it deserves. But what human beings cannot do in words, God has shown forth in events. His kindness has been pleased to reveal his power to us today by a manifestation of events.

†Cf. Rm 1:14

2. The wise of this world deliver beautiful and ornate speeches on trifling matters—the victories of kings, the battles of the mighty, or indeed the course of the stars, even the site of the world. Our fishermen, however, set forth the great and wonderful deeds which they had come to know of God in few and simple words, but in witness to great events. For they realized that they were indebted not only to *the wise* but also to *the foolish,*† not only to the learned but also to the unlettered. And therefore they spoke simply, so everyone could understand, and they supported their statements with such obvious proofs that everyone could grasp them. 3. It behooves us to imitate them and so to choose our words as to

be useful to the simple so as to promote Christ's glory and further their progress.

We told you on another occasion that *Christ came into this world to save sinners.*† Now 'Christ' means 'Anointed'.† Today the force of this anointing has openly been made known. Christ has been born in Judea and immediately the fragrance of that anointing was perceived by men who were in Chaldea. There was fulfilled in our Lord what the Apostle later said of himself and those like him: *We are a pleasant odor to God in every place; for some an odor of life, bringing life, for others an odor of death, bringing death.*†

†1 Tm 1:15
†*Interpretatio* 66 (CCSL 72:142, 17)

†2 Co 2:14–16

4. This has happened today to Christ himself, from whom every *pleasant odor* derives. For what does 'a pleasant odor' mean if not a good report? And what report could be better or more charming than that a little child lying in a manger is God and Lord and the whole world's salvation? This report the pagans heard, as did the Jews. At first the Jews were alive and the pagans dead, but as soon as both perceived this odor the pagans came to life again while the Jews died. For the pagans this odor was life-bearing; for the Jews, death-bearing. 5. For as soon as the kings of which the Gospel speaks learned of the Lord's birth through the star which they had seen in the East, they came with gifts to adore him; while as soon as Herod heard the report of him he plotted with the Jews how to kill him. Then there began in Israel that blindness of which the Apostle says: *Blindness has fallen in part on Israel.*† Then also began to shine that light which the Lord had promised through the prophet to his Church which he was to assemble from the

†Rm 2:25

nations: *Rise up, be enlightened, Jerusalem, for your light has come.*†

†Is 60:1

6. This is the Jerusalem which the Lord Jesus, who is the true and highest peace, is building up out of living stones, the Jerusalem that aspires to the vision of him and believes with utter certainty that it shall find its happiness in that vision. It is holy Church, it is each and every holy gathering, each and every holy soul. This is not new to you. *Rise up*, he said, *be enlightened, Jerusalem*. Rightly is it told: *Rise up*, for it was lying prostrate. Rightly is it told, *Be enlightened*, for it was blind. 7. It was lying prostrate, blind, in darkness, in error, in sin. Therefore it is told: *Rise up*, because he who would raise it up had already stooped down. It is told: *Be enlightened*, because he who would enlighten it was already present. What else does that new star proclaim from the heavens but *Rise up, be enlightened?* The sign of the Lord's birth has appeared in the heavens so that we may rise from the love of earthly things to heaven. And this sign takes the form of a star so that we may know that by his birth we shall be enlightened.

8. But to whom did this star cry out? Not to the Jews, they were blind. Not to bloodthirsty Jerusalem. As soon as it heard of the presence of peace it fell into an uproar and, having lost its peace, sought to kill peace itself. No, doubtless it was to that Queen of the East who hastened *from the ends of the earth to hear the wisdom of Solomon*† whose name means 'Peacemaker'.† And so she is Jerusalem—which means 'Vision of Peace'†—because she came to see the Peacemaker. 9. This queen stands for the Church of the Pagans, for the queen herself was a pagan. The Church is without

†Mt 12:42, Lk 2:31; 1 K 10:1

†*Interpretatio* 63 (CCSL 72:138, 5)

†*Interpretatio* 50 (CCSL 72:121, 9–10) *et passim*

any doubt a queen, reigning as she does over so many nations and peoples. It is of her that David says: *The queen stands at your right hand, arrayed in cloth-of-gold.*† Today this Church begins to be born in [the person of] these pagans who saw the star and understood its significance. Therefore this queen has come today *from the ends of the earth to see the face* of him of whom it is said: *Behold someone greater than Solomon is here.*†

†Ps 44[45]:9

†Mt 12:42; Lk 2:31; 2 Ch 9:23

10. Truly he is *greater than Solomon*, for Solomon was merely the Peacemaker, while this is a Peacemaker who is Peace itself. As the Apostle says: *He is our peace. He has made both [peoples] one.*† So it is that this, our queen, is appropriately called Jerusalem, that is *vision of peace*, because he hastens to her. And this queen of ours is also beautifully called the queen of Sheba.† Now, Sheba means captivity.† 11. Clearly the Church is the queen of Sheba because she organizes and governs well the captivity in which we journey far from that kingdom in which there is no captivity, no unhappiness. That kingdom she will receive on the day of judgment when the Lord says: *Come, you blessed of my Father, receive the kingdom which has been prepared for you.*† And so on. This queen—that is, the holy Church of the Gentiles—before today was lying prostrate; until today she was blind. But today she is told: *Rise up, be enlightened.*

†Eph 2:14

†Cf. 1 K 10:1ff.
†*Interpretatio* 66 (CCSL 72:142, 5) *et passim*

†Mt 25:34

12. Today in [the person of] these three pagan kings she has risen up from that evil routine, from that unclean bed on which she played the harlot with demons. For she used to adore idols, images, and demons. Now she has begun to desire *the most comely among the sons of men*†—that is,

†Ps 44:3 [45:2]

the face of the true *Solomon*. Until today she was blind, but today she has raised her eyes to that wonderful star, as if hearing, *Draw near to him and be enlightened.*† She has begun to seek that true light *which enlightens everyone coming into this world.*† It seems to me that today God is saying: *Let there be light. And light was made.*†

†Ps 33:6 [34:5]

†Jn 1:9
†Gen 1:3

13. He had previously *created heaven and earth, but the earth was waste and empty and there was darkness over the face of the abyss.*† Holy Simeon, who recognized the infant Lord, was heaven. Holy Anna, the prophetess, was heaven. Heaven was Zachary and Elizabeth and those others among the Jews who were spiritually minded. The three kings who, we have said, stand for the holy Church, were still earth. They were earth, they relished nothing but earth. *This earth was empty and destitute,*† empty of truth, destitute of every good work. *There was darkness, too, over the face of the abyss.*† 14. The abyss is the soul on account of the vast depths of its nature. The face of the abyss is the mind. There was darkness over the face of the abyss: the darkness of error, the darkness of heathendom, the terrifying darkness of unbelief. But today those who were earth are told to rise up, those who had darkness over the face of their abyss are told to be enlightened. 'Let there be light' is the same as 'Be enlightened'. When the heathen are enlightened by faith and the knowledge of God, they become light and they hear Paul say: *Once you were darkness but now you are light in the Lord.*†

†Gen 1:1–2

†Gen 1:2

†Gen 1:2

†Eph 5:8

15. But from where does this light come to them? *Rise up*, he says, *be enlightened, Jerusalem, for your light has come*. This is the whole reason

why the holy Church is enlightened, first in those three kings and afterwards in all nations. This is the whole reason—what is said to her through the Prophet: *Because your light has come.*† For *a light has arisen in the darkness.*‡ But for whom? Not for the perverse of heart who remain in their darkness, but for the upright of heart who recognize the light and long to adore.

†Is 60:1
‡Ps 111 [112]:4

16. [The heart that is] empty and a waste is told to rise up—that is, to prepare itself for the things of heaven that are to be desired. And as if to someone who answers: 'I do not see what things of heaven, what things of the spirit I ought to desire', is added: *Be enlightened.* And look how beautifully the two testaments agree in these two lesson—from the prophet and from the Gospel— which are read in the Church today. We explicitly see the Gospel in the prophecy and the prophecy in the Gospel, like a wheel within a wheel.† 17. In the prophecy the holy Church of the Gentiles is told: *Rise up, be enlightened, for your light has come.* In the Gospel the story is told of how there appeared to the same Church of the Gentiles a new star in the heavens which bade it raise itself from the things of earth and invited it to the true light newly born. In the prophecy, *And the glory of the Lord has arisen over you*† is added; in the Gospel is told the story of how the star in which the Lord's glory appeared plainly arose over the kings who then represented the holy Church. But this is the literal sense.

†Gregory the Great, *Homiliae in Ezechielem*, 6.15 (CCSL 142:75, 275–278 and 76–77, 319–325)

†Is 60:1

18. According to the spiritual sense what is meant when the holy Church is told: *For the glory of the Lord has arisen over you?* Before this time the carnal† Jews were glorifying the Lord, but all that

†*Carnales. Carnalis* is usually translated 'physical' here.

glory was beneath them, not beyond them. For all earthly and transitory things, all riches, all worldly honor are surely beneath the human person, not beyond him. But when those carnal Jews glorified the Lord they did so because the Lord promised them the good things of earth. 19. Therefore they had that glory of the Lord with which they glorified him as it were beneath them because the only reward they sought was a temporal one. But today the holy Church is told: *Rise up, for the glory of the Lord has arisen over you*, so that the children of holy Church may turn their heart from the things of the earth to those of heaven and may serve and glorify God not for the things of earth but for the things of heaven. But let us see what comes next in the prophecy and in the Gospel.

20. *For behold*, says the prophet, *darkness shall cover the earth and deep gloom the peoples.*† But the Church of the Gentiles is now told this as if it had been surprised that God showed concern for it and had replied to his previous statement: 'Why are you calling me now? In the beginning you cast me off and summoned the Jews to [do] your work, as it is written: *When the Most High divided the nations, when he separated out the children of Adam, he established the boundaries of the peoples according to the number of the children of Israel. But the Lord's portion was his people, his share of the inheritance was Jacob.*† Among that people there are prophets and just and holy persons pleasing to you. Why therefore are you now calling me?' he asks. 21. I will tell you why: *Because, behold, darkness shall cover the earth.* He calls the Jews 'the earth' because they appreciate and they crave nothing but the earth. This is the earth that darkness will cover, for, as the

†Is 60:2

†Dt 32:8–9

Apostle says: *Blindness in part has fallen on Israel until the full number of the Gentiles comes in.*† Today pagans receive the true light in the presence of which the Jews are struck blind. Now listen to how the Gospel speaks of this darkness and how it describes the Jews as stricken with blindness according to this prophecy.

†Rm 11:25

22. The three kings of whom we have spoken came to Jerusalem and asked: *Where is he who is born King of the Jews?*† As soon as Herod heard those words *he was dismayed.* Why, if not because he was earth and darkness covered the earth? He was afraid of losing his earthly kingdom and therefore when he heard that *a king of the Jews had been born he was dismayed* and blinded. Because all that he sought was an earthly kingdom, he thought that the newborn king would seek only an earthly kingdom. Not only *was Herod dismayed* but *all Jerusalem with him,* because *darkness was covering the earth and deep gloom the peoples.* 23. What was dismayed was the earthly Jerusalem that kills the prophets and stones them. But our mother, the spiritual Jerusalem, the holy Church of the Gentiles, was not dismayed but glad. Therefore the Prophet went on to say: *But over you the Lord will arise and his glory will be seen in you.*† First he said: *The glory of the Lord has risen over you.*† Now however he says: *But over you the Lord will arise and his glory will be seen in you.* And between these two he put this blinding of the carnal Jews. Consider how beautifully the Gospel agrees with this.

†Mt 2:2

†Is 60:2
†Is 60:1

24. Without doubt then the holy Church, whom the Prophet is here addressing, first saw the glory of God beyond itself in the person of the

three pagan kings, when the new star appeared to them announcing that God had been born. Afterwards, the moment they came to Jerusalem, the Jews showed such blindness that, although they considered the one who had been born the Christ, they nevertheless sought to kill him. And again, as soon as the kings left Jerusalem *the star which they had seen in the East went before them until it stood still over the place where the Child was.*†

†Mt 2:9

25. That, perhaps, is why, after the Prophet said of the Jews: *For behold darkness shall cover the earth and deep gloom the peoples*—which surely happened when *King Herod was dismayed and all Jerusalem with him*—he turned at once to our queen and said: *But over you the Lord will arise.* Without any doubt the star which these pagans saw over themselves signifies that our Lord, who had been born, would reign over the holy Church of the Pagans. *And his glory*, he says, *will be seen among you.*

26. Today, brothers, today for sure, the glory of the Lord is seen in the Church of the Gentiles. Was the great glory of the Lord not seen when kings adored that little child, poor and the son of a poor maiden, and offered him gifts? And yet, brothers, this is little in comparison with what is symbolized by the kings and their gifts. Call to mind now the queen of whom we spoke, who *came from the ends of the earth to see the face of Solomon and to hear his wisdom.*† She did not come with empty hands but offered Solomon extremely precious gifts. 27. In these three pagans notice what this queen symbolized, that is the holy Church of the pagans. She brings gifts and they bring gifts. Why? Doubtless the meaning is that throughout the world the holy Church

†Mt 12:42; Lk 2:31; cf. 2 Chr 9:23

was to offer spiritual gifts to our Lord Jesus Christ. Therefore the Prophet goes on to say: *And the nations shall walk in your light and kings in the splendor of your rising.*† Everywhere you see the nations walking in the light of the holy Church. What is the Church's light but that *which enlightens everyone coming into the world?*† 28. The holy Gospel is also the Church's light, like the brightest star shedding its light upon her and enabling her to go *from strength to strength*† so that she may come to Jesus and offer him gold, incense, and myrrh.† Gold stands for faith in his divinity, myrrh for faith in his humanity, incense for faith in the sacrifice which he offered for us to appease God the Father. These are the *gifts*, these are the *perfumes* which our queen, coming *from the ends of the earth*—that is, from all parts of the world—offers to the true Solomon.†

†Is 60:3

†Jn 1:9

†Ps 83:8 [84:7]

†Mt 2:11

†Mt 2:11; 12:42; Lk 11:31; 1 K 10:10

29. Each and every one of us was in Sheba— that is, in captivity. Indeed we were in captivity when we were in the world. We were captives to our vices, to our sins, to the power of the devil, bound with the chains of the worst habits. We were among the Chaldeans, whose name means 'like demons'.† 'Like demons' are those who are unwilling to go to perdition alone but deceive all [the others] they can and drag them into the vices in which they themselves are implicated. Among such [demons] were we, or rather many of us were. But there our soul heard: *Rise up, be enlightened, Jerusalem*. 30. There we heard the report of the true Solomon and we began to long to come to him. But because we were blind and paralyzed, lying prostrate in the desires of the flesh as on a cot, dissipated and sick and incapable of any good work and ignorant of the way *which*

†Ibid. 57

leads to life, each and every one of us had to be told: *Rise up*, so that we might walk; *be enlightened*, so that we might recognize the right way. It was when—through the grace of his visitation—God stirred us to indignation at our sins that he said: *Rise up*. It was when he inspired an attachment to worthy emulation that he said: *Be enlightened*.

31. But why is it that the soul is called Jerusalem while it is in darkness, lying prostrate in its sins, if not because it was destined to pass from agitation to peace? He called it Jerusalem so that by the sound of this name he might by hidden inspiration suggest to it the end to which it was created and the nature with which it was endowed; and so that realizing all this, it might blush at the stench of its vices and turn back in faith to him who is the peace and the glory of all his saints. It is to him that the guiding star leads us, proclaiming him and pointing him out. It proclaims him in its appearing and it points him out by going on ahead and standing still over the house where he is.

32. The star, brothers, the star which leads us to Jesus is sacred Scripture. Behold *our light has already come* because *for us and for our salvation God has become man. He was seen on earth and dwelt among men and women*, so that, by the might of his word and the example of his life he might enlighten *those who are sitting in darkness* and direct them *into the way of peace*.[†] It is no wonder that before the Lord's coming—when they had heard nothing of God, when they did not discern the light of Scripture—the pagans lay prostrate in their sins and in the darkness of their errors. 33. But now lying prostrate in carnal desires and in the darkness of iniquities is a [matter for] great

[†] Lk 1:79; Is 42:7. The Song of Zechariah (*Benedictus*) sung at Lauds.

agitation, *for the true light that enlightens every one coming into this world,* Christ Jesus, *has now come.*† We cannot have further excuse for our sins, for Christ, who takes away the sins of the world and justifies the wicked, now speaks to us openly. *Someone who follows me does not walk in darkness but will have the light of life.*† And what is the *way* by which he walks and *which leads to* him? Let him tell you himself: *Anyone who chooses to come after me must deny himself, take up his cross and follow me.*† The Apostle also points out the way that leads to Christ:, it is, he says, *through many tribulations that we must enter the kingdom of God.*† Again, the Lord tells us in the Gospel: *Blessed are the poor in spirit, for theirs is the kingdom of heaven.*† This is the way by which Jesus walked and by which we shall come to him: the renunciation of our own will, the imitation of Christ's passion, the hardships of the present life, and voluntary poverty. This is the way which sacred Scripture shows us and it is what was meant by the star, which, as we said, appeared to the three kings.

†Jn 1:9

†Jn 8:12

†Mt 16:24

†Acts 14:22; Jn 3:5

†Mt 5:3

35. Be kings, then, [brothers] and let your soul be queen, *the queen of Sheba.* For you are still in Sheba—that is, in captivity. And listen to what sort of captivity this is: *I observe that there is in my bodily members a different law, fighting against the law that my reason approves and making me a prisoner under the law of sin.*† This is Sheba. But control the movements of the flesh in yourselves, *lest sin reign in your mortal body,*† and you will be kings and your soul the queen of Sheba. Thus, with the Gospel of peace to lead you like a guiding star going on ahead, you travel the roads that lead to Christ.† Surely you will come to him and adore him. 36. Yet since it is not right to come

†Rm 7:23

†Rm 6:12

†Mt 2: 9–11

to Christ or to adore him empty handed, prepare your gifts for him. Offer him gold,—that is, true charity. Offer incense—that is, pure prayer. Offer myrrh—that is, mortification of your flesh. Gifts such as these will make God gracious to you, so that he himself will arise over you and his glory will appear in you.† May he deign to grant this, who lives and reigns
through all the ages of ages.
Amen.

† 1 Th 1:10

Sermon Five
For the Purification of Saint Mary

1 SEE YOU GATHERED, brothers, to refresh yourselves with the food *that abides*,[†] the nourishment of God's saving word. As the Lord says: *Heaven and earth will pass away, but the word of the Lord shall endure for all eternity.*[†] *This is the bread that comes down from heaven and gives life to the world.*[‡] You are asking for this bread like children of the Lord Jesus, of whom he himself says: *Allow the children to come to me, for to such as these belongs the kingdom of heaven.*[†] But so that you do not grow faint along the way,[‡] you come and ask to be refreshed, and refreshed with the bread which fills the mind rather than the stomach. May the Lord grant that there may be someone to portion it out to you and that it may not be said of us: *The children asked for bread but there was no one to portion it out for them.*[†] **2.** As it is up to you to ask for bread, so it is up to us to portion it out. We must apportion the bread which God has graciously provided for you on the journey of your pilgrimage so that you can arrive to enjoy the bread which he is keeping whole for you in your homeland with the angels. The bread for your pilgrimage is the mystery of Christ's incarnation, the truth of his teaching and the example of his humility and that of his faithful. The bread of your homeland, by which the angels are refreshed, is the face of God, participation in

[†] Jn 6:27

[†] Mt 24:35; Is 40:8; Ps 118 [119]:89

[‡] Jn 6:33

[†] Mk 10:14; Mt 19:14

[‡] Mt 15:32

[†] Lam 4:4

his divinity and possession of that joy *which eye has not seen, nor ear heard, nor has it entered into the human heart.*†

†1 Co 2:9

†Ps 77 [78]:25

3. So that you may desire this *bread of angels*† more avidly and hasten towards it more eagerly, the Gospel serves you today a [loaf of] bread which will give strength to your spirit along this *road of your exile.*† It sets before you the purification of the Mother of God, our Lady, holy Mary, and the oblation of the Saviour himself. This bread must be portioned out if it is to be eaten, because these matters must be explained if they are to be understood. 4. She purifies herself who gave birth to him who was entirely free from sin, indeed, who was himself capable of purifying the whole world. He offered a sacrifice for himself, who was the sacrifice for the whole world. Why did all this happen? In the first place, because it was not yet time for the Law of Moses to be set aside. Then again because he wanted to show that the Law of Moses was good, inasmuch as he himself *fulfilled it.*† Finally, he wanted to teach us to seek something spiritual in those bodily observances that the Jews carried out.

†1 K 19:8

†1 Tm 1:8

5. Why was it commanded that an infant be circumcised on this eighth day and that the child's mother enter the Temple after forty days, and then with her son and with a *sacrifice?*† Why was it also commanded that all men cut off a part of their flesh—and that very part of which a man is usually most embarrassed? Someone might consider such an observance unseemly, not holy, had the Lord himself not first commanded it down and afterwards carried it out. In fact, it was a holy observance because by this observance man

†Lv 12:1–8

was cleansed from original sin and it signified the faith which we have in the Lord Jesus, the faith by which we are cleansed from all sins. 6. Although there were many holy persons who did not come from *the loins of Abraham*—as, for example, holy Job, yet it was to the descendants of Abraham in particular that the commandment of circumcision was given. The fact that the men of Abraham's race cut away one part of that member by which men beget and are begotten in carnal corruption and pleasure signifies that the Lord Jesus would be born of his lineage but without any fleshly corruption or pleasure. And as those descendants of Abraham cut away that part of their flesh in which lustful pleasure is experienced most keenly, so we, the spiritual progeny of Abraham, ought to cut away all fleshly pleasure. And this [happens] *on the eighth day*. 7. Why? Because *on the eighth day* they were purified by this sacrament from the sin in which they were born through corruption, just as Our Lord, who was born of Abraham's race, by his resurrection on the eighth day—the morrow of the seventh, which is called the Sabbath—having shed all the infirmity of mortality and corruption, raised to immortality and incorruptibility the fleshly nature which he had taken from us and for us.

8. After circumcision there follows purification. Before circumcision both *the woman* and the child were *unclean*. After circumcision they were neither wholly clean nor wholly unclean. For if they were wholly clean they would not need purification or be forbidden to enter the Temple. Yet if they were not tainted with greater uncleanness before circumcision it would not be commanded that a woman who had given birth to an infant

be held to be unclean until the infant was circumcised.† Remember what we said about circumcision and let us portion out this bread in such a way that it will have a good flavor.

†Lv 12:2–4

9. It seems to me that this 'woman' stands for human nature, which by its vices and its sins is *unclean* and expelled from Paradise. There have been some who thought that they could be justified and come to God by their own strength, without faith in Christ. Many eminent philosophers believed this. But they were deluded. They begot sons—that is to say, they behaved manfully by abstinence and contempt of the world and physical continence. They begot sons because they had many disciples. But since they knew nothing of circumcision and the eighth day both those who begot and those who were begotten continued in their uncleanness. 10. So in them neither the mother—that is, human nature—nor the son—that is, their deeds—could possess any cleanness. Therefore the Lord taught us through Moses how this woman and her son ought to be purified. Circumcision on the eighth day is faith in Christ which pertains especially to his resurrection. He died in plain view of everyone. Therefore there is no merit in believing that he died. Merit lies in this: believing that he rose again, something which took place hiddenly. Through this faith we have justice and through this justice cleansing.

11. Therefore the Apostle says: *Christ was given up to death for our misdeeds and he rose for our justification.*† Until a person has this faith he is unclean and whatever he does is unclean, as the Apostle plainly says: *Everything which does not come from faith is sin.*† If *sin*, then unclean. Therefore

†Rm 4:25

†Rm 14:23

'woman', whatever she engenders, whatever she does, *will be unclean* until the eighth day, because human nature in itself and in whatever it does is always in sin until it comes to faith in Christ. 12. *On the eighth day the woman* is cleansed and human nature receives the remission of its sins through faith in Christ's resurrection. Then the child is circumcised because deeds are purified from sin. For example, before faith in Christ [nature] had chastity but this chastity was unclean because it was accompanied by the sin of infidelity. Therefore the child is circumcised on the eighth day because through faith in Christ this chastity is purified from the sin of infidelity. But why is it that this purification leaves the woman as if still unclean so that she has to be purified?

13. There are many kinds of uncleanness. One uncleanness springs from nature, another from the will, another from weakness. From nature comes the uncleanness with which we are born. That is why holy Job says: *No one is clean from sin, not even the infant one day old.*† David, too, says: *Behold, in iniquity was I conceived and in sin did my mother conceive me.*† This is the uncleanness which holy Job had in mind when he said: *Who can cleanse someone born of unclean seed?*† 14. Because of this uncleanness all human beings, when they are born, are children of *hell* and *children of wrath.*† Because of this uncleanness there was circumcision under the Old Law. And it purified men from this uncleanness because it signified faith in our Lord Jesus Christ. This uncleanness by itself was enough to damn a person.

15. But who is there who of his own free will has not added to this uncleanness? Of this

†Jb 14:4

†Ps 50:7 [51:5]

†Jb 14:4

†Mt 23:15; Eph 2:3

uncleanness Scripture says: *There is not a just person on earth who does good and does not sin.*† And if a just person increases this uncleanness, how much more do adulterers, fornicators, murderers, and thieves increase it! And yet baptism—and after baptism, penance—cleanses all these uncleannesses—and that [happens] on the eighth day: through faith in the resurrection of our Lord Jesus Christ. 16. There is yet another uncleanness which springs from weakness. Of this the Apostle says: *I perceive that there is in my bodily members another law fighting against the law of my mind and leading me captive under the law of sin.*† Who is there, brothers, who can boast that he is free from this uncleanness? From it come evil desires and evil pleasures, from it ill-regulated movements in our members, from it the trifles and meanderings of the human heart.

17. Now notice, brothers. You are already purified from those major uncleannesses—that is, from the vices which incur damnation. Your deeds have been purified—as it were, your children circumcised on the eighth day. But can you straightway enter the temple, the temple which is on high in the heavenly Jerusalem? Who can enter that temple as long as he remains in this flesh? *I will pass over*, says David, *into the place of the majestic Tabernacle, even into the house of God.*† 18. But it may be supposed that he was speaking of what was to happen after his death. Yet listen to what follows: *Why are you downcast, my soul, and why do you trouble me?*† Why then was his *soul downcast*, if not because he had come down again from that temple to himself, where he found unhappiness and sorrow. Listen to another who remained constantly in that temple: *Our dwelling*

†Qo 7:21

†Rm 7:23

†Ps 41:5 [42:4]

†Ps 41:6 [42:5]

place, he says, is in heaven.† Therefore, brothers, we cannot go up into that temple the very moment we are purified from our sins by baptism or by confession. Why not? Surely because of certain uncleannesses which cling to us. †Ph 3:20

19. For *who will boast that he has a chaste heart?*† When we wish to raise our heart on high and make the attempt to ascend to that Temple, there come into our hearts thoughts of the evil deeds we have done and the vanities we have pursued. They have not yet been eradicated from our memory and they drag our hearts down so that we cannot ascend to that temple. Therefore we must wait patiently for forty days and look for a sacrifice by which we can be so purified that we may be capable of entering the temple of which we are speaking. †Pr 20:9.

20. This number—that is, forty—signifies the toils and temptations which we ought patiently to endure so long as we are in this life. According to this signification the children of Israel spent forty years in the desert, where they endured many temptations and many labors and so came into the Promised Land. According to this signification, too, Elijah fasted for forty days and so came *to the mountain of God.*† 21. For without any doubt the person who yearns to enter into the heavenly temple—which is symbolized by the Promised Land—and go up to the mountain of the Lord and stand *in his holy place*† must fast and toil and bear with the temptations and hardships of this life, so that he may be purified *from all defilement of flesh and of spirit*† and be numbered among those of whom it is written: *Blessed are the clean of heart for they shall see God.*† †1 K 19:8

†Ps 23 [24]:3

†2 Co 7:1

†Mt 5:8

22. Therefore, dearest brothers, if, after the purification of baptism or confession, we wish to probe into heavenly things with a clean heart and to visit God's temple, we must endure the forty days' purification—that is, we must patiently bear with the labors and temptations of this present life. We ought also to look for a sacrifice. What sort of sacrifice? *A pair of turtle doves or two young pigeons.*[†]

[†]Lk 2:24; Lv 12:8

23. Both of these birds are accustomed to moan, never to sing, and they symbolize the tears and the moanings by which we can be purified from all our vices. To those who still need purification, tears usually well up from two sources: fear and shame. Now there is a third kind of tears which does not so much purify as enrich and refresh and that kind of tears springs from love. But it is of the two kinds by which we can be purified that we have to speak. 24. By the moaning of the pigeon understand the tears which proceed from fear. For the pigeon dwells among human beings where it has constantly to fear traps and snares. By the moaning of the turtle dove understand the tears which are caused by shame. For the turtle dove seems to be a bashful sort of bird which can only have one consort—on account, I suppose, of a sort of natural bashfulness. That is why the Bridegroom in the Song of Songs says to the holy soul: *Your cheeks are like those of a turtle dove.*[†] It is on the cheeks, you know, that shame reveals itself. The holy soul has the cheeks—that is, the bashfulness of a turtle dove—because it is abashed at all other loves but the love of God.

[†]Sg 1:9

25. Someone who for fear of God repents of one's sins and sheds tears offers a pigeon. Someone

who for very abashedness weeps for one's sins before God offers a turtle dove. But why was the commandment given to offer *a pair of turtle doves or two young pigeons?* Because we ought to have a twofold fear and a twofold bashfulness: fear that we may be condemned for the sins we have committed and fear that we may fall into further sins. 26. Now although it is true that the Lord remits all the sins of those who turn back to him and do penance, we should always fear, for we do not know whether our satisfaction is worthy. Again, although a person may feel that he is in a good [state], he can always fall into sin. Therefore we ought always to fear and in this twofold fear weep before God. Then we are offering two young pigeons. 27. Again, we ought to possess a twofold shame: shame because we have defiled and corrupted ourselves by sin and vice; shame because we have been ungrateful for all the good that God has done for us. He has created us, nourished us and given us [our] senses and intelligence. What surpasses everything else, he offered up his own death for us. And yet we have been ungrateful for all this and, in addition, we have paid him back *evil for good and hatred for his love.*† Therefore, brothers, someone is affected by this twofold shame and sheds tears is offering a pair of turtle doves.

†Ps 108 [109]:5; Pr 17:13. Love is *dilectio*.

28. By this offering we can no doubt be cleansed. With this sacrifice we ought to offer our children to God in the temple—that is, commend all our actions with tears to the Lord and carry the whole treasury of our deeds, as if it were our child, into that temple on high, as the Lord commanded: *Lay up treasure for yourselves in heaven.*† To lay up treasure on earth, where *rust and moths*—that

†Mt 6:20

is, pride and vainglory—consume,[†] is to perform one's deeds not in God's temple but in the sight of men and women. 29. Therefore let us lift all our deeds up to God so that as he was *presented in the Temple* today for us, so we with pure minds and actions may be presented to him in that heavenly temple. May he grant us this, he who together
with the Father and Holy Spirit
lives and reigns, God
through all the ages of ages.
Amen.

[†] *Ibid.*

Sermon Six
For the Feast of Saint Benedict

1 KNOW that you are used to welcoming with utter joy the feast days of the saints whenever they occur and that you heighten your fervor by recalling and meditating on their lives and perfections. Yet I think that this feast of our holy Father Benedict means more to you than others and is in some way more welcome—not because it is a greater feast than all others but because he, our own Father, is closer to us than the other saints. *For in Christ Jesus through the Gospel he has given us birth.*† 2. Whatever purity you possess through chastity, all the spiritual delight you take in charity, all the glory you are aware of having† by despising worldliness, by labors, by vigils, by fasts, by voluntary poverty—all this comes through his teaching. Whatever progress you have made in meditation, in prayer, in compunction, in devotion and in the rest of the spiritual exercises, has not all of this been brought about in you—by God's grace—through his ministry and example? Therefore he is closer to you than the rest of the saints, so his feast rightly ought to be for you a day of greater joy.

†1 Co 4:15

†Lit. *in conscientia uestra*

3. *Consider Israel according to the flesh*†—that is, the physical Jews† . By origin they sprang from the great Fathers, Abraham, Isaac, and Jacob, concerning whom the Lord said: *I am the God*

†1 Co 10:18
†*Carnales Iudaei,* contrasted to the *spirituales populi Dei.*

of Abraham, the God of Isaac, and the God of Jacob† —which indeed the Lord said because of their excellence. Yet the Jews themselves glory more in Moses, saying: *We are the disciples of Moses.*† As the Apostle James says in the Acts of the Apostles: *Moses has those who preach him every sabbath in the synagogue.*† Why do these physical Jews have such an attachment to Moses? I think it is because the Lord, through the ministry of Moses, led them out of the land of Egypt and across the Red Sea; because through his prayers they received manna from heaven [and] water from the rock; because by means of his prayer they overcame their enemies;† because from his hand they received the Law which, if observed, would allow them to receive and possess the Land of Promise.

†Ex 3:6; Mt 22:32

†Jn 9:28

†Ac 15:21

†Cf. Ex 17:11–12

5. Surely, brothers, if we clearly see and understand the benefits which the Lord has bestowed on us through our holy Father Benedict, we will plainly see that monks should love him no less than the physical Jews loved Moses. Through the ministry of Moses, the Lord led the Jews out of Egypt, through the ministry of Saint Benedict he has led us out of the world. They were under the domination of Pharaoh, a very cruel king; we were under the devil. They were in slavery to the Egyptians; we, in bondage to our vices. The servants of Pharaoh flogged them, demanding bricks from mud. Perhaps you have forgotten the floggings you suffered in the world.

6. One person was seeking some worldly honor or riches. What a flogging he suffered from these cravings! How fear and envy flogged him! How flogged he was when he could not acquire what he

wanted, when someone else acquired what he so ardently longed for! If he did acquire it however, he was flogged by fear at the thought of losing it and by sorrow when he did lose it! 7. Another person was rushing along, wholly intent on satisfying his own lustful pleasures and desires. How this despicable love, jealousy, and suspiciousness flogged that one! And what happened when those vices were laid bare by someone else? How he lamented! What a flogging his soul took! And, over and above all this, how his own conscience flogged him! And what happened when each person began to reflect on his life and his sins! 8. How often the scourges of his own heart drove him to make resolutions and to say: 'I will never do that again. Never again will I get bogged down in that vice.' And even so the servants of Pharaoh—that is, unclean spirits—pressured us, as if against our own wills, to make mud bricks—that is, to do foul and sordid things. And so we went on building the city of Pharaoh—that is, the devil—in our hearts. Each one [of us] can recall the violence he suffered from his own evil habits and see how, by the grace of God and the teaching of Saint Benedict, he has been freed. He sees that God has given us greater things through Saint Benedict than to the Jews through Moses.

9. If you compare the spiritual delight you often experience in Christ with the manna which the Jews ate in the desert, if you compare the victories which you often gain over your spiritual enemies through the merits and teaching of Blessed Benedict with the victories [the Jews] had over human beings, you will see indeed that the things which you have received are much greater because they are spiritual. Moses established a

law for the Jews and instructed them so that they might enter the Land of Promise and possess it as long as this age endures. Blessed Benedict established for us a law by which, if we observe it, we will enter heaven itself, the Land of the Living, and possess it forever and ever.

10. This law, my brothers, is his Rule. In it he teaches us to offer God spiritual sacrifices, to celebrate the Sabbath spiritually, to build in our hearts a spiritual tabernacle for Christ. If we observe this law we will be, as he himself said, *heirs of the Kingdom of Heaven.*[†] But since we have mentioned Moses and Pharaoh, let us, on this feast of our Father, say something for our edification about their words.

[†RB, Prologue 39]

11. As you know, when the sons of Israel were captive under Pharaoh in Egypt, Moses was sent in God's name to demand that the iniquitous Pharoah set his people free. When he contemptuously refused to do this, he and his people were stricken by the Lord with many and great plagues. Finally, because of the plagues they were enduring, Pharaoh said to Moses: *Go and offer sacrifice to the Lord your God, but in this country.*[†] Moses replied: *Never! It can not be done this way.*[†] And he gave the reason: *We shall sacrifice to our God offerings abominable to the Egyptians.*[†] 12. In Egypt they could not offer sacrifices to God because they were supposed to sacrifice what the Egyptians considered an abomination. Although this might be read as a question—*Can we offer to our God what is abominable to the Egyptians?*—the meaning is the same. Now, because Pharaoh declared: *Go and sacrifice in this land*, Moses said: *Can we offer to our God what is abominable to the Egyptians?* Here

[†Ex 8:25]
[†Ex 8:26]
[†Ibid.]

is understood, *in this land*, and also, *It cannot be done this way*. Where this was supposed to be carried out, Moses indicates, for he adds, *We must go three-days journey into the wilderness to sacrifice to the Lord.*† †Ex 8:27

13. You know, brothers, what Egypt signifies, who Pharaoh is, and who the Egyptians are. Nevertheless, I will state briefly: Egypt is the world; Pharaoh, the devil; the Egyptians, vice and sin. Understand it this way: you were in this Egypt, under these Egyptians, under this Pharaoh. The devil was holding you captive through love of the world, through love of kinsfolk. You were bound by your own cravings. You were held by your evil habits. Brothers, when would he have let you go, if the Lord had not struck him down? 14. But how did the Lord strike him down? Indeed, by your own good will which he gave you, by the good desires which he inspired in you, by the good thoughts which he sowed in your hearts. By all these things the Lord struck down the devil. By all them, the forces of Egypt—your vices and sins—were worn down. Even so, Pharaoh had a hold on you through your evil habits and he did not let you quickly break these bonds of habit. When he saw that your good intention was going to win out, what did he say? *Go and offer sacrifices to your Lord, but in this country.*

15. I would be amazed, brothers, I would be amazed if not all of you have heard this voice, whether through the devil himself secretly in your own hearts or openly through one of his members. 'Do you,' he says, 'want to serve God? Good! But is it necessary to give up your possessions, your churches, your riches? Serve God

here. Do penance here. Serve God with these belongings of yours. Give alms.' I think you will recognize what I am saying. How many have been deceived by this voice, brothers! We are aware of it. We have experience. 16. We know people who have formed a good intention, firmly promised to leave the world and almost did. But then they heard this voice of Pharaoh; they heard and they acquiesced. They began to wish to live as quasi-monastics in the world, but they were deceived. For they fell back into their former vices and added hypocrisy on top of them. No wonder! Great, great indeed, brothers, was their presumption in wanting to do penance in the midst of riches, pleasures, and honors when it was through riches, pleasures, and honors that they had fallen into such horrible transgressions.

17. *Not so*, brothers, *not so*.[†] We must go *three-days journey into solitude* to be able to offer to the *Lord our God* in sacrifice *that which is abominable to the Egyptians*. Perhaps penance itself is an abomination to the Egyptians and therefore we cannot offer this sacrifice in the Egyptians' midst. But first let us see what these three days of journeying are. The first day's journey is leaving the world. The second is leaving our vices and sins and turning ourselves to better ways of living. The third is leaving our own will. Anyone who has made this three days' journey will be able to sacrifice to the Lord what is abominable to the Egyptians.

18. And notice, brothers, there are many who have given up the riches and honors of the world and have withdrawn themselves, as it were, one day's journey from the world. But because they

[†Ps 1:4]

do not yet choose to give up their evil habits, but are as proud as before, as wanton as before, as grasping as before, as angry as before, they have not completed the second day's journey; and therefore they are not fit to sacrifice to God. 19. There are others who do both these things—that is, they give up riches and honors and they abstain from their former sins—but because they go apart by themselves into some forest or some other place, and eat when they choose, fast when they choose, watch when they choose, sleep when they choose, work and rest when they choose, beyond doubt they have not completed the third day's journey. 20. And even those who live in community and seem to have left behind their own will, if they still seek certain freedoms so they can go out when they choose, speak when they choose, work when they choose, read when they choose, and do whatever they can and as much they can according to their own likings, they have not completed the third day's journey either. I am speaking, not about all those who have this freedom, but about those who seek this freedom and take pleasure in it. For some persons sometimes do go out and speak and do these sorts of things, all of which are to them more a burden than a delight and they would more gladly remain in quiet repose.

21. Therefore only someone who has made the three-days journey has thoroughly left Egypt. First of all, just as he once left behind him the riches of the world in an exterior way, so daily, constantly, he rejects them from the depths of his heart. He always stands before the Lord with a spirit free from all cupidity and ambition, saying with blessed Peter: *Behold, we have left all things.*† And then,   †Mt 19:27

correcting his way of life, he manfully resists those vices which dominated him in the world. Finally, he mortifies his own willfulness and depends on the counsel of his spiritual father for whatever he ought to do.

22. And surely, brothers, holy Moses taught the sons of Israel that they actually[†] had to take a three-days journey, at the end of which they would come to the place where they would actually offer sacrifices to God. Our blessed Father Benedict has taught you, however, the spiritual three-days journey and has shown you clearly enough the way by which you will be enabled to complete this three-days journey. For it seems to me that the first day's journey is completed by the way of fear of the Lord, the second by the way of mortification and the third by the way of obedience.

[†] *corporales*, as above.

23. Listen to blessed Benedict as he shows us this way. *The first degree of humility is fear of the Lord*, he says.[†] And, so it seems to me, contempt for riches and honors is the first indication of humility. For as long as a person serves and holds on to the riches and honors of this world, he can perhaps be humble but his humility is thereby not apparent. And therefore, through the first degree of humility a person comes to the first indication of humility. Indeed, each one of you can see this in yourself. 24. For how could you have divested yourself of your riches and possessions, how could you have made this journey, unless the fear of the Lord had been urging you on? The fear of the Lord, therefore, is the way by which this first day's journey is completed. But someone may say: 'How can I, who have left nothing, complete this first day's journey? Because I had nothing in

[†] RB 7.10

the world, I left nothing.' Let anyone who thinks this answer me. When he was in the world did he not crave riches? Did he not, to the best of his ability, acquire what he could? If, therefore, he has given up this cupidity, he has, indeed, completed the first day's journey well.

25. Now let us see the pathway of the second day's journey, and let us willingly run along it. It is the mortification of the flesh. Holy Benedict says: *The second step in humility is that a person not love his own will, nor delight in satisfying the desires of the flesh.*[†] This is clearly the way by which we can accomplish the second day's journey—that is, we will avoid our former vices if we mortify *the desires of the flesh* by vigils and fasts and labor. Let no one say: 'I am strong. I am chaste. I am wise. I have no need of working, watching, fasting.' Is he wiser than Paul? Is he stronger than blessed Benedict? 26. Paul chastised his body and *kept it in subjection,*[†] as he himself said, *in hunger and thirst, in toil and hardship.*[†] And yet he saw *in his members another law fighting the law in his spirit.*[†] Saint Benedict, too, for a number of years lived on bread and water and even so he was barely able to escape the temptations of lust. And he was nearly overwhelmed, as you heard in the readings at Vigils this morning.[†] This is how it was with him, and do you, who are intent on I know not what pleasures and vanities, think that you can escape the lewdness of the flesh? Anyone who wants to complete the second day's journey, therefore, *does not delight in satisfying the desires of his flesh.*[†]

[†]RB 7.31

[†]1 Co 9:27
[†]2 Co 11:27
[†]Rm 7:23

[†]Gregory the Great, *Dialogues*, 2. 2. 1–2 (CCSL 260:136–138, 1–21)

[†]RB 7.31; Gal 5:16

27. But now let us hear what Saint Benedict has to say of the third day's journey. *The third step of humility,* he says, *is that someone, for the love of God,*

subjects himself to his senior in all obedience.[†] In this way, indeed, a person wholly abandons himself and gives himself over to God if *in all obedience he subjects himself* to another so that he cannot eat as he likes nor fast nor labor when he chooses, but [does so] when the other commands and so in all things he follows not his own but the other's will.

[†RB 7.34]

28. Someone who has completed these three days' journeys must offer God a sacrifice of what is *abominable to the Egyptians*—that is, those things which the Egyptians abominate and hate. The Egyptians are lovers of the world, worldlings and libertines. *They rejoice when they do evil and exult in despicable things.*[†] And when they have satisfied their evil desires they rejoice, they are proud; they do not know how to blush nor do they choose to repent. Therefore, *abominable to the Egyptians* are the bitterness of penance, the distress of sorrow, voluntary poverty and worthless self-esteem.[†] These things, *abominable to the Egyptians*, we ought to offer up to the Lord, our God. 29. Let us repent of our sins. Let us mourn and weep for our sins—things we have done and are doing—so that our sins and our vices may be drowned in the tears of penitence as in the bitter and salty waters of Egypt and thus perish and be wiped out. Let us embrace poverty. Let us be vile and worthless in our own eyes. And thus, having truly gone forth from Egypt, we will offer to the Lord our God what is *abominable to the Egyptians* and *our sacrifice will be pleasing* to him.

[†Pr 2:14]

[†Saint Bernard uses the same text of Exodus in the same accommodated sense in his Second Sermon for the Feast of Saints Peter and Paul.]

30. There are, of course, some who after they have left the world continue to take pride in their rank or their clerical status or even in the riches and pomp of the nobility or worldly honor

which they have left behind. They think that they should be honored more than others. They want their superior to call them to his councils and to honor them more than others. They want to have an influence in all his arrangements. If something is arranged or settled without their advice they become indignant and get angry; they think that the superior is despising them out of envy. Such men as these have not yet offered to *the Lord the abominations of the Egyptians*.

31. Yet notice how Saint Benedict teaches us to offer those things which are *abominable to the Egyptians*. After he has taught us by the first three steps of humility the way by which we can complete the three-days journey, he immediately continues [on the subject of] *the abominations of the Egyptians*. *The fourth degree is to follow patiently, with a quiet mind, in the way of obedience even in hard and contrary things, even in the face of injuries.*[†] And in the same vein, [he quotes]: *When they are struck on one cheek they offer the other. When they are forced to go one mile they go two. They sustain false brethren and persecution.*[†]

[†]RB 7.35

[†]RB 7.42f; Mt 5:39ff.

32. These are clearly *the abominations of the Egyptians* because all these things the Egyptians—that is, the worldly minded—abhor. For they deem it is a great disgrace, not only if they suffer injuries patiently, but even if they do not vindicate themselves as much they can. But these sacrifices are pleasing to God. In these sacrifices are slain those things which the world cultivates and loves. Rightly did holy Moses say: *If we immolate in their presence those things which the Egyptians worship, they will stone us.*[†] What do *the Egyptians worship*? Surely riches and honor, gold and silver, the

[†]Ex 8:26

delights of the belly and the gullet. 33. These things *the Egyptians worship*. Any Egyptian having them is proud and exalts himself above others. And those who do not have them venerate and worship and even, as it were, adore those who have them and call them blessed. This is why it is said in the psalm: *May their sheep be fruitful, abounding in their pastures. May their cattle be fat. May there be no breach in their wall nor exile nor outcries in their streets.*† This is the happiness of the Egyptians. And other Egyptians who do not have these things call those who have them blessed and say, as the Prophet adds: *They declare happy the people for whom things are like this.*†

†Ps 143 [144]:13–14

†Ps 143 [144]:15

34. Anyone who chooses to eradicate these things from his heart† while still living among worldly people—that is, anyone who chooses to scorn riches, honors, and amusements and to live simply, soberly, chastely, and religiously—is immediately stoned by the Egyptians—that is, he is abused by his hard-hearted fellow-citizens. One calls him a deceiver; another, a hypocrite. Therefore, you have wisely taken good advice if you gone out of Egypt and come *into solitude* by this three-days journey. But what does it mean, to have come *into solitude*? [It means] to consider this whole world a desert, to desire the Fatherland, to hold on to only as much of this world as is necessary to complete the journey, not as much as the flesh craves. 35. Offer sacrifices, therefore, to God. Put to death within yourselves those things which the world loves. Love to be insignificant for Christ, to be paupers for Christ, to be rejected for Christ. This our blessed Father Benedict teaches us. Follow *his footsteps*, his teaching, so that he may deign to

†Lit. *animus*

recognize you among his own, as the shepherd does his sheep, the father his children, the master his disciples. And by his intercession may you come to the pasture of eternal happiness, to the inheritance of the *children of God*, to the joy of the disciples of Christ, through the goodness of our Lord Jesus Christ, who, as God, lives and reigns
 with the Father and Holy Spirit
 through all the ages of ages.
 Amen

Sermon Seven
For the Feast of Saint Benedict

AS TODAY WE CELEBRATE the passing of our holy Father Benedict, I am obliged to say something about him, especially because I observe that you are eager to listen. Like good sons you have come together to hear about your Father who, *in Christ Jesus, gave birth to you* in the Gospel.† Because we know that he has passed beyond, let us see where he came from and where he has gone.

†1 Co 4:15

2. He came from where we still are, of course, and he has gone on to that place to which we have not yet come. And while we are not physically there where he has gone, we are there in hope and love, as our Redeemer has told us: *Where your treasure is, there also is your heart.*† Thus the Apostle said: *Our dwelling place is in heaven.*† Indeed, Saint Benedict himself, while he lived physically in this world, *dwelt in thought and desire in the heavenly Fatherland.*†

†Mt 6:21
†Ph 3:20

†From *Iste sanctus digne,* an antiphon used in the common office of a confessor (Hesbert 3:3432)

3. So today our Father has passed from earth to heaven, from prison to the kingdom, from death to life, from misery to glory. From this life which can quite appropriately be called death, he has happily passed over into *the land of the living.*† Deservedly do I say he has passed on to *the land of the living* because this life is that not of the living

†Cf. Ps 26 [27]:13, 141:6 [142:5]

but of the dying. All the things which I mentioned earlier—death, prison, and misery—are found in this life. Indeed, all these things are this present life. 4. Now, if it were not death, the Apostle Paul would never have said: *Daily I die for your glory, brothers.*† And again: *Unhappy man that I am! Who will rescue me from the body of this death?*† Very clearly he calls this life 'death' and living in the body, 'dying'. The psalmist bears witness that [this life] is a prison as he says: *Bring my soul out of prison.*† That this life is miserable, indeed misery itself, the daily experience of our own miseries teaches each of us. But blessed David calls it a pool of misery and a mire of mud. With undisguised joy he already proclaimed himself freed from it— because he knew he would be freed: *He heard my prayers and drew me out of this pool of misery and the mire of mud.*†

†1 Co 15:31
†Rom 7:24

†Ps 141:8 [142:7]

†Ps 39 [40]:2

5. Since we know where Saint Benedict passed from and to, let us see now how he passed. For it would be of no profit to those wishing to follow him if they knew only where he passed from and to, unless they also know how he passed. Truly he went through Christ to Christ. *Through faith* in Jesus Christ, which worked in him *through love,* he passed to the vision and contemplation of Jesus Christ by which is satisfied the desire for all that is good. His way therefore was Christ who said of himself in the Gospel: *I am the way, the truth and the life.*† Through Him he passed to Him because He who is *the way* is *life* itself.

†Jn 14:6

6. The most direct way of our Father was the very best way of life. The way of life was his holiness. For, as Saint Gregory has said, *this present life* is nothing more than a kind of *pathway.*† A person

†Gregory the Great, *Moralia in Job,* 23. 24. 47 (CCSL 143B:1179, 42)

who lives well and praiseworthily in that he lives well and worthy of God passes to God and to life eternal. But someone who leads a degenerate life through his degenerate life heads for hell and everlasting death. This is the way of sinners. David speaks of it in the first psalm: *Happy the man who does not follow the advice of the wicked or loiter in the way of sinners.*[†Ps 1:1] 7. Through this evil way one goes to the sinners' wretched death, of which the same Prophet in another place said: *The death of sinners is the worst.*[†Ps 33:22] Very rightly, indeed, he says the death of sinners is the worst because their way is evil. And as the Apostle says: *Evil persons go from bad to worse; erring themselves and leading others into error.*[†2 Tim 3:13] The death of sinners therefore is said to be the worst because as long as they live they become more and more evil until, having reached the depths, they deserve to be cut off and thrown into the fire.

8. But our blessed Father Benedict did not follow this way. He did not lead a degenerate life but held fast to [the way] of which it is said: *The way of the just is straight.*[†Ps 26:7(LXX)] Although *narrow, it leads to life.*[†] The way is narrow at the beginning but afterwards, as blessed Benedict himself teaches us in his Rule, *one runs in the way of God's commandments in the unutterable sweetness of love.*[†RB, Prol. 49] 9. For those who are beginning, [the way] is indeed narrow, as it was for David when he said: *Because of the words of your mouth I have followed harsh ways.*[†Ps 16 [17]:4] But did this prophet, because he found it narrow in the beginning, either abandon or decide that he should abandon it? God forbid! Rather, he held fast until he could make this very different statement: *I have run in the way of your commandments because you have enlarged my heart*[†Ps 118 [119]:32]

10. Blessed Benedict also found the way narrow at the beginning of his conversion. But in the end he found it wide open. Wasn't the way narrow for him when, as we read in his *Life*, he threw himself naked into a thorn bush to avoid consenting to lust?.† But when he found the way narrow, what did he do? Did he ever depart from it? Instead, he kept to it and manfully stood his ground. First he did what later he taught, so he could teach us, his followers, what he himself had done. For as Pope Saint Gregory said of him: *Just as he lived, so he taught. He could not teach other than he lived.*†

†Gregory the Great, *Dialogues*, 2.2. 2 (SCh 260:138, 15–16)

†*Ibid.*, 2.36; SCh 260:242, 10–11

11. How he stood manfully in the way of God we can glean from his own words, since in his Rule he warns anyone *daunted by fear* not to flee the way of salvation.† Experience had taught him that there is no beginning except by the narrow trail. But he was aware that however extraordinarily narrow it might be, it nevertheless led *to life*—as our Lord himself said: *Narrow is the way which leads to life and few they are who walk in it.*† To what life this way leads, our Lord himself teaches in another place, saying: *This is eternal life, to know you, the true God, and Jesus Christ whom you have sent.*†

†RB, Prol. 48; cf. RB 59.6

†Mt 7:14

†Jn 17:3.

12. This is the way by means of which we read that Isaac was made perfect, the way *which leads to the well of seeing and living.*† Of this way the Book of Wisdom says: *The path of the righteous is like the light [of dawn], sparkling and growing to the fullness of day.*† The fear of hell which is labeled servile straitens this way. Perfect charity broadens it. As long as someone is afraid, he suffers difficulty along the way of God and experiences hardship.†

†Gen 24:62

†Prov 4:18

†1 Jn 4:18

13. When, however, he arrives at the *perfect charity which casts out fear*, then, with unmingled joy he cries out with the Apostle: *I have fought a*

good fight, I have finished the course. I have kept the faith.† With David he sings: *I have run in the way of your commandments because you have enlarged my heart.*† Now, someone who has this kind of charity desires with Paul *to be dissolved and to be with Christ.*† Indeed he finds it extremely painful to be separated from Christ any longer and daily with tears repeats those words of the Psalmist: *How much longer will you forget me, O Lord—for ever?*† And with Habakkuk: *How long, Lord, will I cry out and you will not hear; will I, enduring violence, call out to you and you will not save?*†

†2 Tm 4:7

†Ps 118 [119]:32

†Ph 1:23

†Ps 12 [13]:1

†Hab 1:2

14. Along this way, as we said, Saint Benedict passed from death to life, from Egypt to the Promised Land—that is, from the darkness of this world to Jerusalem, which is *a vision of peace.*† And certainly he passed along propitiously because he lived praiseworthily. He passed along this way with Moses, and saw a great vision, not how a bush burned and yet was not consumed,† but how the blessed angels and their equals, the saints of God, forever burn with love and in them that love never grows cold. 15. Let us, too, dearest ones, so pass through this life that we see *that great vision.*† Let us follow *the footsteps* of our holy Father Benedict.† We have a very direct way by which we may arrive there, namely, his Rule and his teaching. If we hold to this as we ought and if we persevere in it, without doubt we too shall arrive there, where he is. That we may do this, may there be granted to us, through the merits and intercession of Saint Benedict, the grace of our Redeemer, Jesus Christ,

†*Interpretatio* 50 (CCSL 72:121,9–10) *et passim*

†Ex 3:3

†1 P 2:21
†Cf. RB 73.3–4

who lives and reigns
with the Father and Holy Spirit,
God, through all the ages of ages.
Amen.

Sermon Eight
For the Feast of Saint Benedict

YOU IN YOUR CHARITY have often heard, dearest brothers, that holy Moses, after he led the children of Israel out of the land of Egypt, built a tabernacle in the desert, using the offerings of the children of Israel.† Some offered him gold; some, silver; some, precious stones and some other things which it is not necessary here to list. But we should reflect on this happening for, as the Apostle said: *All this was done in figure.*†

†Ex 35:20–29

†1 Co 10:11

2. We were in a kind of spiritual Egypt when we were living a worldly life, for Egypt may be interpreted as *darkness*.† Wrongdoings and sins, and obstinacy of mind in these, are *deep darkness*.‡ At one time we were in this [darkness], for by participating in these things we ourselves were made darkness. As the Apostle says: *You were at one time darkness.*† Yet so that we might be *light in the Lord*, <the Lord> gave us a certain Moses, a certain legislator, that is to say, our holy Father Benedict, whose feast we celebrate today. By his wisdom and enterprise we pass through the desert of this world that we may come to the Land of Promise, not that one which the physical children of Israel physically desired but the one which the Prophet hoped for <spiritually> when he said: *I believe I will see the goodness of the Lord in*

†3, *Interpretatio*, 73 (CCSL 72:151, 14) *et passim*

‡Cf. Ex 10:21

†Eph 5:8

the Land of the Living.† Of it the Lord said: *Blessed are the meek for they shall possess the Land.*†

<small>†Ps 26 [27]:13
†Mt 5:4</small>

3. [Benedict] was filled not only with the spirit of Moses; he was also somehow, as someone said, *filled with the spirit of all the just.*† He built a spiritual tabernacle from the offerings of the children of Israel. In his Rule sparkles the gold of blessed Augustine, the silver of Jerome, the double-dyed purple of Gregory,[1] not to mention the jewel-like sayings of the holy Fathers; with all these this heavenly edifice is embellished. 4. You, my brothers, are the tabernacle of God; you [are] *the temple of God.* As the Apostle says: *Holy is the temple of God which you are.*† A temple, because the Lord will reign forever in you. Yet still a tabernacle,† because he is on pilgrimage in you, he hungers in you, he thirsts in you. This tabernacle is still borne along by the ministry of Levites. Some carry it on their shoulders, others with the aid of oxen and carts.

<small>†Gregory the Great, *Dialogues* 2. 8. 8 (SCh 260:166, 73–74)</small>

<small>†1 Co 3:17</small>

<small>†*Tabernaculum* means 'tent', and therefore transportable, as well as 'tabernacle'.</small>

5. They carry the tabernacle who attentively fulfill the precept of our Moses: *Let them most patiently bear one another's infirmities, whether of body or of habit. Let them vie with one another in obedience.*† They carry it on their shoulders who, expecting no earthly recompense, unremittingly reflect on what follows in the same chapter: *Let them prefer absolutely nothing to Christ.*† 6. They carry it, but not on their own shoulders, those who do indeed keep the observances of the Rule but hope

<small>†RB 72.5f</small>

<small>†RB 72.11</small>

---

1. There is a curious anachronism here. Aelred is probably thinking of Pope Saint Gregory I, to whom he has twice referred in the previous sermons. Gregory I, however, had not yet been born when Benedict was building his 'tabernacle' and a reference to Gregory of Nyssa or Gregory Nazianzen, who pre-dated Benedict, would be very unusual for Aelred.

for some transitory thing: dignities, honors, or something of that sort. When they are frustrated in this hope, as it were, in the aid of carts—for by carts temporal honors are represented—they put down the tabernacle and depart. 7. Others also carry it, not on their own shoulders but with the aid of oxen—that is, superiors. For they always want to be commended by their superiors and to have some temporal favor shown to them. So it is that if perchance they hear some harsh word from [the superiors], then, as if frustrated at their aid, they put down the tabernacle altogether or carry it with murmuring. Of them the Apostle said: *There will be a time when they will not bear with sound doctrine but they will turn to fables and with itching ears they will seek teachers to their own liking.*† Just as the adulterer seeks the tingling of lust, so they seek the tingling of adulation. †2 Tm 4:3–4

8. But this, my brothers, this is what tabernacle puts up with as long as it is being carried through the desert of this world, until it is taken into the Land of Promise and becomes a temple instead of a tabernacle, and is dedicated by the true Solomon for *seven days and seven days*†—that is, a twofold rest, a twofold perfection. Then a twofold stole will be given to each—immortality for the body, blessedness for the soul. Yet even now, brothers, if we are spiritual sons of Israel, if we have gone forth spiritually from the land of Egypt, let each of us make our offering and let all of us make our offering for the construction of this tabernacle, and each and every one of us from that in which he abounds. †1 K 8:65

9. *For each one of us has his unique gift from God, one this but another that.*† One person can make †1 Co 7:7; RB 40.1

an offering of more work; another, more vigils; another, more fasting; another, more prayer; and another, more *lectio*[2] or meditation. From all these offerings let one tabernacle be made, so that, as our legislator commands: *No one shall say or presume that anything is his own but all things are common to all.*[†] This is to be understood, brothers, not only of our cowls and robes but far more of our strengths and spiritual gifts.

[†RB 33.6]

10. No one therefore should boast on his own about any grace given by God as if it were exclusively his own. No one should envy his brother because of some grace, as if it were exclusively his. Whatever he has, he should consider the property of all his brothers, and whatever his brother has, he should never doubt is also his. Or that Almighty God can immediately bring to perfection anyone he pleases and bestow all the virtues on any one person. But in his caring way dealing with us he causes each person to need the other and to have in the other what one does not possess in oneself. Thus humility is preserved, charity increased and unity recognized. Therefore each belongs to all and all belong to each. Thus each has the benefit of the virtues while preserving humility by the consciousness of individual weakness. 11. Let our lay brothers not complain that they do not sing psalms or keep vigils as much as the monks do. Nor let the monks complain that they do not work as much as the lay brothers do. For very truly I say that whatever any one person

---

2. *Lectio* has been retained here, rather than 'reading' or 'sacred reading'. *Lectio*, as understood in monastic tradition, is not simply what we moderns mean by reading. It may range from serious study to little more than holding an open book while conversing with God. It is directly ordered to and wholly permeated by the quest for God and aims at the experience of God's indwelling.

does belongs to all and whatever all do belongs to everyone. For just as the members of a single body do not all have the same function yet, as the Apostle says: *The many are one body in Christ, they are each members one of another.*† Therefore let the weak say: I am strong. Because, just as someone else possess the patience of infirmity in him, so he in someone else possess the strength of endurance.

†Rm 12:5; 1 Co 12:12ff; Eph 4:4, 16

12. Beware lest *dying flies* destroy *the sweetness of the oil.*† The sweetness of the oil is the sweetness of brotherly love, which the dying flies—that is, cupidity, envy, and suspicion—destroy. For no one who craves anything of this world loves perfectly. From this craving, envy is born. Whatever someone craves for himself, he envies in others. And usually in the depths of his heart he begins to be suspicious of the person he envies. But now let us compare certain provisions of the Moses of old with the provisions of our modern Moses.

†Qo 10:1

13. The Moses of old established six cities of refuge for the children of Israel, three outside the Land of Promise and three within the Land of Promise, so that anyone who committed unintentional homicide would be safe if he fled to one of them.† There is a physical homicide and a spiritual homicide. For sin indeed is the death of the soul. And this is the worst kind of homicide: to kill oneself by vice or someone else by example. The children of Israel did not have cities of refuge as long as they were in Egypt, not because they did not kill but because they did so more from pride than ignorance. 14. And we, when we were in the spiritual Egypt, sinned, not because we were weak, but because we were proud and we

†Nb 35:11–15, Dt 19:2–10, Jos 20:2–6

enjoy sinning. For us, therefore, there were no cities of refuge. Now although we have left Egypt, *if we say we have no sin we deceive ourselves and the truth is not in us.*† *In many things we all offend.*‡ But whether it happens through weakness and ignorance or through pride is important . For as long as anyone wallows proudly in some sin, even though he seems to have fled from Egypt, the city of refuge is no use to him at all. As the Apostle says: *If we sin deliberately after receiving the knowledge of the truth, no sacrifical victim for sin remains for us.*†

†1 Jn 1:8
‡Jm 3:2

†Heb 10:26

15. It seems to me those six cities of refuge can signify the six general exercises that are provided for us. Three are physical: work, watching, and fasting. These pertain especially to those who are still assailed by physical passions and are still, as it were, outside the Promised Land. They cannot say: *Our way of life is in heaven.*† Three, however, are spiritual: *lectio*, prayer, and meditation. These pertain especially to those whose passions are now weakened and who have passed on to an attachment to the virtues; in these cities they taste *how sweet the Lord is*†—that is, the fruit of the Land of Promise. We have fled to these cities, taking refuge from those who pursue us because of homicide. 16. Who are they? Either the devil or our own cravings. As the Apostle James says: *Each person, lured and enticed, is tempted by his own yearnings.*† The more one sins, the more the very yearning to sin increases. Listen to the Apostle, who intensely feared the enemy: *I see*, he says, *another law in my members, fighting against the law in my mind and leading me captive into the law of sin which is in my members.*† Listen to him fleeing

†Ph 3:20

†Ps 33:9 [34:8], 1 P 2:3

†Jm 1:14

†Rm 7:23

to these cities: *I chastise my body and bring it into submission.*† How? As he clearly said elsewhere: *In labors, in watching, in fasting.*† Listen to Peter calling us to these cities: *Be sober and watch in prayer*† and so on.

†1 Co 9:27
†2 Co 6:5
†1 P 5:8; 4:7

17. What is stated in the law—that a culprit may flee to one of these cities—although it ought to have been commanded in such a way as to be implemented to the letter, is still to be regarded because no one possesses equal grace in all exercises. In time of temptation each person should take refuge in that exercise in which he finds the greater grace. But now we must reflect on what was further commanded, that no one depart from these cities until the death of the high priest.† And who is our high priest, if not Jesus?† 18. We must therefore continue in labors, fasting, and watching until our earthly members are truly mortified, until we bear about in our flesh the death of Jesus,† so that we can say with the Apostle: *With Christ I am nailed to the cross.*† And also: *I carry the stigmata of the Lord Jesus Christ in my body.*† But there is a mortification of the spirit just as of the flesh. Therefore it is written: *Sing to the Lord with harps, with harps*†—that is, with a twofold harp. And so, we must continue as well in spiritual [exercises]. Just as the flesh is killed by wicked passions, so the spirit is killed by depraved thoughts.

†Nb 35:28, Jos 20:6
†Heb 4:14, 9:11
†Co 4:10
†Gal 2:19
†Gal 2:19
†Ps 97 [98]:5

19. If, then, we are buried with Jesus, like him in his death, we shall be his companions also in the resurrection, walking in newness of life.† *When Christ our life appears, we, too, shall appear with him in glory.*† Through the merits and prayers of

†Rm 6:4f
†Cf. Col 3:4

our blessed Father Benedict may this be granted
to us by our Lord Jesus Christ himself, who
with the Father and Holy Spirit,
lives and reigns God
through all the ages of ages.
Amen.

Sermon Nine
FOR THE ANNUNCIATION OF THE LORD

BEHOLD, THE LORD ASCENDS *a light cloud and will enter Egypt and the idols of Egypt will quail before him.*† When Jesus, our Lord and Saviour, was leaving us physically, he promised us the presence of his divinity, the presence of his grace, saying: *Behold, I am with you all days until the consummation of the world.*† But because it was expedient for us always to be mindful of his benefits which he bestowed on us through his physical presence and because he knew that our memory is impaired by forgetfulness, our intellect by error, our attentiveness by cravings, he kindly provided for us that not only would the Scriptures recount his benefits to us, but these benefits would also be re-presented to us by specific spiritual actions. Thus, when he gave over his disciples the sacrament of his Body and Blood he told them: *Do this in memory of me.*†

†Is 19:1

†Mt 26:20

†Lk 22:19, 1 Cor 11:24

2. For this reason, brothers, these feasts have been established by the Church. Because we re-present now his birth, now his passion, resurrection, [and] ascension, that wondrous lovingkindness, that wondrous gentleness, that wondrous charity which he showed for us in all these, will always be fresh in our memory. By means of these [feasts] our faith should develop whenever we hear with our ears and almost see beneath

our eyes what Christ suffered for us, and what he gives us in this life and what he promises us after this life. He suffered death for us, nowadays he forgives us our sins, he promises us eternal happiness after this life.†

†Cf. Aelred, Sermon 26, 9–29; CCCM 2a:210

3. All this—all this liberation which is ours, all this hope which is ours, all this blessedness which is ours—began today. Before this day there was in the world only misery and darkness, but today *the Morning Sun from on high has visited us and a Light has risen for those who sat in darkness and the shadow of death.*† Today our Joseph clad himself in his tunic of many colors, that variegated and beautiful tunic in which he was sent by the Father to visit his brothers and the sheep.† Today he fulfilled what was foretold by Isaiah the prophet, the text with which we began our sermon: *Behold, the Lord ascends a light cloud and will enter Egypt and the idols of Egypt will quail before him.*†

†Lk 1:78f, cf. Ps 111 [112]:4

†Gen 37:3, 12–14

†Is 19:1

4. This, his coming into Egypt, holy Moses greatly desired, as we can understand from his words. For, as you have often heard and read, when the children of Israel were enduring that harsh slavery in Egypt under Pharaoh, God appeared to Moses and commanded him to go down into Egypt and lead his people out from that misery. But although he greatly lamented the captivity which the children of Israel were suffering in Egypt, Moses nevertheless grieved even more over that misery which the whole world was enduring under the devil. And therefore he longed for, he sought out the One who would be worthy not only of leading that people out of Egypt but also of liberating the whole world from hell. 5. Therefore with great feeling he said: *I beg you,*

Lord, send him whom you are going to send.† He knew that God was going to send him, but he was unwilling that the delay should be so long. It was as if he had said: I know, dear Lord, that you are going to send your beloved Son, who is to set us free from this great misery, from this unhappy captivity, and therefore it is perhaps as a sign of that liberation that you will to bring this about first. But what need is there for this? Let him come instead, let him come down, let him enlighten the spiritual Egypt—that is, the darkness of the whole world†—with his dear presence. This longing of holy Moses was fulfilled today.

†Ex 4:13

†*Interpretatio*, 73 (CCSL 72:151, 14) *et passim*

6. Let us consider, therefore, brothers, how great should be our exultation; we see fulfilled what holy Moses with such blazing emotion† longed to have fulfilled. Today <the Lord> mounted *a light cloud* and entered Egypt.† The name 'Egypt', brothers, means 'darkness'.† And what was the whole world before the coming of Christ, if not darkness? It was utterly necessary that this wondrous *light arise in the darkness*—that is, that Christ be born in the world. But, as the Evangelist says: *The light shone in the darkness and the darkness did not comprehend it.*† 7. For without doubt the human mind was so shrouded in and blinded by the darkness of sin that it was quite incapable of concentrating the interior eye on that divine light. So he—that is, mercy himself—acted mercifully and tempered the brightness of his divinity for us with a sort of cloud. That, brothers, that is the [Lord's] most holy flesh which today he assumed from the Virgin's flesh; that is called a 'cloud' because by it the divinity was overshadowed. It is called 'light'† because no wrongdoing weighs it down. Wrongdoing is a heavy thing and drags us

†*Affectus*, usually translated 'attachment'

†Is 19:1
†Jerome, *Interpretatio* 73 (CCSL 72:151,14)

†Jn 1:5

†*Levis*, lightweight, rather than *lumen*, bright..

down into the depths. This is why the prophet saw it sitting on *a leaden weight*.†

[†Zec 5:7–8]

8. This same flesh of his is appropriately enough called a tunic; it was symbolized by Joseph's tunic which was elaborately woven—that is, multicolored and full length, reaching all the way down to his ankles.† That Joseph, brothers, as you have learned from the sacred narrative, was the son of Jacob, the one Jacob loved more than all the others, the one he begot in his old age.† He was the son of Rachel, who gave birth to this child only after being barren for a long time.† All this applies very aptly to our Lord Jesus Christ. For he is the one whom his Father loved more than the others, the one who delights the Father in every way, as he himself declares: *You are my beloved Son in whom I am well pleased.*†

[†Gen 37:23]
[†Gen 37:3; 24:36]
[†Gen 30:22–24]
[†Lk 3:22; Mt 3:17; 12:18]

9. Now the name 'Joseph' means 'growing'.† This name fits no one so well as Christ. For he is that *stone hewn from the mountain by no human hands*‡ that grew into a great mountain and *filled the whole world*.† This is why his Father pronounces the blessing: *Joseph is a growing child, a growing child and fair to look upon*.† Truly he is *fair to look upon, he on whom the angels longed to gaze,*† *at whose beauty the sun and the moon marvel*.† Truly he is fair to look upon. For he is the Wisdom of God‡ of which it is written: *He is more beautiful than the sun and surpasses every constellation*.†

[†Jerome, *Interpretatio*. 80; CCSL 72:160, 22]
[‡Dan 2:45]
[†Dan 2:35]
[†Gen 49:22]
[†1 P 1:12]
[†Antiphon for the Feast of Saint Agnes.]
[‡1 Co 1:24]
[†Ws 7:29]

10. The Joseph of old was born of a barren mother; our Joseph of a virgin. Now between barrenness and virginity there is something common. For although there is in virginity a spiritual fecundity, there is still a physical barrenness. Thus, the privilege of being born of a virgin having been

reserved to the true Joseph, the Joseph of old was born from a barren mother because barrenness shares a certain closeness to virginity. For this reason that prophecy in the book of Wisdom applies quite well to blessed Mary: *Happy is the sterile and undefiled who knows not the sinful bed, she will bear fruit in the sight of holy souls.*† 11. Happy, indeed, was the blessed Mary who, to avoid defilement, chose physical barrenness. She gave little heed to that malediction of the Jews: *Cursed in Israel is the barren.*† Notice, brothers, the utterly beautiful congruence between son and mother. It is written in the law of Moses: *Cursed is anyone who hangs on a gibbet.*† The son did not shun the curse of the cross; the mother did not shun the curse of barrenness. Yet he, by the cross, redeemed us from the law's curse, having for our sake become accursed; and she, because she chose virginal barrenness, has merited virginal fecundity and given birth to the Son of God.

†Ws 3:13

†Source unknown

†Gal 3:13; Dt 21:23

12. Not without good reason then was holy Joseph born of a barren mother. For that barrenness in Rachel prefigured the virginity of our Joseph's mother. Nor is it without significance that 'Rachel' means 'sheep'.† Much more aptly can our Joseph's mother be called a sheep, for upon her fleece came down heavenly rain just as the holy David says: *He shall come down like rain upon a fleece.*† *Fleece, as someone has said, although it belongs to the body knows nothing of the body's passions; so virginity, although it is in the flesh, knows nothing of the vices of the flesh.*‡ 13. *He shall come down like rain upon a fleece.** A fleece can retain the moisture which comes from above but it cannot feel the moisture of carnal pleasure. So too the virginity of blessed Mary obtained the

†*Interpretatio* 9 (CCSL 72:70, 25) *et passim*

†Ps 71 [72]:6

‡Pseudo-Jerome, *Letter* 9:5, in fact, Paschasius Radbertus, *De Assumptione S. Mariae Virginis*, 5:28 (CCSL 56c: 121, 229–231)

* Ps 71 [72]:6

dew which came from heaven but could feel no carnal pleasure. Moreover, what is more befitting the Lamb than that its mother be a sheep? Notice then how appropriately she is called a sheep, who gave birth to the heavenly *Lamb who takes away the sins of the world,*[†Jn 1:29] *who was led like a sheep to the slaughter and like a lamb in the hands of the shearer made no sound and opened not his mouth.*[†Ac 8:32; Is 53:7]

14. Furthermore, the Scriptures say of Rachel: *She had a beautiful face and a charming appearance.*[†Gen 29:17; 39:6] Although it is pleasing to think that the ever-blessed Mary was the loveliest and most beautiful of women even physically, we should nonetheless apply these words to her inner beauty. But who can speak worthily of her inner beauty, if not he who *surpasses all humankind in beauty,*[†Ps 44:3 [45:2]] who so loved, desired, and sanctified her above all other creatures that he not only dwelt in her soul but prepared in her body a dwelling place for himself?

15. *While the king reclined on his couch my spikenard gave forth its scent.*[†Sg 1:2] Without doubt, there, in the bosom of the Father, where he was, he perceived the scent of her virginity. There he reflected on the beauty of her soul and, as a result, on this day he sent his angel to announce his coming, not only into her heart, but also into her flesh. Notice, brothers, what nuptials these are, how heaven-made; in them the bridegroom is God, the bride is the Virgin, and the bridegroom's messenger an angel! 16. In these nuptials the Virgin did not lose her virginity; in these nuptials the bridegroom did not lose his divinity; in these nuptials the angel did not lose its dignity. And yet there is in these nuptials a still greater miracle. The Bridegroom is son and the Bride is mother. He is the bridegroom

because he conjoined the soul of the holy Virgin with his divinity. He is the son because God himself, made man, came forth from her womb like *a bridegroom from the bridal chamber.*† It was therefore right that the angel greeted her saying: *Hail, full of grace. The Lord is with you. Blessed are you among women.*†

†Ps 18:6 [19:5]

†Lk 1:28

17. Reflect, brothers, on the sort of gifts the Son of God sent to his bride. At the moment there comes to mind the gifts which Abraham's son sent by his father's servant to Rebecca, his bride. She too, like Rachel, was a very beautiful virgin who had never known a man.† Abraham's servant found her by the water. There he spoke to her and there he gave her the gifts.† Our loveliest virgin, of whom I am speaking, freely dwelt by spiritual waters—that is, by the sacred Scriptures. To these waters she frequently had recourse, so she could say with the Prophet: *He leads me beside refreshing waters.*† 18. It was there she was found by the angel, the servant of Abraham—not the earthly and mortal but the heavenly and eternal [Abraham]. Accordingly, the Evangelist says: *The angel came into her and said: Hail, full of grace.*† Where was it that he *came into her*? Doubtless where she had hidden herself from the vanities of the world and its cares. She had gone into her private chamber and closed the door and was praying to her Father in secret.† She was *drawing waters* for herself *in joy from the fountain of the Saviour*†—that is, from the sacred Scriptures where she had read about both the virgin's giving birth and of the Saviour's coming.

†Gen 24:16

†Gen 24: 13–22

†Ps 22 [23]:2

†Lk 1:28

†Cf. Mt 6:6

†Is 12:3

19. Perhaps at the time the angel came, she was holding [the text of] Isaiah in her hands;

perhaps she was then studying the prophecy which declares: *Behold a virgin shall conceive and bear a son and his name will be called Emmanuel.*[†Is 7:14] I think that at this moment these [words of the] Scriptures were producing a very appealing conflict in her heart. I think that when she read that it was to come to pass that a certain virgin would give birth to the Son of God, secretly and with some fear she longed that she might be that virgin. But at the same time she considered herself utterly unworthy of being granted such a privilege. 20. Charity conflicted with fear, devotion with humility. At one moment she almost despaired through overwhelming fear; at the next, through the overwhelming desire she drew from it, she could not but hope. First, devotion moved her to presume to it, but then her great humility moved her to hesitate. It was then, when she was in this [moment of] hesitation, this wavering, this longing, that *the angel came into her and said: Hail, full of grace.*[†Lk 1:28]

21. Abraham's servant, as Scripture says, gave Rebecca *golden earrings and bracelets.*[†Gen 24:22] It is of these earrings that the friends of the true Bridegroom speak, one of whom is Gabriel who is now addressing Mary. And they say to the Bride: *We will make golden pendants for you.*[†Sg 1:10] Pendants are the same as earrings. They are ornaments for the ears, just as bracelets are ornaments for the arms. And indeed this servant of the great Abraham, this angel Gabriel, adorned the ears of this Virgin of ours with a lovely ornament when he said: *Hail, full of grace.*[†Lk 1:28] He adorned her arms with a beautiful golden bracelet when he said: *The Lord is with you.*[†Lk 1:28] 22. He whose coming the angel was announcing can quite appropriately be called a bracelet, for,

just as a bracelet has neither beginning nor end, so in his divinity he neither begins nor ceases to be. This bracelet adorned the arms of this virgin of ours because she often carried, cradled in her arms, the Son of God to whom she had given birth. Amidst all these riches and delights the blessed Mary remained utterly chaste, not only in the flesh but also in the mind. This is why it says in the Song of Songs: *You are beautiful and fair, utterly chaste in the midst of delights.*† †Sg 7:6

23. Physical corruption is wantonness, mental corruption is pride. It is no great achievement to preserve chastity in destitution or humility with no other virtues. For no one can succumb to carnal vices and take pride spiritually. We are not now speaking of the pride by which worldly, carnal persons pride themselves, of course, but of that which assails perfect and holy persons. As it is a great achievement to preserve integrity in the midst of material wealth and physical delights, so it is without any doubt the height of achievement to feel nothing of this pride in the midst of spiritual gifts.

24. What thoroughly imbued the blessed Mary was indeed true chastity of the mind. Listen then to how humble she was in the midst of all those spiritual gifts which she had above all other humans. Mary said to the angel: *Behold the handmaid of the Lord.*† And now listen to the Evangelist: *Rising up*, he says, *Mary set out in haste for the hill country, to the home of Zachary and greeted Elizabeth.*† Let us also add this: *Joseph also went up to Bethlehem together with Mary, his betrothed wife, who was pregnant.*† Reflect in all this on her wonderful humility.

†Lk 1:28

†Lk 1:39–40

†Lk 2:4–5

25. She—filled with God, greater than the world,

higher than heaven, more fertile than Paradise, the splendor of virgins, the glory of women, the praise of humankind, the gladness of angels, she whom the Son of God chose to be his mother—called herself a handmaiden. She whom the angel greeted subjected herself in great obedience to a workman. She—the queen of heaven, the mistress of the angels, who bore God in her womb—greeted her kinswoman humbly because she was older than herself. How very right it is then to say of blessed Mary: *You are beautiful and fair, utterly chaste in the midst of delights.*† If we can appraise this beauty well we shall see that what was said of Rachel applies to no one more aptly than to the mother of our Joseph: *She had a beautiful face and a charming appearance.*† †Sg 7:6

†Gen 29

26. Scripture tells us in addition that \<Jacob\> loved Joseph more than his other sons *because he had begotten him in his old age.*† Moses was a son of God. David was a son of God. And all the prophets and all the saints are sons of God. But *who in the clouds shall be equal to the Lord, who among the sons of God shall be like God?*† They are all beloved but none so beloved as our Joseph. Him he begot *in his old age.* [God] is that Ancient of Days of whom Daniel speaks: *As I looked thrones were placed and an Ancient of Days took his seat.*† The agedness of God—or old age or longevity—it is nothing other than his eternity. 27. In his eternity the Eternal begot this Joseph of ours coeternal and consubstantial with himself. He is *the brightness of eternal light, the flawless mirror of God's majesty, and the image of his goodness.*† It is not surprising then if God the Father does not love those who are his sons by grace as much as [he does] the One who is his Son by nature. This

†Gen 37:3

†Ps 88:7

†Dan 7:9

†Ws 7:26

Joseph of ours, moreover, although in the flesh he was born after many other sons of God, is still the *firstborn* of all. As the Apostle states: *He is the firstborn of all creation.*† *Only-begotten* of God, *the firstborn from the dead.*†

†Col 1:15
†Jn 1:18; Col 1:18

28. In signification of this, Scripture says of the Joseph who was the type [of Christ] that, although Ruben was the firstborn according to the flesh, the rights of primogeniture were accorded to Joseph.† That is why John the Baptist says of our Joseph: *After me there comes a man who was made before me.*† It is as if he said: Although according to the flesh I may have been born first, he is still *the Firstborn*. As far as human beings are concerned, God grows old for them when the love of God cools in their hearts and charity grows cold. God had already, so to speak, grown old for this world because everyone had gone astray, *had become worthless* and there was *not one who did good.*†

†1 Ch 5:2

†Jn 1:30

†Cf Ps 13: 3 [14:1], 52:4 [53:1].

29. Now, his father made Joseph a *many-colored tunic*. This is the cloud of which we spoke a short time ago, the most holy flesh of our Saviour. It is then a cloud because he used it to temper the brightness of his divinity for us; a tunic because he appeared in this world, as it were, clothed with flesh and, when he chose, he laid the flesh aside like a tunic and, when he chose, he took it up again. 30. Long ago he made a tunic for Adam, the disobedient. but it was of skin. For our Joseph, who obeyed him in everything, *he made a tunic of many colors*. The skin tunic, generally made from dead animals who inhabited this earth, showed him to be of the earth. The many-colored tunic, which in its beautiful variety [of hues] bore some likeness to the heavens, signified that this Joseph is

of heaven. Thus the Apostle says: *The first man was of the earth and earthly; the second man was from heaven and heavenly.*† 31. Superbly indeed is that tunic said to be many-colored, for our Lord Jesus Christ was adorned with the complete variety of the virtues, even in his human nature. The tunic is said to be full length—reaching to his ankles, the end of the body—because till the very end. his holy flesh remains free from corruption As the Psalmist says: *You will not allow your Holy One to see corruption.*†

†1 Co 15:47

†Ps 15 [16]:10

32. Let us then, brothers, take off Adam's tunic of skins—that is, *the works of darkness*. And since today *the true Day has illumined us, let us walk with decency, as befits the day: no revelling or drunkenness, no promiscuity or licentiousness, no quarreling or jealousy.*† For all these things belong to that skin tunic which we must take off if we wish to put on the many colored tunic, about which the Apostle immediately goes on to add: *But put on the Lord Jesus Christ.*† Regarding the various colors of this tunic he exhorts us elsewhere *as God's chosen people, holy and beloved, to put on compassion, kindness, humility, gentleness, patience.*† 33. This is that beautiful variety of virtues which first and foremost our Lord Jesus Christ put on and which every Christian must put on. Because our Joseph's tunic was not only many colored but—as it is written in the Gospel—woven of *one piece from top to bottom;*† after listing that beautiful array of diverse virtues the Apostle goes on without pausing to speak of the seamless texture of the tunic: *Above all have that charity which is the bond of perfection.*† Yet just as this variety signified that Jesus was filled with all the virtues, so *the light*

†Rm 13:12f.

†Rm 13:14

†Col 3:12

†Jn 19:23

†Col 3:14

cloud[†] signifies that he was devoid of and utterly unburdened by vices.

[†] Is 19:1, above, paragraph 6.

34. We can also understand that *light cloud* as blessed Mary, through whom our Lord came *into Egypt*—that is, into this world. She can well be called a cloud in that she was filled with the rain of spiritual grace. She was light in that none of this world's burden weighed her down. It was this cloud which the Lord mounted and entered into Egypt—that is, the weakness of this world, according to the prophecy we have already cited: *Behold the Lord will mount a light cloud and enter Egypt.*[†]

[†] Is 19:1

35. *And*, he says, *the idols of Egypt will quail before him.*[†] Thanks be to God, it has already happened: the idols of Egypt have quailed before him. The idols have been banished from the world. There are few or none now who adore stones and wood, as almost the whole world did before Christ's coming. But, brothers, if only men and women were as ready to cast all the idols out of their hearts as they are to cast them out of their homes! Anyone who loves money more than God neglects God and worships an idol. For what is money but an idol, bearing the image, not of God, but of a human being? But this has nothing to do with us. What then? Need we fear nothing from these idols? If only it were nothing!

[†] Is 19:1

36. But although Jacob has left *Mesopotamia in Syria*, although he has gone up to Bethel, yet he has in his company a wife *who stole* Laban's *idols*.[†] And as for us, although we may have left the world as Jacob left Mesopotamia, we still have our

[†] Gen 35: 1ff

sensuality and carnality which, like that woman, retains memories of the world and images of the life we have left behind. So it is that that part of our memory which God alone should hold these idols of Egypt occupy and claim as their own. On account of these idols Laban—that is, the devil—pursues us. And, since he cannot claim us by means of the riches of the world, delicious banquets, drunkenness, lusting, quarrelling and antagonisms, he tries his utmost to unsettle us through the illusions these idols cause. 37. What then is to be done? Even if we cannot wholly expel them we should cover them over as much as possible. For *blessed are they whose wrongdoings have been forgiven, whose sins have been covered over.*† Let us with vigils, <labor>, fasting, and assiduous prayer cover over whatever failures may be ours through this instability of mind, these wandering thoughts, and memories of this sort. And *since charity covers a multitude of sins*† let us work at it with our full attention. Thus the devil will find nothing of his own in us. For by these virtues we will be made one with Him in whom he found nothing.†

†Ps 31 [32]:1

†1 P 4:8

†Jn 14:30

38. Let us apply ourselves with full concentration to becoming spiritual clouds so we may overflow with the dew of heavenly teaching. Let us be light, so that, free from the dregs of cravings, we may soar high above this world on the wings of the virtues. For if our soul is like this, *the Lord* will see fit to mount upon it as if *on a light cloud* and enlighten our Egypt—that is, the darkness of our heart. He will expel all the idols of which we have spoken. He alone will possess our soul. He alone will dwell there.

39. But since these idols usually arise from the curiosity which tends to divert our attention to outward things, let us together with the blessed Mary enter the inner room and as far as possible hide ourselves within ourselves. And *with the door closed*,[†] let us beseech our Lord Jesus Christ that he, who today deigned to assume our nature, may according to his will and our advantage prepare us and so guard our life that he will remain always in our hearts, he who
>with the Father and Holy Spirit lives and reigns
>>through all the ages of ages.
>>>Amen.

[†] Mt 6:6

Sermon Ten
For Palm Sunday

ALTHOUGH THE RECURRENCE of this day which all Christians celebrate with such devotion and attention is enough to arouse our hearts to devotion, we ought nonetheless to discharge our duty of [giving you] a sermon, not only because the Passion of the Lord is going to be read out to us but also because our salvation will be remembered. That way, everything will be provided us, nothing at all will be omitted which can inflame our minds to the love of God. First of all, brothers, notice that two things are set before us today concerning our Lord Jesus Christ: the greatest glory which the Jewish people showed him on this earth; and the greatest outrages which the same people heaped upon him.

2. As you heard just a little while ago from the Gospel, and will shortly hear again,[1] when our Lord arrived in Jerusalem seated upon an ass, *a large crowd went out to meet him.*† *Some spread their clothes along the road, others cut branches from*

†Jn 12:12–13

---

1. In cistercian usages the sermon is preached in the monks' Chapterhouse after the celebration of the office of Prime. Earlier in the day, at the end of the office of Vigils, Aelred, as abbot, would have sung the Gospel relating Our Lord's triumphant entrance into Jerusalem. At the beginning of the procession before the community Mass, celebrated a few hours later, the deacon would then sing the same Gospel.

the trees and strewed them in his path, and both those in front of and those following him cried out: Hosanna to the Son of David. Blessed is he who comes in the name of the Lord.† The same Gospel also relates what you have not yet heard but, please God, you will hear shortly: how the very same people heaped outrages on the Lord. For by them he was bound, buffeted, spat upon, and finally condemned to the death which from their viewpoint was totally ignominious.

†Mt 21:8–9; Mk 11:9

3. But think quite carefully about what I said. 'The same people', I said, not 'the same persons'. For those who welcomed the Lord with such honor were Jews and those who inflicted such outrages on him were also Jews. Yet the latter were not the same as the former. Once upon a time the Lord showed both to the prophet Jeremiah through a sort of likeness. He said to him: *What is it you see, Jeremiah?* And he answered: *Figs, good figs, very good ones; and bad ones, very bad ones, which cannot be eaten because they are bad.*†

†Jer 24:3

4. Now, they are called good figs who showed the Lord so much sweetness in their love, such tenderness in their service, that, like the very sweetest figs, they were worthy of being eaten by him—that is, of being united with his Body, his holy Church. That is why Jeremiah says of these good figs: *These were like figs usually are at the beginning of the season.*† For they were as it were the first fruits of the holy Church. Of them the Apostle says: *You have come to the Church among the first whose names were written in heaven.*†

†Jer 24:2

†Heb 12:22–23

5. Those who retained none of the sweetness of charity or the tenderness of devotion, but became very bitter through jealousy, hatred, and malice

can very aptly be called rotten figs. They are not at all worthy of being eaten by the Lord—that is, of being drawn into his Body. They are the vine which he says through Isaiah: *I looked for it to bear grapes and it produced thorns.*† Thorns indeed it produced, so bitter, so pungent, that they even brought forth blood from that holiest body.

†Is 5:1,4; Gen 1:12, 3:18; Heb 6:8

6. And as the Prophet spoke of good and bad figs, he called both of them figs but he made a distinction between them. Some he called good, others bad. In the same way, both those who today cried out *Hosanna to the Son of David* and those who cried out *Crucify him, crucify him* were Jews but between them there is a great difference. This difference, brothers, is indicated quite clearly in the Book of Joshua.

7. When the children of Israel were about to cross the Jordan to enter the Promised Land according to the Lord's command, the Levites went into the river first, carrying the ark of the Lord. As soon as the ark entered the water, the waters were divided. The upper part piled up like a wall, while the lower part flowed away into the sea.† That ark, brothers, signified the Lord.

†Jos 3:14–16

8. In the ark were *Aaron's rod which once budded and the tablets of the Covenant and a golden jar containing the manna.*† All of these are found very beautifully in our Lord. In him is Aaron's rod— that is, priestly power—which first blossomed but then dried up among the Jews. But in our Lord Jesus Christ it flowers eternally. As the Psalmist tells him: *You are a priest for ever according to the order of Melchisedech.*† In him are the tablets of the Covenant—that is, perfect knowledge. As the

†Heb 9:4

†Ps 109 [110]:4

Apostle says: *In him all the treasures of wisdom and knowledge lie hidden.*† 9. In another place the Apostle says: *The head of Christ is God.*† And in the Song of Songs it is written of him: *His head is of the finest gold.*† The golden jar can therefore be understood as his divinity. Therefore the Apostle says: *In him all the fullness of the godhead dwells in bodily form.*† And indeed it contains manna— that is, the bread of angels, the refreshment of holy souls. This is the bread of which it is written: *Blessed is the one who will eat bread in the kingdom of God.*† This is the bread which the Lord himself will serve, after the day of judgement, to all who are his own.

†Col 2:3
†1 Co 11:3
†Sg 5:11
†Col 2:9
†Lk 14:15

10. Indeed, quite beautifully is it recorded that these three things were in the ark: the rod, the tablets, and the manna. The rod with which he chastises us, the tablets by which he instructs us, the manna with which he feeds us. With the rod he beats us lest we become proud. With the tablets he instructs us, that we may love him. With the manna of his sweetness he feeds us lest we grow faint along the way. 11. This is the rod with which he threatens certain people, saying: *I will punish their wrongdoing with the rod and their sins with stripes.*† This is the rod for which the prophet longed when he said: *Correct me, Lord, but yet in moderation and not as justice demands.*† These tablets the Lord promises us by saying: *I will put my law in their minds and write it on their hearts.*† These tablets were desired by the one who said: *Instruct me in the path of your righteousness.*† This manna the Lord promises us when he says: *Come to me all you who labor and are heavily burdened and I will refresh you.*† In this spiritual food exalted

†Ps 88:33 [89:32]
†Jer 10:24
†Jer 31:33
†Ps 118:[119]:27
†Mt 11:28

the person who said: *The Lord is my shepherd and I shall not lack anything.*†

†Ps 22 [23]:1; Gen 48:15

12. So the ark in the Jordan [stands for] Christ in Judea. The Jordan, which was in the Promised Land that the Lord himself promised and gave to the Jews, represents the Jews. Now, notice how the water divided by the ark refers to what we are presently considering. Reflect on those about whom you sang a little while ago: *When the Lord entered the Holy City, < the children of the Hebrews, foretelling the resurrection of life with palm branches, shouted: Hosanna in the highest>.*† These are the upper part of the water, [the part] that stood still. It stood in *the law of the Lord*,‡ in the way of his commandments, in exultation at his praise, in the sweetness of his love.

†The responsory for Palm Sunday (Hesbert 4:6961)

‡Ps 118 [119]:1, 32; Ps 1:2

13. And aptly [is it called] the upper part. For it belongs to *the Jerusalem which is above, which is free, which is our mother.*† Upper, indeed. It does not bend its heart to the earth. And so it cries out: *Hosanna in the highest.*† These [children] are called progeny (*pueri*) because they are pure (*puri*). Pure from malice, pure from envy, pure from avarice. It is these the prophet exhorts when he says: *Children, praise the Lord, praise the name of the Lord.*† They are the true Hebrews—which means 'over-leaping'.† They had leapt over all that is perishable, all that is transitory. They rejoiced, they exulted only in the praises of their Creator, their Saviour. 14. It was indeed fitting that in their hands they carry palms, which is the sign of victory, the sign of peace. For they acknowledged him as their unconquered king who, as it is said in the Apocalypse, *rode forth conquering that he might conquer.*† They acknowledged the true

†Gal 4:26

†Mt 21:9

†Ps 112 [113]:1
†*Interpretatio* 35 (CCSL 72:103, 16) *et passim*

†Rv 6:2

Solomon, the Son of David, in whose kingdom is perpetual peace and everlasting rest. These are the waters of the Jordan which, in the presence of the ark, retained the sweetness and savor which they derived from their sources—that is, from their origin in the prophets and patriarchs—without any admixture of bitterness. Therefore they deserved to taste the potency of eternal sweetness and delight and to manifest the glory of the resurrection in their deeds.

15. Going out to meet the Lord with palms, they proclaimed the resurrection to life, for the saints *will come with exultation carrying the sheaves*† of their good works, carrying the palms of the victories they have scored over the devil. Then—at that resurrection, that is—the Lord will enter *the holy city, the heavenly Jerusalem.*† He will enter it with the children of the Hebrews, who at that resurrection will come out to meet him; as the Apostle says: *We who are left alive will be caught up in the clouds to meet Christ in the air; thus we shall be forever with the Lord.*† 16. Then indeed they will truly be progeny (*pueri*), because perfectly pure (*puri*), not only from the contagion of sin but even from all corruption. Then they will truly be Hebrews—that is, those who perfectly overleap not only the danger of death but even the fear of death. Then confidently they will carry palms of victory with great exultation and assurance, saying:, *Where, death, is your victory? Where, death, is your sting?*† And truly, brother, it was fitting that the resurrection to life should be proclaimed by those for whom the Lord was to be not ruination but resurrection, just as holy Simeon prophesied of him: *Behold, he is set for the ruination and the resurrection of many and for a sign which will be rejected.*†

†Ps 125 [126]:6

†Responsory for Palm Sunday (Hesbert 4:6961)

†1 Th 4:17

†1 Co 15:55

†Lk 2:34

17. [Simeon] says three things: ruination for some, resurrection for others, and a sign of rejection. Already in this division of which we speak, notice how Jesus is for some resurrection, for others ruination. For those surely who proclaimed the resurrection to life, who in their deeds manifested the resurrection that was to be, who very manifestly declared themselves to be already risen in spirit, who hoped they would be restored to life by him on the day of judgment, for them without doubt Jesus was set to bring resurrection.

18. Notice now the other part of the Jordan's waters, [the part] which at the presence of the ark of the Lord flowed away into the sea. Today, this holy ark, which we commended to your loving [consideration] a little while ago, appeared in the waters of the Jordan—that is, among the jewish people. So it is that the good part profited by this and became better and stronger. By the same event, the other part—the scribes and the pharisees—plunged into a greater bitterness as if into the sea. Whatever they had brought with them of that natural source from which they had come forth was swallowed up in the brine of the sea. 19. All information about the Scriptures, all knowledge of the Law, all understanding of prophecy—all this the bitterness of envy and ill-will consumed in them. Hearing the din of the people praising [the Lord], seeing the wondrous honor they accorded him, and inflamed with rage because they could not stop the people, they railed at the object of these demonstrations, saying: *Do you hear what these people are saying?* He gave them this excellent answer: *I tell you, if they keep silence the stones will shout aloud.*†

†Lk 19:40

20. That, brothers, is what has now very clearly been fulfilled. The Jews keep silence, the stones shout aloud. The prophet's statement has been fulfilled: *The bricks have fallen but we will build in hewn stone.*† Who are these bricks but those Jews of clay and earth who have fallen from the holy building of the patriarchs and prophets? It is to them that Jesus *is set for ruination.* For what could have cemented them in more securely made them fall even more miserably.

†Is 9:10

21. But while those who rejected *the firm* and solid *foundation* go to ruin, Jerusalem is being built up with living stones, hewn stones that, fastening themselves to Christ, the most solid of stones who has *become the key-stone,*† take their very name from him. Well, Jews, what have you gained? What you then wanted has happened. The children of the Hebrews in the natural order do not shout now, they do not shout *Hosanna to the Son of David.* Yet does that mean that the greeting is not shouted? Kings shout it, emperors shout it, men shout it, women shout it, youth shout it, virgins shout it, children shout it, old men shout it.

†1 P 2:5–7

22. Notice, you wretches, notice, you blind, how thousands upon thousands come out to meet him today with palm branches. Notice how many thousands today lay before him not their clothes but their very bodies.† Hear, if you are not deaf, how many thousands of men and women today shout, sing, celebrate, supplicate: *Hosanna to the Son of David. Blessed is he who comes in the name of the Lord.*† Thus is fulfilled what the holy David said: *The sinner will see and grow angry, he will gnash his teeth and despair.*† 23. There you have,

†In the course of the chanting of the Passion of our Lord Jesus Christ on Palm Sunday, cistercian monks prostrated themselves full length on the floor of the church.

†Mt 21:9

†Ps 111 [112]:10

brothers, all that the Jews today can do amidst such praises accorded to Christ. They can grow angry, they can gnash their teeth, they can be consumed with envy, but *the desire of the sinners shall come to nothing.*† Christ is adored, praised, acclaimed because, the bricks of clay being silent, the living stones cry out. Our Jesus is destined therefore for *the ruination and the resurrection of many*, the ruination of the bricks, the resurrection of the stones. *And,* he says, *as a sign that will be rejected.*† This is the sign which he has now lifted up in the midst of the nations—the sign of his passion, the sign of his cross.

†Ibid.

†Lk 2:34; Is 9:10

24. It is the sign that the whole world had rejected, a scandal to the Jews, a folly to the Gentiles. *We*, says the Apostle, *preach Christ crucified, a scandal to the Jews, to the Gentiles, however, a folly.*† And notice, brothers, how quickly this sign was rejected. On the very day on which the sign was put up, as you have heard in the Gospel, Pilate gave it a title: *This is Jesus of Nazareth, King of the Jews.*† It was immediately rejected. For the Jews said: *Do not write 'King of the Jews'.*† 25. Christ's cross triumphed over this rejection. Where the godless thought it was they who had triumphed over Christ there, it was instead Christ who appeared the victor. The sign of his victory was fastened to the cross itself and, what is more amazing, it was fastened there by his very enemies. The enemies who plotted his death now vie with one another to give him glory: *Do not write [that]*, says the pharisee. *What I have written, I have written*, says Pilate. And look! Now both Pilate and pharisee have passed away but what Pilate wrote has not been erased.

†1 Co 1:23

†Jn 19:19; Mt 27:37

†Jn 19:21

26. Does a wondrous joy not arise in your hearts, my brothers, when you perceive before you the sign of the Cross, still glorious with that inscription? Still now there can be read on the cross of Christ: *Jesus of Nazareth, King of the Jews.* All to no avail was the rejection of the godless. This rejection on the part of the Jews was followed by rejection on the part of the pagans. Even emperors take up arms against the cross of Christ, philosophers debate, orators inveigh, even the dregs of the populace howl. What shall I say? Against one wooden gibbet the whole world everywhere was fighting. 27. But now, brothers, reflect on the omnipotence of our Lord Jesus Christ, reflect on Wisdom. By means of that gibbet—and nothing was more despicable, nothing more vile, nothing more hateful, nothing more horrible, for what is more vile than a cross on which robbers were hung, men guilty of sacrilege executed, parricides put to death?—by means of that, I tell you, the Lord subjugated emperors, made fools of the wise, instructed the simple and unlearned, glorified the poor, and of all of them together worshipers of the gibbet.

28. Look, brothers: on the forehead of kings there is no [sign] more magnificent, on the hand none more impressive, on the breast nothing more salutary. All that rejection has come to an end. Would that what is true of the voice was also be true of behavior. Yet many and,—what is more to be regretted—even those who profess the cross of Christ, reject that cross. Not indeed by what they say but by what they do. Listen to the Apostle: *As I have often told you and now tell you with tears in my eyes, there are many whose way*

of life makes them enemies of the cross of Christ.[†Ph 3:18] Who are they who reject the cross of Christ if not those who are the enemies of the cross of Christ? And who are they? *Those,* he says, *whose God is their stomach.*[†Ph 3:19]

29. My sons, I address you as my brothers, as men who not only adore the cross of Christ but have also made profession on it. You have not only made profession, but are lovers of it. You I address. Let anyone feel as he will, judge as he will, flatter himself as much as he will. In the cross of Christ there is nothing weak, nothing soft, nothing delicate, nothing that coddles flesh and blood. 30. Let the cross of Christ itself be, as it were, the mirror of the Christian. In [the light of] the cross of Christ let each person examine his life, whether the way he lives conforms to the cross of Christ. And to the extent to which anyone shares Christ's cross, let him count on sharing Christ's glory. But anyone who spurns the bitterness of Christ's cross should stand in fear of not being admitted to the sight of the Crucified. Realize, my brothers, how greatly you should rejoice, you who have crucified yourselves with Christ. 31. *It is the truth I am telling you,* brothers. *I do not lie.*[†1 Tm 2:7; Rm 9:1] Our order is Christ's cross. Therefore, brothers, hold fast to these two things: that you do not depart from the cross of Christ; that when you are placed on the cross, you do nothing against the cross of Christ. To speak more plainly, this means: persevere in your order and, persevering in the order, do not knowingly do anything contrary to that order. In this way you will beyond any doubt follow Christ to the place where he went from his cross.

32. It gives me great delight, brothers, to speak at length of Christ's cross which is our glory, our life.[†] But due measure must be observed, especially because we have to devote more time [today] to the Divine Office. For that reason, let us turn to our Lord Jesus Christ and implore his mercy, that he may deign to look *upon this family of his for which he did not hesitate to be given into the hands of evil men and to undergo the torments of the cross.*[†]

>Together with the Father and Holy Spirit
>he lives and reigns,
>God through all the ages of ages.
>Amen.

[†] Antiphon for the feast of the Exaltation of the Holy Cross (Hesbert 3:3954), cf. Gal 6:14

[†] Collect for the Holy Week liturgy of the Cistercians

Sermon Eleven
For the Feast of Easter

LIKE NEW-BORN INFANTS, *crave spiritual milk that you may grow up to salvation, if indeed you have tasted how sweet the Lord is.*† The Apostle exhorts you, brothers, to desire milk and such milk as will enable you to grow, and to grow up to salvation. But listen to what he adds: *If indeed you have tasted how sweet the Lord is.* And that milk, what is it supposed to signify, if not the sweetness of Jesus Christ? Why then does he exhort us to desire milk if we have already tasted how sweet the Lord is? It would seem then, brothers, that the Apostle is speaking here of two sorts of sweetness.

†1 P 2:2–3

2. Perhaps one sort is that which you have tasted in these days and therefore he confidently exhorts you to desire the other sort of sweetness which is symbolized by milk. That in these days you have tasted how sweet the Lord is is credible, especially you who have seen and reflected on, as if in the presence of Jesus Christ on his cross, you who have seen those holy arms outstretched as if to embrace you, you who have contemplated those sweet breasts laid bare, as if to refresh you. 3. All this, brothers, though it happened once and for all—for, as the Apostle says, *Christ was offered once to take away the sins of the multitude*†—yet you have seen it all far better and more clearly with

†Heb 9:28

the eyes of your heart than many saw it with their physical eyes then, when it happened. In all these things you have tasted how sweet the Lord is. Sweet, humble, meek, merciful, gentle, and caring. How much sweetness he showed at that supper which he celebrated with his disciples before his passion!

4. At that supper he told his disciples: *I have longed with great longing to eat this Passover with you before I suffer.*† This is that sweet food with which the Jews mixed gall, as holy David prophesied: *They gave me gall in my food.*† This was fulfilled literally when *they gave him wine to drink mixed with gall.*† But because that gall was given him as a drink, not as food, it would seem that in these words the prophet intended us to consider not only the literal sense but also its inner meaning. 5. With that sweetest food, which he took so sweetly and so humbly with his disciples, the Jews mixed gall. They corrupted with their money one of his very own disciples who had come with the others to share this food. They robbed him of love and with the gall of malice rendered him bitter through and through. For what were those good disciples of his if not his food? In them he took delight. Their love and devotion fed him. And what was that traitor Judas among them but gall mixed into good food?

†Lk 22:15

†Ps 68:22 [69:21]
†Mt 27:34

6. At that supper the old Passover which the Jews were accustomed to celebrate came to an end and the new Passover which we celebrate began. How could he have shown us greater sweetness than by leaving for us his own body and blood as a memorial of himself? For he willed that the price which he paid for us once should always be

before our eyes.† With a wondrous affection he willed that his body and blood be not only our ransom but also our food.

    7. Does it not seem to you, my brothers, that he very explicitly fulfilled at his supper what the prophet David said: *There is in the Lord's hand a cup of foaming wine, full of spices. He has poured it from one to another.*† For after he had celebrated that old Passover which the Jews were accustomed to celebrating with the flesh of a lamb and blood, *Jesus took bread* and giving it *to his disciples* said: *This is my body.* And afterwards he [gave them] the cup, saying, *This is my blood.*† Notice the cup in the Lord's hand. What is this cup but the established usages of the Law? This cup was full of *foaming wine*—that is, pure wine. 8. This wine is the spiritual meaning contained in those usages of the old Law. It is wine because it gave joy to the human heart.† It is wine because it inebriated those who understood it. It inebriated them with the love of God. It inebriated them so much that they forgot themselves and loved God alone, desired only him. Was David not inebriated with this wine when, as if drunk, he took off his clothes and exposed himself to dance before the ark of the Lord?† Was Isaiah not inebriated with this wine when, as he himself bears witness, *he walked naked and barefoot* in the sight of all the people?

    9. But, although this wine was pure in itself, yet because certain physical observances were still mixed with it, *the cup in the Lord's hand of foaming wine* is *full of spices.* Reflect on that Lamb which our Lord at this supper held in his hands. Notice there that established usage of the law like a cup in the Lord's hand. In this cup—that is, in this

usage—there was pure wine—that is, a spiritual meaning. Notice, on the other hand, the bread and wine, as it were another cup. In this cup there was not at first that spiritual wine. 10. Now notice how he poured the wine that was in the one cup into the other. What was the wine in the old usage? The lamb symbolized the body of Christ, the lamb's blood the blood of Christ. There you have the wine in the first cup. But *he poured it from one to the other*. Let me tell you how. *He took bread* and said: *This is my body*. He also took wine and said: *This is my blood*.† There is the change. †Mt 26:26 The lamb that contained in symbol Christ's body and blood is left empty. The other cup has been filled because the bread has become the body of Christ and the wine the blood of Christ.

11. Let us notice yet more. That lamb represented the Lord's passion. This is why the command was given that as a memorial of the Lord's passion every year that lamb should be slaughtered.† The †Ex 12:1–14 commemoration of the Lord's passion in the lamb was like the wine in the cup. But God *has poured it from one into the other*, for he has transferred the commemoration of his passion, which was previously in that lamb, to the sacrament of his body and blood which he has now given to his disciples, saying: *Do this in memory of me*.† 12. Here †1 Co 11:24 there was a certain mixture on account of physical observances, for although the lamb symbolized the body of Christ, it was not really the body of Christ, but a lamb. In our sacrament there is no mixture, for after the consecration our sacrament is no longer the substance of an animal and it is not the bread and wine [that it was], but it is really and truly the body and blood of Christ. Yet because the prophet foresaw in spirit that the physical Jews

would refuse to abandon these dregs of physical observances he added: *Yet its dregs have not been drained.*† The wine has been taken away and the dregs still remain. 13. Therefore he says: *All sinners on earth must drink,*† but other dregs and other wine. Before the coming of the Lord and his passion the Jews alone drank from this cup, but what they drank was spiced wine, not pure. The pagans did not drink from it and therefore not *all sinners* drank. Christ came, suffered for us, rose from the dead, ascended into heaven and look, you see *all sinners on earth* drinking from it. *All*—that is, Jews and pagans. But the Jews drink only the dregs and we drink only the wine. They have the lamb which has lost all flavor of meaning. We have that Lamb who took away the sins of the world [and] in whom is the expression of truth itself.

†Ps 74:9 [75:8]

†Ps 74:9 [75:8]

14. Notice further how *he poured from one into the other.* In the old Passover, according to the prescription of the Law, with the lamb's flesh they ate unleavened bread with wild herbs.† There you have the cup in the Lord's hand. What wine was in this mystic cup? The connotation of unfeigned humility. For what is leaven but pride? This is why the Apostle exhorts us: *Rid yourselves of the old leaven.*† Truly pride is the old leaven. For it came into existence when angels were first created. That leaven made one of them so swell up that he sought to be like God, so corrupted him that from being an angel he became the devil. That leaven made a human being so swell up that she wanted to be like God,† so corrupted her that she became *like the senseless beasts.*† The unleavened bread, like the wine, was the exercises of humility, for this is indeed what it signified. 16. Now notice

†Ex 12:8

†1 Co 5:7

†Gen 3:5
†Ps 48:13, 21 [49:12,20]

our Lord, how he *rises from supper*, how he *girds himself with a towel*, how he *washes the feet of his disciples*. By this he took the meaning of humility which the unleavened bread had had and transferred it to this sacrament.† For he said: *Do you understand what I have done for you? You call me 'Master' and 'Lord', and rightly so, for that is what I am. If I, your Lord and Master, have washed your feet, you also ought to wash one another's feet.*‡ This washing is not only the sign of an important reality, about which this is not the time to speak, but it is also a manifest exercise of humility.

†The early Cistercians, like many theologians of the time, considered the foot washing a sacrament instituted by Christ.
‡Jn 13:13–14

17. Listen, brothers, how at that supper he offered you not wild herbs but wine—that is the meaning of those herbs. What is the meaning of wild herbs if not the bitterness of this life and its persecutions? For wild herbs are extremely bitter. That is why, among the many other things he said in his last discourse, the Lord also added this: *If they have persecuted me, they will persecute you also.*† And again: *In this world you will suffer distress.*† Why should we who are daily tried in the bitter hardships of this life any longer physically seek those wild herbs?

†Jn 15:20

18. It would take a long time, brothers, to explain everything that was done physically in those ancient observances, and which the Lord has bidden us to celebrate spiritually. For our Lord commended these and many other sacramental rites to you three days ago and in all of them you were doubtless able to taste how sweet the Lord is, so that now you ought to be longing for that other sweetness which the Apostle signified by milk.

19. What then? What could the remembrance of the Lord's passion effect in your hearts? What was

it like to see our utterly sweet Lord bound, spat upon, buffeted? How Isaiah fed on this sight—not of course that he saw it happening but he told about it as if it were happening. *As many were astonished at you,* he said, *so will his appearance be dishonored among men, his comeliness among the sons of men.*[†Is 52:14]

20. *Many were* indeed *astonished* when he fed five thousand people with five loaves and two fishes. *Many were astonished* when he gave light to the man born blind. *Many were astonished* when he restored Lazarus to life. They *were astonished*, they praised him, they heaped honor on him. Great was that honor but no less [great] was the outrage which they perpetrated on him later. That is why the prophet says: *His appearance will be dishonored among men.* 'Dishonored' means without honor.[†*Inglorius . . . sine gloria.*] 21. And his appearance was indeed dishonored when his face was covered and spat upon. His comeliness was without honor when they crowned him with thorns, when they scourged him and struck his head with a reed. It was without glory, but, as the Prophet says, *among the sons of men.* Now, among the sons of God all this outrageous treatment is great honor. To such an extent was this all honor, in reality, that the same Prophet says: *We saw him and there was no attractiveness in him and we desired him as a man degraded.*[†Is 53:2–3. *Aspectus . . . despectum.* A parallel not possible in English.] As such Isaiah desired him. Why? He saw that all that degradation would be the salvation of the human race and the honor of Christ himself.

22. This the Apostle shows clearly when he says: *He humbled himself, becoming obedient unto death, even the death of the cross.*[†Ph 2:8] Look at the degradation. But listen to what comes next:

Therefore God exalted him[†] and so on. Saint David prophesied the same: *From the torrent along the path he will drink and therefore he will hold his head high.*[†] He drank *from the torrent* because he tasted the bitterness of this life but it was *along the path*—that is, in passing. His sufferings were soon finished, his death was soon transformed. Therefore he held *his head high*. For it was because he died that he rose again and he was glorified because he rose.

†Ph 2:9

†Ps 109:7

23. Now, what sweetness was your heart able to imbibe when, with your inner eye, you saw the Lord carrying his cross? Who can appreciate that humility, that meekness, that patient endurance? Indeed, *he was led like a sheep to the slaughter, like a lamb before its shearers he was silent and did not open his mouth.*[†] How sweet it was to reflect on the, as it were, still fresh wounds of Christ, to stand as it were by his cross, to see the tears of his mother, to hear that sweet voice [say]: *Father, forgive them for they know not what they do.*[†] What hope for the forgiveness of our sins does not surge up in us when we hear him praying so sweetly even for his enemies. 24. But this sweetness was not that of milk but that of wine. For while on the one hand it tasted sweet, on the other it had a bite. The sweetness lay in affection and devotion but at the same time a certain tender sadness and compassion gave it that bite. You should not be able to look at those sweet hands being pierced with nails so hard without sadness, albeit sweet. Nor, similarly, on the piercing of his feet with iron and the wounding of that most tender side with the lance. Nor should you be able to behold those dear sweet tears of our Lady without compassion, however sweet.

†Is 3:7

†Lk 23:34

25. Therefore, you who have tasted this biting wine—that is, the remembrance of the Lord's passion—now crave milk—that is, the gentleness of his resurrection. And it is rightly milk, for there is no sadness mixed in with it. The angels exult, the apostles give glory, the holy women take delight in that blessed sight. Alleluia everywhere, praise everywhere, joy everywhere! 26. What <a joy> already to see him eating and drinking with his disciples, him whom previously you saw hanging on the cross; to kiss with great gladness those sweet wounds at which a little while earlier you wept with such compassion! *This is the day which the Lord made. Let us exult and be glad in it.*† [†Ps 117 [118]:24] This is the day blessed Abraham saw in spirit, *saw and was glad.* For as the Lord says in the Gospel: *Your father Abraham rejoiced to see my day; he saw it and was glad.*† [†Jn 8:56]

27. As the holy Fathers interpreted this, Abraham saw the Lord's day then, when he gave a hospitable welcome to the three angels who were types of the holy Trinity. For he welcomed them, as Scripture relates, *under a tree* and he waited on them to show them honor.† [†Gen 18:4–8] In them *he saw this day, saw it and was glad.* To provide for their needs he killed the finest and tenderest calf and served them hearth cakes along with milk and butter. Notice, brothers, this great mystery.† [†*Sacramentum.*] For it would seem that these things had little savor. Their [meaning] is obscure. But in them our Lord Jesus Christ was, as it were, hidden. He lies there concealed. 28. But let us go with these holy women the evangelist speaks of today.† [†Mk 16:1–2] Let us go *to the tomb* of the Scriptures. Let us go with the aromatic oils of dutiful devotion. Let us seek our Lord here. Let us seek him with faith,

with devotion, with charity. For these are the ointments we have to bring to this tomb if we want to find Jesus. But *who will roll away the stone for us from the entrance to the tomb*[†]—that is, the covering of this passage of Scripture—so that we may be able to find what we are looking for? May his angel, his grace, come to our assistance.

†Mk 16:3

29. What tree is this? It is the one from which hung the bunch of utterly sweet grapes that yielded the wine which today gladdens the whole world.[†] Think of the bunch of grapes which the children of Israel carried on a wooden pole.[†] What is the bunch of grapes on the wooden pole, if not Christ on his cross? Today, my brothers, the whole world is nourished with that wine which flowed from this <bunch of grapes>. For what Christian today does not drink Christ's blood? 30. Back then what did Abraham see in that prize calf, if not the sacrifice offered for the salvation of the whole world. It was indeed the prize calf. By its death it redeemed the whole world, with its flesh it refreshes the whole world, with its horns it triumphed over the devil and his angels,[†] with its hooves it does not stops dislodging earthly desires from our hearts.

†Ps 103 [104]:15
†Nb 13:24–25

†Mt 25:41

31. But now what shall we say about the hearth cake? What is bread baked in ashes? What is this bread? Is it perhaps that of which the Jews—as it is written in the book of the prophet Jeremiah—said: *Come, let us put wood into his bread.*[†] Note, wood again, again the cross of Christ. And what is the bread, if not the body of Christ? *The bread that I shall give*, he said, *is my flesh for the life of the world.*[†] Then what is bread in ashes? Hearth cakes, when they are cooked, are covered with ashes.

†Jer 11:19; 18:18

†Jn 6:52

And what are ashes, if not earth. Don't you think that Christ's burial is very explicitly signified here? The bread in the ashes is therefore the body of Christ in the heart of the earth. 32. But why is the number three mentioned here? Abraham ordered that three measures should be used to make the hearth cakes. Why was this, if not because he saw in spirit that, *as Jonas was three days and three nights in the whale's belly*,[†Mt 12:40] so Christ's flesh was three days and three nights in the earth? As the calf which he slaughtered represented the Lord's passion and the hearth cake his burial, therefore, the milk is to be understood as the sweetness of his resurrection.

33. There was every need, brothers, that his disciples, who were still infants, should be nourished with this milk. So little were they that during his passion they fled and abandoned him.[†Mt 26:56] So little was Peter that, because of the remark of a lone serving girl, he denied him.[†Mt 26:69–72] It was necessary therefore that, like infants, they should see his resurrection even with their physical eyes, and so, as it were, having been nourished with a kind of milk, that they might be capable of believing things unseen, of contemplating the invisible. 34. How lovely it is that he willed that the women announce his resurrection to the disciples.[†Mt 28:7] For it falls to women to provide milk to little ones. In this there is also another significance. Those who are in charge of little children and sick people must, like mothers to their children, give them this milk with great compassion and deference. Until the little ones have been nourished with this milk they must not show them solid food—that is, the deep things of the godhead. Such a person was Paul who said: *As to little ones in Christ, I gave you milk to drink, not solid food.*[†1 Co 3:2]

35. With good reason Abraham, when *he saw these things, exulted*. And you, brothers, who see these things, exult! Crave this milk, crave it and taste it. Thrive on it and thrive *to your salvation*. For the apostle Paul says: *If with your lips you confess that Jesus is Lord and in your hearts you believe that God raised him from the dead, you will be saved.*† But we ought to understand here that faith *which works through love.*† Obtain it from this milk—that is, extract the richness of love for Christ from this remembrance of the Lord's resurrection. 36. This was the meaning of the butter we mentioned a little while ago. For, just as butter is obtained from milk, so from the remembrance which we ought to have of the Lord's resurrection, of the time he spent with his disciples, of the way in which they touched his wounds,† of the tears that the women shed at his tomb,† we should, as it were, grow fat with love for him.

37. Let us be *like new-born infants*.‡ Infants in innocence, in simplicity. Once we have put off the old man who we had been, who was crucified with Christ, as Christ has risen from the dead through the glory of the Father, may we, having been crucified with him and buried to all the desires of this world, deserve to rise to a new life. And in the future resurrection may we deserve to rejoice with him for ever.† May our Lord Jesus Christ himself grant us this,
>who lives and reigns
>with the Father and Holy Spirit,
>God, through all the ages of ages.
>Amen.

†Rm 10:9

†Gal 5:6

†Lk 24:39; Jn 20:27

†Jn 20:11, cf. *Benedictus* antiphon for Holy Saturday (Hesbert 3:3826)

‡1 P 2:2

†Rm 6:4–6

Sermon Twelve
For the Feast of Easter

AT THE TIME WHEN the sons of Israel were leaving Egypt, it was prescribed in the Law that a lamb was to be slaughtered and eaten. This was called the paschal feast† †Ex 12:1–14
It was also prescribed that for seven days they should eat unleavened bread—that is, [bread] without leavening.† And this was called the feast of unleavened bread, and not only the feast of unleavened bread, but also the pasch.† The Evangelist brings this out when he says, *The festival of unleavened bread, called the pasch, was approaching.*† The first feast, when they killed the lamb, was called only the pasch; this latter was called both the pasch and the feast of unleavened bread. 2. It seems to me, then, that the first feast symbolizes the Lord's passion and the latter his resurrection. That the first symbolizes the Lord's passion is sufficiently well known. In it the true Lamb was slain and by his blood we have been saved from the hand of Pharaoh—in the spiritual sense, the devil. The feast is called the pasch—that is, the passing over—because Christ at his passion passed over from this world. As the Evangelist says: *Before the day of paschal feast Jesus knew that his hour had come to pass from this world to the Father.*†

†Ex 12:15–20

†Lv 23:6

†Lk 22:1

†Jn 13:1

3. Yet let us take a look at how the other feast symbolizes the Lord's resurrection. And first of

all let us reflect on how profoundly that [divine] majesty humbled himself and to what depths he descended for us. He who was the creator, made himself a creature. He who was Lord, made himself a servant. He who was rich, made himself poor. He who was great, made himself little. *And the Word was made flesh.*† He was bread and he fed the angels. But he did not feed us. And so we were wretched, because a rational creature is always wretched if she is not fed this bread. 4. We were, however, so weak that in no way could we taste that bread in all its purity. We had within us a corrosive leaven that robbed us of our pristine strength. We had become so unlike that pure and untainted bread that we could not taste it at all. This leavening which we had within us was twofold. We had within us the leavening of mortality and we had within us the leavening of iniquity.

†Jn 1:14

5. You see now how far removed we were from that bread in which there was neither mortality nor iniquity. How were we to ascend to it? How were we to taste it? What things are so contrary to one another as mortality and immortality, iniquity and justice? We are mortals and sinners; he is immortal and just. How were we to come together? He saw this, he who is caring and merciful saw this. Because we could not ascend to him, he came down to us. He took upon himself one part of our leavening and so adapted himself to our weakness. 6. He did not take to himself the whole leaven that was in us, but a certain part of it. If he had taken on the whole of it he would be as we are and he would not be able to help us. If he had taken none of it he would be so distant from us that we would not be able in any way to

approach him. And so we would remain forever in our wretchedness. We have said that there was a twofold leavening in us: mortality and iniquity. The one he took on and by it was made like us. The other he avoided so that he could profit us.

7. The leavening of our mortality therefore he accepted, and abode in the purity of his justice, so that he would be the sort of being[†] who could come down to us and yet remain the sort of being to whom we ought to ascend. You see now, brothers, how that pure bread is leavened for our sakes. To this leavening of mortality belongs hunger, thirst, sorrow, misery. All of this our Lord took on himself. He chose to take on this leavening, but he was not obliged to remain in ferment.[†] 8. First he showed this leavening in himself through a wondrous compassion and then he purged himself of this leaven through a wondrous charity. He purged himself of this leavening in such a way as to show his wonderful charity for us. He knew that we had not only leavening which was extremely bad, but also a leavening which was far worse and death-dealing, which prevented us from uniting ourselves to this bread which is truly pure and untainted. Therefore he willed to purge himself from the leavening of mortality in the way in which we have to purge ourselves from the leavening of iniquity.

9. We ought to know that our iniquity is the cause of our mortality. And therefore when we are fully purged of iniquity we will doubtless also be purged of mortality. We ought meanwhile to realize that our iniquity is twofold. It comes from the nature in which we were born and from the evil will which we later brought to it. From

[†] *Talis* in Latin.

[†] *. . . fermenta suscipere . . . in fermento remanere.*

both of these the Lord purges us. He offered for us a sacrifice—his own blood—and through this sacrifice we are purged. 10. And therefore what we suffer now from the corruption of our nature is no longer iniquity but infirmity. From the corruption of our nature come the impulses of concupiscence which we suffer unwillingly. From this come the impulses of lust, anger, pride, ambition. But if we do not consent [to them], God does not impute them to us, because that pure sacrifice was offered to offset the corruption of our nature. Note, then, by the workings of his compassion in us in baptism we are purged of all sins, both those which came from nature and those which we added voluntarily.

11. But have we kept ourselves in that untainted state? What then shall we do? He has taught us how we are to be cleansed. In the same way as he was purged of the leavening of mortality we ought to be purged from the leavening of iniquity. Doubtless, he could somehow have purged himself of mortality without suffering pain. But since we cannot be purged of our iniquity except by temporal pains, he willed to provide an example for us.

12. Remember now that we said that our Lord Jesus Christ is bread. Think of him before the passion. Notice that he was, as it were, bread with leavening in it. He was hungry and thirsty, he wept, he slept, he felt tired. All these things belong not to the leavening of iniquity but to the leavening of infirmity and morality. By all of them he demonstrated the compassion and the charity he had towards us. All of them are various kinds of medicine that were characteristic of our infirmity.

All of them, because they were characteristic of us in that he did not possess them himself, he took them on from us. 13. But in us they are all mixed with sin. For our hunger and thirst are usually accompanied by evil obsessions, our sadness by complaining and despair or bitterness, our sleep by looseness, and our lethargy and laziness by listlessness. But our Lord untangled them and separated them. He rejected the sin and took on the infirmity. For a short time he hid what was his own and took upon himself what was ours. That is why Isaiah said: *That he may accomplish his work, his alien work; that he may accomplish his work, his work was foreign to him.*†

†Is 28:21

14. *That he may accomplish his work.* What work? Many are the works of our Lord, but here he is speaking of a particular work which belongs especially to him. The angels, the archangels, and all the powers of heaven are his work. *Heaven, earth, the sea and all that they contain*† are his work. But we know how he accomplished these works; he did not undertake alien works to accomplish these. *He spoke and they were made.*† What then is this work of his that is so special, so singular, so wonderful, so unheard of? 15. Let us listen then to what Scripture says: *His mercies are above all his works.*† I see three types of work that belong to God. There is the work of his wisdom, the work of his mercy, and the work of his judgement. The work of his wisdom: *heaven and earth and everything that they contain.*† The work of his judgement: *to render to each one according to his deeds.*† But *his mercies are above all his works.*‡ Therefore the work of his mercy is especially his work. It is his own work, his proper work, in

†Ex 20:11; Ps 145 [146]:6; Ac 14:14

†Ps 32 [33]:9; 148:5

†Ps 144 [145]:9

†Ex 20:11; Ps 145 [146]:6; Ac 14:14
†Rv 22:12
‡Ps 144[145]:9

which there appears to the utmost his goodness, his charity, and his kindness.

16. His work is in keeping with his name. What name? You know his name. What is the sound, the savor, the fragrance of his name? *Oil. Your name is oil poured out.*† Why oil? Because his name savors of charity, it savors of mercy. How does that dear name of Jesus sound? It sounds our salvation, for he is my God and my Jesus—that is, my Saviour, my well-being, and therefore my mercy.† 17. He accomplished the work of his wisdom when he created the world. But he had not yet accomplished the work of his mercy. For the work of mercy corresponds to those who are wretched. He accomplished the work of judgement when he hurled the devil out of heaven for his pride. He accomplished the work of judgement when he expelled a human being from paradise for disobedience. Yet in these works he demonstrated his wisdom and power. He willed to show his mercy as well, *for his mercies are above all his works.*† Therefore the work of his mercy is properly said to be his work.

†Sg 1:2

†*Interpretatio* 77 (CCSL 72:156, 11) et passim

†Ps 144 [145]:9

18. But how would he accomplish this work if not by saving the wretched? Therefore the work of our salvation is the work of his mercy—that is, the work that is properly *his work.* What is the property of the Saviour—that is, Jesus—if not to save? What does the prophet say? *That he may accomplish his work, his alien work.*† As you know, brothers, our Lord Jesus Christ is *wisdom*, he is *strength*, he is *life*.† What is the opposite of wisdom and as it were foreign to it? Without doubt, folly. And what is the opposite of strength?

†Is 28:21

†1 Co 1:30; Jn 11:25; 14:6

Without doubt, infirmity. Similarly the only thing opposite death is life. 19. Reflect now on how our Lord took on himself a work which was alien to him so that he might be able to accomplish his own work, that is, the work of his mercy. He who was wisdom willed to be, as it were, foolish. He who was strong willed to be infirm. This is why the Apostle says: *The folly of God is wiser than the wisdom of human beings and the infirmity of God stronger than human strength.*[†] *That he may accomplish his work, his alien work*, bread hungers, the fountain thirsts, strength grows tired and life dies.

[† 1 Co 1:25]

20. But how does he accomplish his own work by means of this alien work? It is his hunger that feeds us, his thirst that inebriates us, his weariness that refreshes us, his death that brings us life. Our spiritual repletion, our spiritual inebriation, our spiritual refreshment, our spiritual vivifying is all the work of his mercy. By means of this alien work he accomplishes everything. Wisdom accomplishes this by means of folly, as the Apostles says: *Because the world did not know God, it pleased God that through the folly of preaching those who believed were saved.*[†] 21. Therefore, as we said, wisdom accomplishes this its work by means of folly, strength accomplishes it by means of weakness, bread accomplishes it by means of hunger, the fountain accomplishes it by means of thirst, might accomplishes it by means of weariness, life accomplishes it by means of death. *That he may accomplish his work, his alien work; that he may accomplish his work, his work that was foreign to him.*[†] In order that he might accomplish the work of his mercy, the work of his wisdom and the work of his judgment became foreign to him.

[† 1 Co 1:21]

[† Is 28:21]

22. We said that the angels are the work of his wisdom. Listen to what he himself said when he was arrested by the Jews. Peter wanted to defend the Lord and struck somebody with his sword. Then the Lord said to him: *Do you suppose that I cannot appeal to my Father who would send me more than twelve legions of angels?*[†] He could have had all the angels with him and they would have destroyed those who sought to arrest him. But he did not choose to do so. For in order to accomplish his work, that marvelous work he had resolved on, he willed that the very angels should be as it were foreign to him and not fight against his enemies.

[†]Mt 26:53

23. Human beings are also the work of his wisdom. Listen to what he told Pilate: *If my kingdom belonged to this world my followers would be fighting to keep me from being betrayed into the hands of the Jews.*[†] He did not choose to have anyone with him, nor angels, nor human beings, nor any other creature. Therefore, in order to accomplish his work, his own work was foreign to him. Therefore he said: *I have trodden the winepress alone.*[†]

[†]Jn 18:36

[†]Is 63:3

24. *Alone,* he says. *Alone,* because his own work was *foreign to him.* The angels were foreign, because they were not present. Human beings were foreign, because they did not fight. The heavens were foreign, because they did not strike his enemies with lightning. Earth was foreign because it did not swallow them up. The sea was foreign because it did not drown them. Even his work of judgement was foreign to him, as he said: *I do not pass judgement on anyone.*[†] And again: *God did not send his Son into the world to judge the world.*[†]

[†]Jn 8:15
[†]Jn 3:17

25. *That he might accomplish his work, his alien work.*† *That he might accomplish* the work of his mercy, he accepted the leaven of our mortality, something clearly foreign to the purity of his divinity. At length the time came when he willed to rid himself of this leavening. He applied fire—that is, his passion. In his passion all that leavening was destroyed, all corruption and all mortality were destroyed, and today he rose from the earth, unleavened bread, pure bread.

†Is 28:21

26. You see now why it was prescribed that, after the lamb had been slaughtered, the bread the Jews ate had to be without leavening. Because before the passion of the Lamb—our Lord Jesus Christ—doubtless his flesh—which is our refreshment, our bread, as you know, since we eat that flesh under the appearance of bread—before his passion, I say, that flesh was mortal. It could be hungry, it could be thirsty, it could grieve; it could die. But after the passion it rose immortal, impassible, and incorruptible.

27. Well, brothers, let us celebrate the feast of unleavened bread. Let us eat this bread without leaven. Our bread is the body of our Lord. It is without leavening because, as the Apostle says: *Christ, once raised from the dead, is never to die again.*† If we would eat this bread which is without leavening, we too must be free of leavening as the Apostle commands. A little while ago you heard what he said: *Get rid of the old leavening.*† This leavening, as we have said above, is sin. 28. Yet how are we to purge ourselves of it? Surely our Lord has taught us. In the same way as he himself rid himself of the leavening which he had taken upon himself for our sakes we must rid

†Rm 6:9

†1 Co 5:7

ourselves of the leavening which corrupts us. It was by way of insults, reviling, scourging, the cross and death that he came to the resurrection. At his resurrection he was rid of the leavening and now the flesh which he offers us is pure, immortal. What shall we think, brothers? Can we come to resurrection by any way other than that which he followed? Anyone who thinks to is wrong.

29. But you ask which resurrection is meant. We read of two resurrections in Scripture. John says in the Apocalypse: *Blessed is the person who has a share in the first resurrection.*† The first resurrection is that of souls, the second that of bodies. Our Lord effects both of them in us by his one resurrection. He could not rise in his soul because he did not die in his soul. He rose in the body because he died in the body. 30. We who have undergone death in body and in soul must rise in body and in soul. First in the soul, afterwards in the body. At the resurrection of the body our Lord put aside the leavening of mortality. By the resurrection of our soul we put aside the leavening of iniquity. But if he arrived at the resurrection of the flesh by way of life's hardships, much more do we need to arrive at the resurrection of the soul by way of those hardships, so that we may be put aside the leavening of sin by the resurrection of the soul and, as the Apostle says, *be [bread of] a new mixture.*†

†Rv 20:6

†1 Co 5:7

31. The old *mixture* was sin, with which we were all mixed and leavened. The new mixture is of the blood of our Lord Jesus Christ, with which we were mixed and thereby purified from the evil leavening. As flour, when mixed with water,

combines with it and forms a single mass so, when we have water poured over us at baptism we became, as it were, one mass with Christ. As the Apostle says: *As many form one loaf, we are one body in Christ.*†

†1 Co 10:17

32. Yet because, through our own negligence, we have contaminated ourselves after that purifying, let us flee again to Christ's blood; that is, let us imitate his passion so that we may be able to share his resurrection here in soul and on the day of judgement in both body and soul. Because this cannot be brought about by our own efforts let us implore his mercy that he himself might deign to act in us,
Jesus Christ our Lord,
who with the Father and Holy Spirit
lives and reigns, God
through all the ages of ages.
Amen.

Sermon Thirteen
For the Ascension of the Lord

FOR SOME TIME NOW we have been keeping before our minds the resurrection of our Lord Jesus Christ, for the same length of time as he spent in the world after his resurrection. Today we celebrate the day on which he showed us openly that all the things which he did and suffered in this world he did to lead us from the death into which we fell through Adam to true life, and to raise us up from this exile to our homeland for which we were created—that is, to heaven.

2. He died for our sins and *he rose for our justification*[†] and he ascended into heaven for our glorification. Through his death we received the *remission of our sins*.[‡] For what we could not do he accomplished in satisfaction for our sins. Through faith in his resurrection we are justified. Infidels, pagans, and Jews knew about and accepted his death, although they did not want to believe in his death. But his resurrection, because they could not see that, they did not want to accept.[†] 3. Our faith, however, merits justification and awaits a great reward because we believe something we cannot see. This is why the Lord said to Thomas, *Because you have seen me, you have believed, blessed are they who have not seen and have believed.*[†] That blessedness which we are awaiting, however, he

[†] Rm 4:25. *Justificatio* will ordinarily be translated as 'righteousness' here
[‡] Eph 1:7; Col 1:14

[†] Aelred makes a distinction between *credere* ('accept') and *credere in* ('believe in') which is hard to maintain in English.
[†] Jn 20:29

willed to show forth today in his own person by ascending into heaven. He did this so that we might be certain that we, who are his members, may ascend to where he, who is our head, has ascended.

4. Therefore, dearest brothers, we ought to celebrate this day with great joy because there can be no greater glorification of the human person than what has been shown to us today. This nature of ours which had been so depraved and degraded that it was even compared to brute animals—as the Prophet says, *Man, when he was in honor, did not understand and became comparable to stupid beasts*†—[this nature] was in our Lord Jesus Christ so exalted that every other creature is beneath it and even the angels adore it as something beyond them.

†Ps 48:13 [49:12]

5. As you have often heard, after his resurrection Our Lord willed to remain in this world in bodily form for forty days† for many reasons. He wanted to confirm his resurrection and to demonstrate in many ways that he truly rose from the dead in the flesh. Therefore, he often ate and drank with his disciples and he openly showed them his wounds.† And when the apostle Thomas was unwilling to believe that the other apostles had seen him, he allowed Thomas to touch his *side and his hands*.† By his bodily presence he wanted to reassure his disciples, grieved beyond measure during his passion and almost in despair, and to prove to them on the authority of the Scriptures that it was necessary for him to die and to rise again. Moreover, he opened for them the meaning of the Scriptures that they might understand them.†

†Ac 1:3

†Ac 10:42

†Jn 20:27

†Lk 24:45

6. Yet—and we should notice this—before his passion and resurrection he fasted for the same length of time that he chose to be physically with his disciples after the resurrection.† By his fasting he commended to us the value of the physical affliction which we ought to endure in this life. By his physical presence which he revealed to his own after his resurrection, we are able to understand the consolation of his utterly sweet presence which we will experience after our own resurrection. Both were commended to us over the same length of time because it is in the measure to which we bear affliction for Christ in this life that we shall receive consolation in the [life] to come.

†Mk 1:12

7. Besides this, after his resurrection our Lord willed to commend great mysteries to our attention by means of certain physical signs. During these days he appeared to his disciples as they were fishing and at his bidding they hauled to shore *a net full of great fishes, a hundred and fifty-three*†—which symbolizes the happiness of those who at the future resurrection will be presented to Christ the Lord by his ministers. The meal, too, which he willed to have with his disciples signified that banquet at which we shall eat and drink *at his table in his kingdom.*†

†Jn 21:11

†Lk 22:30

8. During these days he gave his disciples, who were still on earth, the Holy Spirit whom afterwards he sent from heaven.† And by this twofold giving of the one Holy Spirit he commended <to us> love of God and of neighbor. Yet the number 'forty days' still signifies deep mysteries. Yet those of you who are in the habit of reading the commentaries of the holy Fathers have no need

†Jn 20:22

to hear much about that, while our lay brothers, I think, would prefer to hear about something else. Therefore, I do not wish to say anything more on that subject.

9. And so, after [our Lord] had completed everything for which he willed to dwell so long on earth, on this day on which he willed to ascend into heaven, he appeared to them and ate with them. As Luke says in the Acts of the Apostles, *While he was eating with them he told them not to leave Jerusalem*[†] and so on. How happy were those who shared this meal! Yet, as the Evangelist says, *He reproached their incredulity and hardness of heart, because they had not believed those who had seen him after he had risen from the dead.*[†] 10. Often after his resurrection he had appeared to his disciples and eaten and drunk with them. But at this final appearance, when he chose to ascend into heaven, there were many, I think, who had not seen him before but had only heard from those who had seen him and they had doubted just a little. Therefore the Lord *reproached their incredulity*. And he did it in an extremely beautiful way. On the one hand he scolded them; on the other hand he reassured them. And he scolded them most when he promised them great things; as it is written, *He commanded them not to leave Jerusalem but they were to wait for the promise of the Father, which, he said, you have heard through my mouth. John, indeed, baptized with water; you, however, will be baptized with Holy Spirit within a few days.*[†]

11. We read in the Book of Kings that when Elijah was taken up in the chariot of fire, he left his cloak to Elisha. And the spirit of Elijah was bestowed

†Ac 1:4

†Mk 16:14

†Ac 1:4

doubly on Elisha.† The prophet Elijah signifies our Lord and Elisha the apostles and the disciples of the Lord.† The fact that Elijah was taken up into heaven signifies the ascension of our Lord. But because Elijah was only a human being, he needed the help of another. Our Lord, who was true God, ascended into heaven by his own power‡—as the Evangelist said, *It happened, when he blessed them, he parted from them and was borne into heaven.*†

12. Elijah's cloak signifies the holy Church; as the holy patriarch Jacob said of our Lord, *He will wash his mantle in wine, his cloak in the blood of grapes,*† because with his own blood he purified the holy Church.‡ When Elijah mounted his chariot he left Elisha his cloak,† and when our Lord ascended into heaven he commended his Church to his disciples. For he said, *Go forth into the whole world, preach the Gospel to every creature*†—that is, to the whole human race, Jews and Gentiles, wise and unwise,† rich and poor, all of whom make up the holy Church.

13. But what does it signify that Elijah's spirit came to be doubly with Elisha?† Our Lord in a certain place said to his disciples, *Someone who has faith in me will do what I am doing and will do things greater than these.*‡ Many indeed were the things which our Lord did by himself when he was physically on earth. Yet, after he ascended into heaven, he did much more, so to speak, through the apostles and his other disciples. 14. By himself he converted but a few Jews. Through the apostles he caused the whole world to believe in him. Many sick persons were healed by touching *the hem of his garment.*† But, which seems greater, he cured many by the mere shadow of Peter.‡ Therefore it can be said that Elijah's spirit was bestowed

†2 K 2:9–15

†Cf. Bernard, Sermon 3.5 on the Ascension; SBOp 5:134, 3–4
‡Gregory the Great, *Homilies on the Gospels*, 29:5; PL 76: 1216 CD; CS 123:231
†Lk 24:51

†Gen 49:11
‡Pseudo-Origen, *On Genesis*, Homily 17:8; CCSL 20:197, 5–10.
†2 Kgs 2:13

†Mk 16:15

†Rm 1:14

†2 K 2:9, 15
Cf. Bernard of Clairvaux, *Sermon for the Feast of the Ascension*, 3.5
‡Jn 14:12

†Mt 14:36; Mk 6:56

‡Ac 5:15

doubly on Elisha since, as far as the conversion of men and women is concerned, he converted many more through the apostles than through himself. 15. When Elisha himself, of whom it is written that the spirit of Elijah was bestowed on him doubly, came to the Jordan and struck the river, it did not part. As soon as he uttered the name of Elijah, saying, *Where is the God of Elijah now?* the waters parted.[†2 K 2:14] Thus, although the apostles seem to have done more than the Lord did by himself on earth, yet they did it not in their own name or by their own power, as our Lord did, but in the name of their Master and by his power.

16. That the spirit of Elijah was bestowed doubly on Elisha after Elijah was taken up can also be understood [to mean] that the Spirit of God, who was present in the apostles before the ascension, was bestowed doubly on them after the ascension because the grace they received from Holy Spirit after the ascension was greater than they had before. 17. The grace which Elisha is said to have had—that the holy apostles, as we said a while ago, twice received the Spirit of our Elijah—that is, our Lord Jesus Christ—can be further understood to mean the Holy Spirit. First, when [our Lord] on earth appeared to them and *breathed on them and said, Receive Holy Spirit.*[†Jn 20:22] And later, from heaven, when *tongues, divided like flames of fire, appeared to them and rested above each one of them.*[†Ac 2:3] We shall celebrate the memorial of that day, God granting, in a few days' time.

18. When that pleasant meal was over, the Evangelist tells us, *he led them out to Bethany.*[†Lk 24:50] Bethany is a village situated on the Mount of Olives.

'Bethany' means *house of obedience*.[†] Note the beautiful symbolism here: first he ate with them and then *he led them out to Bethany*.[‡] It is those whom he is accustomed to refresh with spiritual food that he makes truly obedient. Nor ought we to overlook that it says *He led them out*. For it is the one whom the Lord has led out who truly goes up to Bethany. 19. First, [he leads men and women] *out* of the world, when he causes them to love *neither the world nor what is in the world*.[†] He leads them *out* as well from their evil deeds and habits when he makes the wanton chaste, the impatient peaceful, the proud humble. And again he leads them *out* from their very self—that is, from self-will—so that they may always have in their heart what the Lord said, *I have not come to do my own will but the will of him who sent me*.[†] Someone whom he has led *out* like this he does indeed bring *to Bethany*. *To Bethany* which is on a hill and not on any hill, but on the Mount of Olives.

[†]*Interpretatio*, 60; CCSL 72:135, 26–27
[‡]Lk 24:50

[†]1 Jn 2:15

[†]Jn 6:38

20. There is a Bethany in a valley. Bethany, as we said, means *house of obedience* and connotes the heart obedient to God's precepts. Then the *house of obedience* is in a valley when someone seems to be obedient in order to be able to obtain something earthly. Again, just as there are good hills—of which it is written, *I lift up my eyes to the hills, from where help will come to me*[†]—so there are bad hills, which are spoken of when the Lord says of the devil, *for him the hills bear grass*.[†] 21. One of these [bad hills] is the hill of pride on which there sits the one *who sees all that is lofty and is king over all the sons of pride*.[†] On this hill some people have their Bethany—that is, their heart, which [only] seems to be a *house of obedience* because whatever they do they do

[†]Ps 120 [121]:1

[†]Jb 40:15
[†]Jb 41:25

in order to receive glory from men and women. Jesus, the teacher of humility, does not come near this Bethany, but rather comes to the [town] on the Mount of Olives.

22. Mount of Olives means *rich with oil*. For *the mountain of God is a rich mountain*.[†Ps 67 [68]:16] By the Mount of Olives charity is signified, for it is more excellent than the other virtues. In it abounds the spiritual oil by which the wounds of our souls are healed and through which the light of truth illumines us. It is the nature of oil that, if it is put into other liquids, it rises to the top. And therefore the Apostle, after he had spoken of other virtues, when he wished to speak of charity began by saying, *And now I will show you the best way of all*.[†1 Co 13:1. Cf. Augustine of Hippo, *On John*, Tractate 6.20; CCSL 36:64, 2–7] 23. Therefore, dearest brothers, if we want with our spiritual eyes to see Jesus ascending into heaven and if we want to arrive in heaven with him and through him, we ought to go forth in mind and in contemplation from this world. We ought also, if we can, to raise our hearts from the physical senses and take up *the bright weapons of obedience*.[†RB Prol. 3] We ought not to set the reward of our obedience in the valleys—that is, in earthly and base things—nor on the hill of pride, lest the Lord say of us, *Amen, I tell you, they have received their reward*.[†Mt 6:2, 5] But our obedience ought to be on the mountain of oil, on the mountain of charity, so that whatever we do, we do for the love of God.

24. Then *he led them out to Bethany and blessed them with uplifted hands*.[†Lk 24:50] O how happy were those who were of that company and were found worthy to be blessed by those hands. *And he blessed them with uplifted hands*. Notice, my brothers, what a heritage our Lord left us when

he departed from this world: not gold, not silver, not any earthly thing, but his blessing. 25. And so that we be not too cast down by his physical departure from us, let us hear what he told them according to another Evangelist. *Behold, he said, I am with you unto the end of the ages.*† How then did he depart from us? Surely as far as his physical presence was concerned. As far as his divinity is concerned, he is always with us. By his loving providence he always surrounds us. *And it happened, as he blessed them he departed from them and was carried up into heaven.*† 26. *If God is for us, who is against us? It is God who justifies; who then can condemn? It is Christ Jesus, who died and, more than that, who rose again, who is at the right hand of God, who pleads our cause.*† We ought therefore, dearest brothers, to take a bold stand against the devil and his snares and to have great hope in our Lord Jesus Christ. For how can they perish for whom Christ prays, for whom he displays in the sight of his Father those wounds which he suffered for us? And therefore our hope ought to be fixed firmly on him.

†Mt 28:20

†Lk 24:51

†Rm 8:31, 33f

27. We read in the Old Testament that, after the people of Israel left Egypt with Moses at their head, the Amalekites, a savage race, came and did battle against them. Moses sent an army against them, while *he himself went up on to a mountain to pray* for them and raised his hands to the Lord.† And *it came to pass that* while he kept his hands raised, the people of Israel were triumphant but whenever he lowered his hands Amalek started to win. Why was it, do you think, that *the raising of his hands* possessed such grace? Without doubt God usually takes more account of the mind's attachments than of the body's postures.

†Ex 17:8–16

28. Why was it then? Did his prayer have no effect before God unless he raised his hands? That *lifting up of his hands* had such an effect that their enemies could not withstand the Israelites. The reason why this *lifting up of hands* had such force was that it signified the raising of the hands of him who said in the psalm, *The lifting up of my hands is like an evening sacrifice.*[†] For, when evening had already come upon the world, his sweetest hands were stretched out on the cross and there was offered up that evening sacrifice that took away the sins of the whole world.

[†Ps 140 [141]:2]

29. So that *raising of* Moses' *hands* signified the passion of our Lord Jesus Christ who *went up on to a mountain to pray*[†] because he ascended into heaven to plead our cause with the Father.[†] There he lifts up his hands so that Amalek—that is, the devil—will not be able to vanquish us. For there he appears *in God's sight on our behalf*[†] and represents to him the passion that he underwent for us. 30. As for us, brothers, as long as we are in this wretched life which is *a trial upon earth,*[†] as long as *our fight is against the principalities and powers, against the rulers of the dark things of the world, against the spiritual forces of evil in the heavens,*[†] we need to have our Lord lifting up his hands within us—that is to say, that the remembrance of his passion continually present in our minds. 31. We can be quite sure, my brothers, that as long as the memory of his passion is in our heart, as long as our hope is directed to where *Christ is pleading our cause at the right hand of the Father,*[†] the spiritual Amalek—that is, the devil—will not be able to vanquish us. And therefore, my brothers, let us see that this attachment, this remembrance, does not through some negligence on our part grow

[†Mt 14:23]
[†Jn 3:13; Heb 7:25; Rm 8:34; 1 Jn 2:1]
[†Heb 9:24]
[†Jb 7:1]
[†Eph 6:12]
[†Col 3:1; Rm 8:34]

lukewarm in us. For then we shall immediately grow faint and our enemy will gain the upper hand and cause us distress.

32. So then, our Lord ascended to the Father today, while the disciples watched in amazement and exultation,† though an exultation mixed with sorrow. They exulted because he in whom they had placed their hope was possessed of such power that by his own might he could penetrate heaven. They exulted, knowing that where he had ascended they also would come to be, as he had said to the Father before his passion, *I will that where I am they too may be with me.*† 33. They exulted because the pride of the Jews had been confounded, because they saw ascending into heaven the one whom the Jews, when they stood at the cross blaspheming and wagging their heads, had thought unable to come down from his cross. They exulted because they were shortly to receive the Holy Spirit as Jesus had promised and by her consolation they would be braced against all temptations. Chiefly they exulted seeing angels *clothed in white who asked them, Men of Galilee, why stand there looking up into heaven?*† †Jn 20:17; Ac 1:9–10

†Jn 17:24

†Ac 1:10–11

34. Appropriately are they called Galilaeans—that is, emigrants†—implying that they were moving away from the physical observances of the Law to things spiritual. Before the Lord's passion they had been told: *Do not take the road to Gentile lands and do not enter any Samaritan town but go rather to the lost sheep of the house of Israel.*† Now a kind of emigration is enjoined on them. The Lord tells them, *Go forth to the whole world and proclaim the Gospel <to every creature>.*† †*Interpretatio*, 64; CCSL 72:140, 25

†Mt 10:5–16

†Mt 16:15

35. *Men of Galilee, why stand there looking up into heaven?*† Small wonder! Although they were exulting for all the reasons I have mentioned, they felt no slight grief at his departure, which had just taken place. For his physical presence was extremely agreeable to them. In it they took great delight. What had brought them such delight while they possessed it certainly could not be given up without sorrow. Therefore they did what they could. They looked up into heaven, whither he had ascended. With their eyes at least they followed him whom they loved.

†Ac 1:11

36. The angel asked them, *Men of Galilee, why stand here looking up into heaven? This Jesus who has been taken from you up into heaven will come in the same way as you have seen him go.*† There is great comfort here. *He will come in the same way.* How? With the same flesh, with the same comeliness, with the scars and the wounds that he conveyed to heaven. *They will look upon him whom they pierced.*† The Jews will see the face which they veiled.† They will see him at whom they wagged their heads in contempt.‡

†Ac 1:11

†Jn 19:37
†Lk 2:64; Mk 14:65
‡Mt 27:39; Mk 15:29

37. We too, dearest ones, shall see our poor Lord whom we paupers follow, but we will see him not poor, not veiled, not hidden, not mute. *Our God will come openly, our God, and he will not be silent.*† He was hidden to the Jews who veiled his face. He spoke not to the pharisees who blasphemed him. But *our God will come openly, our God, and he will not be silent.* And we, my brothers, let us hear the blasphemers unperturbed. Let us patiently endure persecutors. Let us be silent at insults. *Our God will come openly* and so on. 38. Let it be our sole concern: to remain attached to him with our whole heart, our whole mind, our whole

†Ps 49 [50]:3

strength,† recognizing who our Head is, where our Head is. Let us live as befits the members of that Head, with our minds fixed not here where our lower part is, but there where our Head has today ascended, beseeching God, the Father almighty, to deign to give us his grace, so that all the attachment of our devotion may be directed to where our very substance, Jesus Christ our Lord, is with him,

†Mk 12:30

> with whom he lives and reigns
> in the unity of Holy Spirit
> through all the ages of ages.
> Amen.

Sermon Fourteen
For the Nativity of Saint John Baptist

SOMEONE WHO SPEAKS THE WORD of God to others ought to aim not at how he can vaunt his own knowledge but at how he can build up his hearers. With a motherly compassion for weaker intellects therefore he ought, I might say, prattle to them, descending to the use of baby talk. But my own intellectual limitations make it necessary for my hearers to stoop to the insignificance of my comments. 2. For this, my brothers, I confess I blush not a little. But again, I summon up some nerve when I consider Zachary, the father of the man whose feast we celebrate today. He, when he wanted to communicate the name of John, he who had previously been mute, in the very act of communicating it, became extremely eloquent.[†] And perhaps we, if we begin to speak about John, will not be altogether speechless.

[†Lk 1:63f]

3. But what shall we say about him or how shall we praise someone who was praised by angelic authority before he was born and who in the womb, into which he came by the way infected with sin, was by an inexpressible grace made a most worthy dwelling place of Holy Spirit?[†] Nor should we overlook that a priest was chosen to be his father, the temple chosen to be the place where his birth was foretold, the name to be

[†Lk 1:15ff]

conferred on him conferred by an angel.† Not even the hour at which this happened should be overlooked. For its was at the hour of *the incense offering.* †Lk 1:5ff

4. Would that we, too, my brothers, might be among those priests to whom the apostle Peter says, *You are a chosen race, a royal priesthood.*† Would that our hearts might become the *temple of God,* as the Apostle says, *The temple of God is holy, and you are that temple.*† Perhaps at the hour of *the incense offering,* the hour of salutary compunction, when *our prayer rises like incense in the sight* of the Lord,† an angel, a messenger of divine grace, will appear to us. For 'John' means 'the grace of God'.† 5. And this name is aptly conferred at the command of an angel to him who, while still in his mother's womb, recognized that inexpressible grace by which *the Word was made flesh.*† Afterwards with his finger he pointed out that same *Word made flesh.* He was the wonderful preacher of God's grace. By his words he opened the doors of the kingdom of heaven even to publicans and harlots,† doing violence, as it were, to heaven's purity by their conversion. This is why the Lord says in the Gospel what you have just heard: *Ever since the coming of John the Baptist the kingdom of heaven has been suffering force and the violent are carrying it away.*†

†1 P 2:9

†1 Co 3:17

†Ps 140 [141]:2

†Cf. *Interpretatio,* 69 (CCSL 72:146, 17)

†Jn 1:14

†Mt 21:31

†Mt 11:12

6. Before John's day there was brought to bear on the kingdom of heaven violence which the kingdom of heaven surely did not suffer from before the days of John. For till then the cherubim with the whirling sword kept wretched Adam, sulking beneath his fig leaves, away from the entrance of Paradise† and to some degree frustrated his

†Gen 3:7, 24

efforts to do it violence. Until then those seven women who ate their own bread and dressed in their own clothes still suffered reproach.† They suffered reproach as they went about looking for some one man whom they could all lay hold of and they did not find him. 7. Individually they did indeed lay hold of various men and women, but there was no one person they could all lay hold of together who would take away their reproach—until that one man came. [He could] because he was unique, because he was singular—for he, I say, was singular until he came over—this one man who was encompassed by a woman.† His wife was our human flesh which in the virgin's womb, as in his own bridal chamber, divinity by a marvelous dispensation took to wife. In the other children of Adam human nature long remained sterile. In this lordly man it has borne sevenfold. That is to say, it accomplished all the workings of Holy Spirit <for> in the Lord himself the fullness of divinity dwelt in a wondrous way because in him it dwelt physically.†

†Is 4:1

†Jer 31:22

†Col 2:9

8. This is the one man all those seven women laid hold of together—that is, the seven graces of Holy Spirit,† which truly do not need bread or clothing. What is the food of Holy Spirit? The Lord says in the Gospel, *My food is to do the will of my Father.*† The Son's *food* then is *to do the will of the Father.* The food of Holy Spirit is the same. This is the food in which she delights: to inspire men and women to do *the will of the Father.* 9. Her clothes are the saints. In their hearts this divine fire is nurtured and, as it were, is warmed. Whence it is said, *And with all of these you shall be clothed as with garments.*† Even before the coming of John the sevenfold Spirit was clothed with these garments

†Is 4:1

†Jn 4:34

†Is 49:18

and with this bread she was fed to her great delight. With the aid of the grace of Holy Spirit, some shone with the spirit of wisdom, others with that of understanding, others of counsel, others of fortitude, others of piety, others of knowledge and others of fear.† †Is 11:2f

10. What *reproach* then did Holy Spirit suffer in these seven women? She conferred justice on men and women and they did not render back the recompense of justice. For what is the recompense of justice? The kingdom of heaven. Therefore the force of justice demanded the kingdom of heaven for itself. But the kingdom of heaven did not give way to this force until he came who took away the reproach and—with the cherub and the whirling sword taken away— opened the portal of Paradise to those who with some force, crucifying *their flesh with its vices and passions*, claim justice for themselves.† †Gal 5:24

11. But what does it mean: *Let us bear your name?*† Let this man Jesus be wisdom, let him be understanding, let him be counsel, let him be fortitude, let him be knowledge, piety, fear. For it is also written, *You are our fear.*† Let Jesus then be all this, and with a wondrous wisdom let him set aside the cherubim and the whirling sword. The cherubim seems to me to be divine justice, which excluded proud and disobedient persons from Paradise until they were released from their pride by humility, from their disobedience by obedience. Because they were released by our Jesus, the justice that excluded was taken away and the justice that admitted took its place.

†Is 4:1 Lit. Let your name be called down upon us.
†Cf. Gen 31:42 (?)

12. But what was that whirling sword? I hear the Lord mention a sword in the Gospel: *I have come*

to bring not peace but a sword.[†] By the sword, therefore, he wanted to signify something that is contrary to peace. And what is so contrary to peace as discord? There surely it expresses a good, if indeed it can be called good. But here, it seems to me, the sword signifies that discord which by the sin of the first man was brought about between God and humankind, between angelic and human nature, between heavenly and earthly creation. Therefore, this sword is said to be whirling because eventually by God's grace it was to be taken away. For the true Solomon, the true peacemaker,[†] came and by the blood of his cross *restored peace to all things in heaven and on earth*.[†] And because this amazing grace began to be preached *from the days of John, from the days of John the kingdom of heaven has suffered violence and the violent have taken it away*.[†]

13. The kingdom of heaven can also be taken to mean purity of heart,[†] to which we can attain only by subjecting ourselves to some violence. Of this kingdom the Lord says: *The kingdom of God is within you*.[†] And the Apostle: *The kingdom of God is not food and drink but justice and peace and joy in the Holy Spirit*.[†] It was by means of certain force that the same Apostle strove to carry off this kingdom. For he says, *I chastise my body*[†] and so on. The first to teach this violence in the Gospel was John, first by the example of his way of life and then by the word of preaching, saying: *Produce fruits worthy of repentance*.[†] 14. We do *produce fruits worthy of repentance* if, in the same way as we present the members [of our body] at the service of injustice and evil, we put them at the service of justice and holiness[†] *so that sin shall not reign in our mortal body*[†] but justice and peace and joy in

the Holy Spirit†—*that is, the kingdom of God. We produce fruits worthy of repentance* if, renouncing the works of the flesh by which the devil reigns in men and women, we tear open the earth of our heart with the plough of compunction, so that the fruits of the Spirit—charity, joy, peace, and the others listed by the Apostle†—spring up in it. By what force we come to these fruits the same Apostle shows in the next verse, saying: *Those who belong to Christ have crucified their flesh with its vices and obsessions.*† †Rm 14:17

†Gal 5:22

†Gal 5:24

15. Does John not show the same thing by his example? From his very infancy, so to speak, he was fearful of being contaminated by the sordidness of the crowds that milled around him. Like that most chaste of birds, the turtle dove, borrowing wings of purity and innocence, he took flight into the hidden places of the desert.† There he showed that the first step towards this heavenly kingdom is contempt of the world. For *anyone who loves the world does not have the love of the Father in him.*† Where there is no love, however, the kingdom of God cannot exist. Aptly therefore is it said of John, *And he was in the desert until the day when he appeared publicly.*† †Ps 54:7–8 [55:6–7]

†1 Jn 2:19

†Lk 1:80

16. And we, brothers, if *we are eager to have the kingdom of God within*† us, we must fly away to a spiritual desert and our hearts must be *a trackless and waterless wasteland,*† so that in it the Lord may appear and there establish his kingdom. It must be a *wasteland* so far as the occupations of this world are concerned, so that *the world may be crucified to us and we to the world.*† It must be *trackless* so far as spiritual beasts—that is, unclean spirits—are concerned, lest they say to our soul: *Lie down* †Lk 17:21

†Ps 62:3 [63:1]; Ex 3:1f; Ac 7:30

†Gal 6:14

that we may walk over you.† It must be *waterless,* having no rivulet of harmful pleasure, so that *our soul* may have nothing to do with *the water that lacks substance.*†

17. About contempt of one's own flesh, what shall I say? The Gospel tells us, *His clothing was of camel's hair.*† There you see what kind of garments bedeck Christ's soldier. It seems to me that this man even by his clothes cries out, *Woe is me, that the time of my sojourn is lengthened*† and *I am a stranger among you and a exile like all my fathers.*† It is from *camel's hair* that sackcloth, which is the garb of penitents, is made. What he was later to preach by his word, [John] thus first showed by his example: *Do penance, for the kingdom of heaven is at hand.*† Now let us also hear about his amazing abstinence. His food was *locusts and wild honey.*† By his garb he trampled on the delicacy of the body; by this food, on gluttony.

18. This is the violence by which *the kingdom of heaven* is carried off. *This is the force it has suffered since the days of John.*† For from now on it is not against Canaanites and Perizzites† in the flesh that we have to fight so we may secure their earthly kingdom by force; it is against those most savage enemies of all, our physical passions, so by driving them out of the recesses of our hearts, we may prepare a temple and a kingdom in the land of our heart for the true Solomon *by crucifying our flesh with its vices and lusts.*† 19. This force to possess the kingdom of heaven had been neglected by those of whom Paul said: *As I have often told you and now tell you with tears in my eyes, there are many who walk as enemies of the cross of Christ.*† What is meant by being *enemies of the cross of*

Christ is made clear when he adds: *Their stomach is their god and they glory in their private parts.*† †Ph 3:19
This then is to be an enemy *of the cross of Christ*: to ally oneself with the gluttony of the stomach and the sensuality of the body. By these words he expresses those two vices to which nearly the whole world surrenders: gluttony and lust. Add to them pride and avarice and you will have the four wheels on which the devil infiltrates nearly the whole universe.

20. As for the heavenly flights of the locusts and the sweetness of spiritual honey,† since this †Cf. Mt 3:4
sermon has already been long, we will leave them to your own meditations. I had almost skipped over the *leather belt*† which symbolizes the virtue †Mt 3:4; Mk 1:6
of chastity. In the excellence of this virtue, purity of heart consists above all. Although it is of little or no use without the other virtues, just as they are of little or no use without it, still the absence of any other is easier to bear for a time than the absence of chastity. 21. Indeed, it has a prerogative which gives it a special luster among the other virtues: not only is it, like them, concerned with a quality of the soul but it invests the corruptible flesh itself with a certain real incorruptibility. It gives it a foretaste of some of the delights of the future resurrection. Then *people will not marry or be given in marriage, but they will be like the angels of God.*† Among all the other virtues this is the †Mt 22:30; Lk 20:35
one which merits the company of the angels, the approach of Holy Spirit and, even more intimately, the embrace of *the fairest among the sons of men.*† †Ps 44:3 [45:2]
John, it says, *had a leather belt around his waist.*† †Mt 3:4

22. He became an extremely energetic practitioner of evangelical perfection even before he

heard of it. Almighty God grant that we may travel along the way he showed, that *by following the exhortations of so great a prophet we may come safely to him whom he foretold,*
our Lord Jesus Christ,[†]
who lives and reigns with God the Father
in unity with the Holy Spirit
through infinite ages of ages.
Amen.

[†] Cf. Gregory the Great, Prayer for the Vigil of the Nativity of Saint John the Baptist, used in the cistercian breviary: *Oratio in vigilia nativitatis sancti Ioannis Baptistae; Corpus Orationum,* 7, n° 4492. CCSL 160F:89

Sermon Fifteen
For the Feast of the Holy Apostles Peter and Paul

YOU REALIZE FULL WELL, my brothers, that it is the custom, according to the statutes of our Order, that on this feast, as on a number of others, we should hear something that will edify us. As people in secular society usually add something to their menu on feast days over and above what they have at other times, so in the same way it is laid down for us that for our well-being on feast days we should add to what we do at other times so that we may be edified by someone's comments. 2. And is there anyone, my brothers, who will not take pleasure, especially on this feast which we celebrate in honor of the holy apostles Peter and Paul, in hearing or speaking something about them? Indeed, all Christians, and especially all religious, who love Christ and his Church ought willingly to speak and hear of those who are the fathers of the Christian religion, the pillars of holy Church, and the mountain on which the Church is built. As the Prophet says: *Its foundations are upon the holy mountains.*† They are also the *torches of this world.*† As the Lord says: *You are the light of the world.*†

†Ps 86 [87]:1
†Cf Ph 2:15
†Mt 5:14

3. Brothers, we ought to love and praise all Christ's apostles and all his saints, but these two

most of all. For one of them is the prince of all the apostles and the head of holy Church and to his care the Church of Christ has been quite specially commended. The other is particularly our apostle, we who are gentiles. As he himself says: *He who made Peter an apostle to the circumcised also made me an apostle among the gentiles.*† And elsewhere: *As long as I am the apostle of the gentiles I will honor my ministry.*† In them we can see quite openly the wonderful works of the Lord and how marvelously he accomplishes his will in whom he wills and as he wills. 4. For who can not wonder and rejoice that our Lord chose some poor, unlearned, and illiterate fisherman and through him overcame all the wisdom of the world; that he laid kings and emperors and all the pride of the world at his feet, as it were, so that now that dead fisherman is more honored than a live emperor? Who could bring this about, brothers, but God alone? This is why Saint Paul the Apostle says: *Brothers, behold your vocation. Not many of you were wise according to the flesh, not many noble, not many powerful. But God chose those the world counts stupid to confound the wise . . . so that no flesh may glory in his sight.*†

†Gal 2:8

†Rm 11:13

†1 Co 1:26–29

5. For if he had first chosen the wise of this world and others through them, they could think that their wisdom had been a great boon to God. Again, if he had first chosen the rich and the powerful of this world and others through them, they could think that their riches and their power had benefitted God. And therefore in his marvelous wisdom he first chose the poor and unlearned and those who were of no account in the eyes of other people and through them subjected the whole world to himself, so that

whatever was done was credited to God alone and not to any human being. 6. Further, against those poor and unlearned persons he allowed the whole world to rage: kings, princes, and emperors, who by means of laws, torture, and a thousand ways of inflicting death, strove to destroy them and to extirpate our faith. And all these things those poor ones overcame and in the midst of all this they gained the whole world. This will enable you to see, brothers, how blind and stubborn are the Jews and those who persist in paganism, who cannot understand that no one could do these things, *save God alone.*† †Mt 2:7; Lk 5:21

7. But since the Jews first brought the false charge that *none of the pharisees or rulers believed in him but only the mob, ignorant of the law,*† notice how Christ vanquished their folly by his wisdom and frustrated everything they tried to do. Observe, *he believed in him.* Yes, he who was *a pharisee and had sat at the feet of Gamaliel,* he who, *without any quarrel,* lived *according to the justice which comes of the law,* and, what is more astonishing, who zealously persecuted *the Church of God.*† How was it, brothers, that [Paul] came to believe in him? 8. The other apostles, who were *simple and unlearned,* were called in a simple way. But it was when this proud and conceited, puffed up and haughty man was raging more than ever and loathing Christ and his people that he was, not won over by wheedling words but laid low by the awesome power of the very One whom he thought was dead.† †Jn 7:48f

†Ph 3:5f; Ac 22:3

†Ac 9:1ff

9. If then anyone says that those fishermen would have been ready to believe instantly anything they were told, that person ought to reflect on

how this persecutor, this man who longed with such zeal to keep the old law, was converted without any [show of] human wisdom. He should reflect, too, that, if Jesus Christ could easily attract unlearned fishermen, how could these same unlearned men, even in the throes of such persecutions, convert so many of the wise and powerful to what they themselves believed? As for us, brothers, let us praise the wonderful works of the Lord and take delight in discerning in this fisherman the wisdom of our Lord and in this persecutor praise his power.

10. These are the clouds which water the whole world with their spiritual rain—that is, with the preaching of the Gospel—that it may produce *good fruit* and, in what was once the seed-ground of vice, give rise to virtues.† Some say that when clouds converge one with another, thunder and lightning usually result. Let us notice now how these clouds converged and what sort of thunder and lightning was the outcome.

†Mt 3:10

11. Saint Paul says somewhere: *After three years I went to Jerusalem to see Peter and I stayed with him fifteen days.*† And again he says: *Then fourteen years later I went up to Jerusalem again and conferred with them about the Gospel.*† Again, a little further on: *James and Cephas*—that is, Peter—*gave me their right hands*† and so on. Mark how these clouds converged there and how immediately the thunder of our Lord's Gospel rumbled throughout the world and everywhere a blaze of miracles burst forth. 12. If, however, that convergence or collision of clouds ought to signify some opposition, let us listen to Paul saying: *When Peter came to Antioch I opposed him to his face, because he was*

†Gal 1:18

†Gal 2:1f

†Gal 2:9

reprehensible.† Notice, brothers, Paul's wonderful freedom, Peter's wonderful humility. The one was ready to oppose his superior for the sake of truth; the other humbly yielded to the truth which he heard from his junior.

†Gal 2:11

13. These are the fountains which water the Lord's paradise and quench the thirst of the holy Church with a pleasant drink. Of these fountains the Psalmist says: *In the churches bless the Lord God for the fountains of Israel. There is young Benjamin in ecstacy; the princes of Judah their leaders, the princes of Zebulun, the princes of Naphthali.*† Saint Paul the Apostle was *of the tribe of Benjamin*, as he himself openly states† and therefore he is signified by Benjamin. 14. And so it is that in the blessing of Benjamin, the Patriarch Jacob declared: *Benjamin is a rapacious wolf who will seize his prey at evening, yet in the morning will divide the food.*† That is an obvious prophecy of how Paul first raged against the Church and afterwards fed the Church with spiritual food. How this Benjamin was in ecstacy the same Paul explains when he says of himself: *I know a man who fourteen years ago was caught up into Paradise, whether in the body or out of it, I do not know; God knows.*†

†Ps 67:27–28 [68:26–27]

†Rm 11:2; Ph 3:5

†Gen 49:27

†2 Co 12:2ff

15. But we should not overlook the fact that, as we find in the Book of Genesis, the holy Joseph loved Benjamin more than the rest of his brothers. When they came to Egypt, where, as you have often heard, he by then enjoyed great power, he chose not to confess to them who he was until Benjamin came with them. He went further, giving them this prohibition: They were in no way to have the nerve [to try] to look upon his face unless they brought Benjamin

with them. Almost all Christians realize that holy Joseph signified our Lord and that the anguish he suffered at the hands of his brothers signified the sufferings which our Lord endured at the hands of the Jews.† 16. To all intents and purposes his brothers killed Joseph when they threw him into the well. That is why he says in the psalm: *They put me in a deep pit, in darkness, in the shadow of death.*† Again, that they slaughtered a goat and Joseph escaped† signifies that Christ was slaughtered as a victim for sin† but he escaped with his life nonetheless, for he rose on the third day.† Joseph, whom his brothers declared to be dead, reigned over Egypt, while our Joseph, whom the Jews boasted of having slaughtered, reigned over the people of the Gentiles.

17. This story suggests many things we could talk about but it is our intention to speak especially about those holy apostles whose feast we are celebrating. Notice then that our Joseph is still openly selling grain†—that is, wisdom, knowledge, and spiritual teaching—to the Egyptians—that is, the Gentiles. And his brothers according to the flesh do not know it and are therefore dying of hunger and thirst. For they are the evil vine upon which the Lord forbade the clouds—of which we spoke a little while ago—to rain. This is what he had threatened through the Prophet: *I will command my clouds that they pour no rain upon it.*† 18. And why, brothers, do they suffer this hunger? Surely, because they do not have Benjamin—that is, Paul—with them, for without him they cannot look upon the face of Joseph. And almost all Egyptians recognize Joseph. And he feeds them. But he does yet not want to reveal himself to his brothers because they do not have Benjamin

with them. But the time will surely come when they will have Paul with them—that is, when they will follow his teaching—and then our Joseph will no longer be able to contain himself.† Then he will show the depths of his fondness† for his brothers also. Because, when *the fullness of the nations* have entered, then *the whole of Israel will be saved*.‡

†Gen 45:1
†Lit. bowels of his loving kindness (*viscera pietatis suae*)
‡Rm 11:25f

19. Benjamin is also interpreted to mean *son of the right hand*.† The right hand usually signifies power. Accordingly, Benjamin is called *son of the right hand* as he is the son of power, because it was not some preaching or any human enterprise that engendered Saint Paul in the faith of Christ, but divine power laid him low. Now the other apostles, as they were called in a simple way, so quite simply *they followed*.† But where Paul raged more savagely and persecuted Christians yet further afield, there the power of God suddenly laid him low so that in the very same place and at the very same hour, he was first hostile to Christ and then totally obedient to him. *This is a change wrought by the right hand of the Most High.*† *Great sins* were forgiven him,† not because he had loved greatly but so that he might love greatly.

†Gen 35:18

†Mt 4:18ff

†Ps 76:11 [77:10]
†Lk 7:47

20. Previously there was no name he hated so much as the name of Jesus Christ; afterwards nothing seemed so sweet to him as that name. He loved Christ so much that he was unwilling any longer to bear the name which he bore at the time he was persecuting Christ. It was as if he hated that name because by that name he was a persecutor of Christ. Therefore, just as he renounced the mind-set of the persecutor, so he wanted to relinquish the name as well. And it was not straightaway at his baptism that he was

named Paul; that is quite clear from the Acts of the Apostles.† It was when Christ began to be more fully his delight that he despised his very name and all that he had been previously begun to be something. 21. For who can say or even conceive how much Paul loved our Lord? That sweet name, the name of Christ, was always in his heart, always on his lips, so much so that he could hardly utter a word without always adding that name. As you read and hear in his epistles, in almost every verse he always inserts: *in Christ Jesus*† or *in Christ Jesus our Lord*‡ or *through Jesus Christ our Lord*.† Previously he rejoiced when he could put any of the Lord's disciples in bonds or cast them into prison or stone them;† now when he suffers all these things, he glories all the more.† And therefore he says: *I find happiness in my infirmities, in insults, in hardships suffered for Christ.*†

†Ac 13:9

‡Rm 3:24 et passim

‡Rm 6:11 et passim

†Rm 4:24 et passim

†Ac 9:1f; 7:58ff

†2 Co 11:30

†2 Co 12:10

22. But now let us say something about blessed Peter. There are some who say that just as the verse we quoted a little while ago—*There is young Benjamin in ecstacy*†—affirms that Paul sprang from the tribe of Benjamin,‡ so the next verse—*The princes of Judah are their leaders, the princes of Zebulun, the princes of Nephthali*†—would have it that all the other apostles are born of these three sons of Jacob—that is, from Judah, Zebulun, and Nephthali. Yet since we do not know from what tribe Peter sprang, to show our devotion by speaking of him, let us see how that blessing which Jacob bestowed upon Nephthali can be appropriated to the blessed Peter. 23. For he said: *Nephthali is a well-watered field, a deer that is sent, giving utterance to words of beauty.*† We can well say that the blessed Peter was a well-watered field, whom no evil fluid of lustful pleasure nor any

†Ps 67:28 [68:27]

‡Rm 11:1, Ph 3:5

†Ps 67:28 [68:27]

†Gen 49:21

physical delectation wash away. But the Father in heaven saturated him with heaven's dew. As our Lord told him: *Blessed are you, Simon Bar Jonah, because flesh and blood did not reveal this to you but my Father who is in heaven.*† He can well be called a deer.

†Mt 16:17

24. A deer has the habit of killing serpents and the blessed Peter with wonderful sagacity destroyed the spiritual serpents—that is, the vices—which first began to sprout in the Church. It was he who smote Ananias and Sapphira with the deer's horns—that is, with his power and might—on account of their avarice and fraud; the one like the other he killed with two blows as with two horns.† He also as if with his spiritual horns put Simon Magus to flight from east to west and furthermore threw him down from the air, and he died.† 25. Deer also have the habit of climbing the highest mountains, and Peter climbed up on the mount with the Lord. And he, with the two sons of Zebedee, saw: the Lord transfigured and Moses and Elijah speaking with him†—something the other apostles were not able to see. And because of the supreme delight he experienced at the beauty he saw in the Lord, he said: *Lord, it is good for us to be here.*† He could say then with the Prophet: *As a deer longs for the fountains of water, so my soul longs for you, O God. My soul thirsts for God, the living fountain.*†

†Ac 5:1–11

†Ac 8:18–24

†Mt 17:1–3

†Mt 17:1ff

†Ps 41:2f

26. This is the thirst he endured once when he was on board ship with the other apostles and saw our Lord *walking on the sea*. As soon as he heard that it was the Lord, he could not bear the thirst he felt to go to him and so he said: *Lord, if it is you, bid me come to you over the water.*† Let

†Mt 14:26ff

us reflect now, brothers, what faith, what love he bore in his heart. Great faith it was to believe that he, mortal and corruptible man that he was, could walk on the waters by the Lord's command alone. Great love it was that could not wait in patience for the Lord to come to them in the boat but wanted to go to him over the sea. 27. Great love, I think, made him forget himself. And therefore he was in some way outside himself when he walked on the sea. For as soon as he returned to himself *he got frightened* and therefore began *to sink*. Yet this happened by God's providence, so that the power of the Lord would be shown by his walking on the sea and Peter's weakness through his being allowed to sink. And indeed it was not fitting that in one and the same miracle they be equal, the disciple and the Master, the servant and the Lord, he who was only man and He who was both God and man.

28. At another time, after the resurrection, when Peter was fishing with seven of his fellow disciples, as the Evangelist tells us, *Jesus stood on the shore*. And as soon as Peter heard that *it is the Lord, as the deer longs for the fountains of water, he wrapped his tunic about him—for he was naked—and plunged into the sea. The other disciples came on in the boat.*[†] Brothers, notice that wonderful love! *The disciple whom Jesus loved* was there and yet he waited patiently for the boat to reach the shore. [Peter] could not restrain the wonderful ardor of divine love he had in his heart. The wondrous thirst he had for coming to [Jesus] scarcely allowed him to cover that part of his body which is not fittingly seen.

†Jn 21:4ff

29. The Patriarch added in blessing Naphthali: *Give utterance to words of beauty.*[†] Once, as you

†Gen 49:21

have just heard from the Gospel, Jesus asked his disciples: *Who do people say that the Son of Man is?* They answered: *Some say John the Baptist; others, however, say Elijah; still others say Jeremiah or one of the prophets.* And the Lord asked them: *And you, who do you say that I am?* At once Peter gave utterance to that most beautiful of all phrases, saying: *You are Christ, the Son of the Living God.*† 30. O what a beautiful phrase! And lest we should think that he did not have a heartfelt conviction of this truth but uttered this opinion about Him because of the great love with which he loved him, the Lord replied: *Blessed are you, Simon Bar Jonah, because flesh and blood did not reveal this to you but my Father who is in heaven.*† Here we are openly taught that he did not say just something from his own opinion but something he had learned from divine revelation. 31. And beautifully is he called Simon Bar Jonah. Simon means *obedient*,† Bar Jonah means *son of the dove*.‡ Indeed, anyone who is truly obedient, anyone who is, through simplicity and meekness, a son of that dove which came down upon the Lord Jesus at his baptism, that person is without doubt *blessed*; he, without doubt taught by the Father, can proclaim our Lord Jesus by a true and open witness and love him with a perfect love.

†Mt 16:13ff

†Mt 16:17

†*Interpretatio*, 71 (CCSL 72:148,4)
‡*Interpretatio*, 60 (CCSL 72:135, 22)

32. What we have already said enables us to recognize how very much both men—Saint Peter and Saint Paul—loved Christ. This may lead someone to ponder which of them we are to suppose loved him the more. We can show that Saint Peter loved Christ more than the other apostles who were with him For after that fishing expedition of which we earlier spoke, when the Lord had eaten with his disciples, he said to Peter: *Simon Bar Jonah, do you love me more than these?*† As

†Jn 21:15

Saint Augustine says, the Lord asked this because he, who saw his heart, knew this to be true.† 33. Although all the disciples were not present, there was present the one in regard to whom some doubt might arise—that is, Saint John. We could think that he loved Christ more, because Christ loved him more. But our Paul was not then among the disciples of Christ and therefore the question may be asked whether he loved the Lord more. If we consider their labors, Paul labored for Christ *more than them all.*† If we look at their manner of dying, Peter suffered the more bitter death for Christ.

†Augustine, *Tractates on the Gospel of John*, 124:4 (CCSL 36:683, 20–27)

†1 Co 15:10

34. Brothers, who dares to affirm anything in this matter? We know that both of them loved Christ greatly and were loved greatly by Christ. And therefore let us love and let us honor both of them, and let us praise the Lord for the life and death of both. Because the life of both affords us the nourishment of teaching and the death of both an example of patience. What else can I call them but two seraphim? Seraphim means *fire*† and without doubt both burned wondrously with the love of God. And both gently enkindled the love of God in the hearts of others. Nonetheless we can find some differences in their love.

†*Interpretatio* 50 (CCSL 72: 121–122, 24–25)

35. Now in the love by which Peter loved the Lord there is commended to us a certain amiable affection which we should feel for Christ's humanity. It was this fervor and love—of which we spoke a little while ago—that Peter had for Christ's humanity, as we can show from the Gospel. Once, when the Lord spoke to his disciples about his passion and said that he was to be betrayed and killed, Peter loved him so tenderly and found his

physical presence so sweet that he said: *Be kinder to yourself, Lord; let this not happen.*† 36. Again when the time came at which he willed to suffer and the Jews came with the betrayer to arrest him, an excited Peter *snatched up a sword,* wanting to prevent from happening what the Lord himself wanted to happen.† This to be sure he did out of the very strong attachment of love he had toward Christ's humanity.

†Mt 16:22

†Jn 18:10f

In Paul, however, there is commended to us that love which we should have for the recognition of Christ's divinity. So it is that Paul himself says: *And if we have known Christ according to the flesh, we now know him so no longer.*†

†2 Co 5:16

37. We can be quite sure that both—that is, Peter and Paul—especially after having received the Holy Spirit after the Lord's ascension, recognized and loved our Lord Jesus Christ perfectly, in so far as a human being can. Yet since some people are so weak as to be quite unable to raise themselves to the recognition of divinity, while others are so strong that they can contemplate even what is divine and heavenly, the weak have the example of Peter for giving themselves to a kind of tender love of Christ's humanity and the strong have in Paul certain levels of contemplation by which they mount to gaze upon the things of heaven.

38. Our Lord provided beautifully that these two fathers of our faith would suffer in the same city, be put to death by the same tyrant, and on one and the same day would both finish their course, and both at the same time would come to him whom they so perfectly loved. There reigned in Rome an emperor who had the whole world

under his sway and to him the whole world paid tribute. The Lord beautifully provided that the princes of our faith should take possession of that mistress of the world, Rome, and consecrate it with their blood, so that where once the princes of error reigned, there henceforth the princes of truth would reign. 39. And then it was made clear that those who had already conquered the head of the world would thereafter subject all the members to their laws. We, brothers, see this already achieved. Furthermore, that earthly empire has for the most part already passed away, yet our princes' empire endures. The two consuls who used to govern the Roman Empire are no more, but these, our two consuls who instruct the christian empire with their doctrine and protect it by their intercession, still remain.

40. They are the rams in the flock of our Lord Jesus Christ and it is up to us, the sheep, to follow their lead. Let us see and reflect more attentively on the way by which they have gone ahead and let us follow them. If a dying sheep would return to the flock which the *good Shepherd left on the mountains* to seek the one lost sheep,[†] it would need to follow those rams whom this Shepherd orders should be followed. But by which way have they walked? Listen, please, to the way Paul walked.: *In labor, hardships, in many watches, in hunger and thirst, in many fasts.*[†] And again he says: *Who is weak and I am not weak? Who is scandalized and I do not burn?*[†] 41. This is clearly the way of charity by which we need to travel: *In labor and hardships, in watches and fasts*. All of this is endured for God's sake. To afflict oneself like this pertains to the love of God. To be weak with the weak, to burn with the scandalized pertains to love of

[†Mt 18:12, Lk 15:4, Jn 10: 11ff]

[†2 Co 11:27]

[†1 Co 11:29]

neighbor. Let us hear too what Peter says: *Christ suffered for us leaving you an example that you might follow in his footsteps.*†   †1 P 2:21

42. Notice, my brothers, that if we want to follow our rams *we need to enter the kingdom of God through many tribulations.*† Let us therefore with full alacrity bear the labors and temptations of this life for Christ because *if we suffer with him we will also reign with him.*† And, as Saint Paul says, if we are his companions in his passion we will be likewise in his consolation.† Through the prayers of Peter and Paul may this be granted us by our Lord Jesus Christ,
    who lives and reigns
  with the Father and Holy Spirit,
   God, through all the ages of ages.
       Amen.

†Ac 14:21; Jn 3:5

†Rm 8:17; 2 Tm 2:12

†2 Co 1:7

Sermon Sixteen
For the Feast of the Holy Apostles Peter and Paul

YOU ARE GATHERED TODAY for an amazing spectacle. Something is said to be a spectacle when a multitude of men and women hasten together to see something wonderful or unusual. And what do we think, brothers—that men and women of the world have spectacles and we are without spectacles? Let us lift up our eyes. Let us look at the arrangement of this world,† the beauty of the sun and moon, *the order of the stars,*† the varieties of flowers and the flavors of the fruits and, as a certain sage remarked, *the force of the winds and the rage of the beasts,*† the properties of the herbs and the potencies of [various] stones. And let us say with the Prophet: *You have delighted me, Lord, in the things you have made!*† And again: *I have gone around and I have offered sacrifices in the tabernacle*† and so on.

†Ws 7:17
†Ws 7:29; Jer 31:35

†Ws 7:20

†Ps 91:5 [92:4]
†Ps 26:6 [27:5]

2. What did he go around and how did he go around? He went around the world by assiduous meditation and began to recognize the Creator in created things and he understood that he is beautiful, who made such beautiful things, good who made such good things, wise who arranged everything in such order.† And seeing this he

†Ws 8:1

exulted there wherein he had constructed a *tabernacle* for his Lord. For he did not *give sleep to his eyes nor slumber to his eyelids until he had found a place for the Lord, a tabernacle for the God of Jacob.*† †Ps 131 [132]:4–5
He chose not to resign himself to inactivity or to sleep until he had banished vices and wicked passions from his soul, that there he might make a place of the Lord and a tabernacle of his God. 3. In this tabernacle therefore he sacrificed to God an *offering of praise*† when he considered [God's] †Ps 26:6 [27:5]
wonderful works. For when he saw them, how did he cry there within, how did he give voice? Without doubt *all his bones* said: *Lord, who is like you?*† All this holy David saw and even so, as if all †Ps 34 [35]:10; Ex 15:11
these were nothing, he said: *God is wonderful in his saints.*† This is the spectacle for which you are †Ps 67:36 [68:35]
gathered today. God is indeed wonderful in the creation of the world, but more wonderful still in the conversion of Paul. The God who lighted up heaven is wonderful, but far more wonderful is the God who so lifted up Peter.

4. This spectacle was foreseen with delight by the prophet who says: *Who are these who fly like the clouds?*† *Who are these*, he asks, *who are they?* One †Is 60:8
is a rowdy† and the other a persecutor.‡ What †See Jn 18:10
an amazing spectacle: they *fly like the clouds*. Peter ‡1 Tm 1:13
flies. Who is not amazed? But why *like the clouds?* Notice, brothers, we can see three things in a cloud: darkness, lightning, rain. But darkness is always evident in a cloud. Lightning is not always, but is sometimes, evident. Yet rain is always in a cloud even though sometimes it does not rain. Then *who are these who fly like the clouds?* They are dark, but even so they send forth rain and lightning.

5. Brothers, let us say something about the darkness of these clouds. In the darkness there is a sort of blackness, in the splendor of lightning there is a sort of beauty. There comes to mind now the utterance: *I am black but comely.*† The darkness is exterior, the beauty within. All physical things are exterior, all spiritual within. The physical things pertain to this world, the spiritual to heaven. Let us see now what this exterior shine is and then we will understand what the exterior darkness is. 6. The luster of this world is found in amusements, in riches, in honors, in renown, in knowledge. You can easily recognize that this is an exterior—this is, a this-worldly luster. Notice now what the exterior darkness is, that which is in fact contrary to these. Notice now: poverty, hardship, obscurity, disgrace, foolishness, vileness. This is the darkness which is evident in these clouds, as one of them—that is, Saint Paul—said: *Mark your calling, brothers, for not many of you were powerful* and so on. *God has chose the ignoble of the world,*† the obscure of the world, the needy of the world.

[The rest of the sermon is missing]

†Sg 1:4

†1 Co 1:26ff

Sermon Seventeen
ON THE FEAST OF THE HOLY APOSTLES PETER AND PAUL

WHEN THE RICH of this world are at war they usually rouse their soldiers to fight not only by words but also by promises. When they see them acting without much wisdom or prudence, they usually point out to them their enemies' strength. When they see them falling back because the demand is excessive, they usually spur them on with promises. So our Lord, because he knows how crafty and powerful our enemy is, encourages us to be be strong and says: *Be strong in war and battle against the ancient serpent.*[†] And because he sees that in this war the demand [placed on us] is very great, he promises us a great reward and says: *And receive the eternal kingdom.*[†] Great is this war, strong is this enemy, but great is the reward. Be then *strong in war.*

[†] *From an antiphon for the commemoration of apostles (Hesbert 3:2684)*
[†] *Ibid.*

2. It is a great war, a great war. No one may feel secure. As long as one lives, even if one lives well, it is war. This is why holy Job says: *Human life on earth is a warfare.*[†] For someone who does not take part in spiritual warfare here should be called not a human being but a beast. If someone does not fight against the pleasures and desires of the flesh[†] but consents to them, then indeed he lives not like a human being but like a beast. Indeed,

[†] Jb 7:1
[†] Cf. Gal 5:16

you know, brothers, that from the day you came here and began to serve Christ, you entered a place of battle. That is why Solomon says: *Son, you have entered to serve the Lord, be strong and prepare your soul for temptation.*[†Si 2:1] This is the battle. Be then *strong in war*.

3. The saints whose feast we are celebrating today had a twofold battle—that is, an interior one and an outward one. We have only one—that is, the interior one. But Saint Peter, as you know, had to do battle not only spiritually against the lion *that prowls around looking for someone to devour*[†1 P 5:8] but also outwardly against Simon Magnus,[†Ac 8:18ff] against the despicable Nero, against the tortures and persecutions of evil people. And Paul, too, speaks of the outward battle: *Battles without and fears within.*[†2 Co 7:5] And again: *If I battled against wild beasts at Ephesus.*[†1 Co 15:32] About the interior battle he says: *I see another law in my members fighting the law of my mind and taking me prisoner under the law of sin.*[†Rm 7:23] But they had heard well the voice of their Leader who had said: *Be strong in war*. Therefore they fought well, they conquered well, and today they received the reward of victory.

4. And you, brothers, *be strong in war*. Do not desert the place of battle. For this is a place of battle. Hold fast in this castle of yours, in this house of yours, and let each one [of you] hold his place well and defend it. For there are various places in this castle and it has been established who shall keep one place and who another. Let no one therefore allow the enemy to enter through that part where he is stationed. The cloistered monks have one place, the officials have another, superiors another. Let each guard his own place

well. Let him keep watch in so far as he can lest the enemy gain entry.

5. The place of the cloistered, which they ought to defend and guard against enemies, is the regular observance. They ought to see to it that the enemy does not find some opening in the regular observance through which he can enter. They ought to be observant lest there be some indolence in their labor through which the enemy might enter and shatter that great wall which usually protects us from those worst of these enemies, spiritual weariness[†] and sadness. 6. They ought diligently to take care lest some excess destroy our abstinence, lest too much sleepiness shorten our vigils. These are two excellent towers by which we are defended against the fiery darts of lust and therefore they are to be guarded carefully lest in them the enemy discover some opening. Silence, too, ought to be diligently guarded. For if there should be a breach here and it breaks down, the enemy immediately enters by means of quarrels, rivalry, and discord.

[†] *Acedia*, the classical vice against which all monks traditionally are warned.

7. The place of the officials is charity, mercy, the care of guests and the poor, and the other things like this. They ought, therefore, to guard their place and not allow the enemy to enter either through harshness or through avarice. Let them see to *good not only before God but also before all men and women,*[†] *so that in all God may be glorified.*[‡]

[†] Rm 12:17
[‡] RB 57:9; 1 P 4:11

8. Now the place of superiors is judgement and discipline. This place they ought to guard in such a way that judgement is not harsh nor discipline relaxed. But let them so watch over everything that the enemy may not find any opening in the

complaints of the community on account of their faulty administration nor again any opening in undue freedom because of their remissness. Since in all these things war is being waged, the Lord therefore urges everyone, saying: *Be strong in war.*

9. Now, the vices of curiosity and pleasure-seeking are liable to assail those in the cloister. For some, when they see themselves released from external affairs, are liable to keep too curious an eye on the activities introduced by those who are engaged in them, and so to pass judgement on all their words and deeds and thus come to despise the very people whom they should most honor and to overrate themselves. 10. Then they devise schemes in their heart, give free rein to their imaginations and say: 'Oh, if I were abbot—or prior or cellarer or porter, I would not involve myself in earthly matters. I would do this and that.' In such muttering practically the whole of their time is spent In this way arise [feelings of] envy against superiors and unfounded reports. If they see—or think they see—superiors make some mistake, they make the matter as public as they dare. Without a doubt they incur that curse by which Noah cursed his son who laughed at his father's shame.† This vice is liable to assail most especially those who think themselves to be of some consequence.

11. There are others who, because they are remiss about themselves, do not much care about others. Since they themselves are free from outward cares they surrender themselves to idleness and lethargy. Unable to go out and about physically, they wander in spirit among worldly desires and physical pleasures, and are content to

†Gen 9:21ff

remain in the monastery only in body. Of these the Prophet says; *The enemies saw her and they derided her sabbaths.*† A sabbath, as you know, is a rest. But the enemies mock the sabbath of those who put up an outward show of repose while inwardly they are continually engrossed in worldly and disgraceful things. 12. Clearly what has to be taken into account here is the way in which thoughts are entertained. For if someone who is aware of all these thoughts in himself is *strong in war* and fighting *against the ancient serpent* who instills such thoughts, he loses nothing as a result but rather wins a crown. For sin lies, not in suggestion, but in consent. But because thoughts of this kind are very violent and greatly harass their victims, we need to hear the Lord saying, *Be strong in war.*

†Lam 1:17

13. As for the officials—by which I mean cellarers, porters, and guestmasters—they are usually assailed by covetousness, avarice, and sadness. For many officials are either overly cautious or naturally grasping. When they see their reserves gradually diminishing they become too greedy for what they do not possess or they avariciously hold on to what they do have, or they distribute what they do have with a kind of sadness. Against all these temptations it is necessary that they be strong and fight steadfastly. May they take up a firm faith to counteract covetousness, generosity against avarice, and cheerfulness against sadness. Let them take up God's commandments and promises as if they were missiles [to be directed] against the enemy, the ancient serpent who suggests those things. 14. Against that fear and <that> covetousness let them set what the Lord says: *Do not be anxious saying, what shall we*

eat or what shall we drink or what shall we wear?[†Mt 6:31] To be well noted here is what the Lord promises us. Beyond doubt it is those things which we need—that is, what is necessary—food and clothing. You see therefore that the Lord did not promise us what is superfluous. Let us be confident then, for as long as we do not seek what is superfluous but [only] what is requisite, God will provide it. And if sometimes he withdraws something necessary to the body, he does it for the greater good of the soul. To overcome that sadness let them hear the Apostles: *Not with sadness*, he says, *or out of necessity, for God loves a cheerful giver.*[†2 Co 9:7] Let them *be strong in war*. Let them fight against temptations. To the best of their ability, let them provide what is necessary in fair measure and lay aside all anxiety.

15. Superiors, who are in a higher place, must beware especially of two temptations: pride and vanity. It is pride if they think themselves better because they are more highly placed. It is vanity if they delight in their position and preen themselves on it. Let them also then *be strong in war* and fight with the ancient serpent. Against pride let them set the words of Scripture which say: *The higher you are, the humbler you must be in everything.*[†Si 3:20] And again: *Have they made you the prince? Be as one of them.*[†Si 32:1] Against vanity, however, by which the mind takes pleasure in superior rank, let them ponder what is written: *Judgement is harshest on those in high places.*[†Ws 6:6] And: *The powerful powerfully suffer torments.*[†Ws 6:7] 16. Since therefore there is no one serving God in any place, in any rank, in any dignity, against whom the ancient serpent does not fight, let us all hear: *Be strong in war and fight against the ancient serpent.* As I said at the

beginning, when secular leaders see their soldiers behaving less than prudently, they point out to them the strength and craftiness of the enemy. So here we are told two things about our enemy: he is ancient, it says, and he is a serpent.

17. When we are told that he is ancient what is being pointed out to us is that he is used to this sort of fighting and therefore is extremely astute. So it is we should guard ourselves carefully and vigilantly. He has no other concerns—not food nor clothing nor sleep—nothing but deceiving human beings. In this he has exercised himself from the beginning of the world up to the present moment. Brothers, he has learned a great deal about this art and therefore it is essential that we be vigilant. 18. For the serpent, as you know, is extremely slippery and anywhere he can first poke his head in he easily enters entirely. Such is this enemy of ours. Wherever he can first poke his head—that is, cause an evil thought be to accepted—he easily introduces his whole body—that is, the act of sin. Therefore, it is essential that we always reflect on all the movements of the heart so that this serpent may not be able to intrude something unclean or something contrary to reason. For, as our Lord says, in the heart is the root and, as it were, the head of all our deeds: *From the heart*, he says, *come evil thoughts, fornication, adultery and blasphemy.*[†] †Mt 15:19

19. We ought to reflect on that to which we are called. We ought to observe that the men and women of this world give us their lands and their property so that they may be protected by our prayers and reconciled to God. Therefore it is essential that in purity of life and the practice of

good works we surpass those who put such trust in us, lest it be said of us: *Blush, Sidon, says the sea.*† This is without a doubt what happens when those who bear the name 'religious' become worse than worldlings. For then in comparison with the sea—that is, the world—Sidon—that is, relgious life—blushes for shame.

†Is 23:4

20. But since fighting daily—indeed without interruption—against the flesh and thoughts and *against spiritual evils*† is very hard work, it is essential that we always look to the reward that is promised us. Therefore, after having exhorted us to warfare and made known our enemy's astuteness and malice, [the antiphon] immediately consoles us with [the prospect of] reward, saying: *And receive the eternal kingdom.*† 'The kingdom of God' we should understand in two ways—that is, in this life and in the life to come.

†Eph 6:12

†From the antiphon for feasts commemorating apostles (above, n. 1)

21. For in this life without a doubt we can and we should have within us the kingdom of God. For the Apostle says: *The kingdom of God is not eating and drinking but justice and peace and joy in the Holy Spirit.*† If we persevere in this warfare and do not consent to vices we shall have within us yet in this life the kingdom of God—that is, justice and peace and joy. Justice as a result of our virtues, peace arising from the harmony of flesh and spirit when they agree in what is good, joy from the witness of a good conscience. 22. This kingdom also follows that ineffable [reality] *which eye has not seen, nor ear heard, nor the human heart conceived.*† Accordingly, the Lord will say on the day of judgement: *Come, blessed of my Father, receive the kingdom that has been prepared for you*

†Rm 14:17

†1 Co 2:9

since the world was made.[†] May he who made the promise deign to lead us to its fulfillment, Jesus Christ, our Lord,
    who with the Father and Holy Spirit,
lives and reigns through all the ages of ages.
        Amen.

[†]Mt 25:34

Sermon Eighteen
For the Feast of the Holy Apostles Peter and Paul

YOU REALIZE, BROTHERS, that among all our Lord's apostles and martyrs these two whose feast we are celebrating today seem to have a certain special dignity. No wonder. To them in a quite special way the Lord commended the holy Church. For when Saint Peter confessed that the Lord himself was the *Son of God*,† the Lord answered him: *You are Peter and upon this rock I will build my Church, and to you will I give the keys of the kingdom of heaven.*† Moreover the Lord made Saint Paul more or less [Peter's] equal, as Paul himself says: *God who made Peter an apostle to the circumcised also made me an apostle among the nations.*†

†Mt 16:16

†Mt 16:18–19

†Gal 2:8

2. These are the ones whom the Lord promised to holy Church through the Prophet, saying: *In the place of your fathers sons have been born to you.*† The Fathers of the holy Church are the holy patriarchs and prophets who first taught God's law and prophesied the coming of our Lord. But before the Lord's coming prophets ceased to be on account of the sins of the people. Our Lord came anyway, and in place of the prophets he chose the holy apostles. He fulfilled what the prophet said: *In the place of your fathers sons have been born to you.* 3. And notice how he shows that

†Ps 44:17 [45:16]

the dignity of the apostles is greater than that of the prophets. For the prophets were princes of one people and lived in one nation, in one part of the earth. And of the apostles he says: *You will make them princes over the whole earth.*† What land is there, brothers, in which the power and the dignity of these apostles are not found? Kings, earls, rich and poor, all today praise and glorify these holy friends of God. Why—if not because the Lord made them *princes over the whole earth?*

†Ps 44:17 [45:16]

4. And we, brothers, in so far as we can, let us praise these holy apostles and friends of God and our fathers and *princes*. Let us praise them and let us so prepare ourselves that we may be able to praise them worthily. Then shall we be able to praise them worthily, if we strive to imitate their life. Let us imitate their fortitude, their utterly holy life and their noble perseverance. Without any doubt, brothers, they had great fortitude. For they are the pillars which the Lord made firm, as it is written: *The earth has melted and all who live in it. I have made its pillars firm.*†

†Ps 74:4 [75:3]

5. When *has the earth melted?* Notice, brothers: before our Lord came upon earth the whole earth was frozen and hard. It was frozen because it had no warmth of charity,† but was in the cold grip of iniquity. It was hard, for it had none of the suppleness of piety and kindness. Our Lord came, however, and set *fire to the earth*† to counteract the cold, as he himself says: *I have come to set fire to the earth and what do I will but that it burn?*† This fire thawed the cold and the earth began to melt and to stream with tears. 6. But what does *all who live in it*† mean? *All* were melted, brothers. Yet [there are] some resembling her who says in the Song

†Mt 24:12

†Lk 12:49

†Lk 12:49

†Ps 74:4 [75:3]

of Songs: *My soul melted.*† But [there are] others resembling [those] the Prophet describes: *Like wax melting before the fire, may sinners perish before the face of God.*† Some were melted by repentance, others by envy. 7. We can understand 'the earth' here as the holy Church, which says what we said a short time ago: *My soul was melted*† by fire in the presence of our Lord. *And all who live in it*† ought to live in the Church in that way—that is, in true faith and charity. They were indeed all melted by the fire of divine love. *The earth has melted and all who live in it. I have made its pillars firm.*†

†Sg 5:6

†Ps 67:3 [68:2]

†Sg 5:6
†Ps 74:4 [75:3]

†Ps 74:4 [75:3]

8. The pillars of this earth are the holy apostles, especially those two whose feast we are celebrating today. They are the pillars which uphold the holy Church by their teaching, by their prayers, and by the example of their patience. These are the pillars our Lord made firm. For at first they were very weak, quite unable to hold up either themselves or anyone else. And this was our Lord's great way of working. 9. For if they had always been strong, someone could think that it was from themselves they had this strength. Therefore our Lord willed first to show what they were like of themselves and then he made them firm so that everyone might know that all their strength came from God. Again, because they were to be the Fathers of the Church and doctors to cure the sick, in order to know how to have compassion on the infirmities of others, they first experienced infirmity in themselves. Therefore, he made firm the pillars of the earth—that is, of the holy Church.

10. The one pillar, Saint Peter, was very infirm when the comment of a single maidservant

unmanned him.† Afterwards [the Lord] made this pillar firm. First, when he asked him three times: *Peter, do you love me?* and he three time answered: *I love you.*† It was as if by denying him three times Peter had somehow lessened within himself the love of our Lord and consequently this pillar collapsed and cracked. Similarly, by professing his love three times, this pillar was made firm. And it should be noted that the Lord, when Peter answered: *I love you*, immediately said to him: *Feed my sheep.*† As if he said: In this way demonstrate the love you have for me, *feed my sheep*. Accordingly, brothers, someone who says he loves God without wanting to *feed his sheep* speaks falsely.

†Mt 26:69–70 and parallels

†Jn 21:15ff

†Jn 21:17

11. But someone will say: What has this to do with us? This is a matter for bishops, for abbots, and for priests who have the care of souls. True, it is their concern, brothers, but it is also yours. For Christ's sheep are fed in two ways—that is, by word and by example. Certainly, brothers, there are many prelates in the Church who can quite ably feed Christ's sheep by their words, but because they live badly they would feed them better if they kept silent or withdrew <from them> and if they provided them an example of humility, poverty, abstinence, chastity, and the other virtues. 12. He does better who does both. Someone who cannot do both does better to feed by example than by word. For if it is only by his words that someone can be of profit to others, he is doing harm to himself. If he cannot do both, by example he can profit them and himself. Therefore, brothers, if you love our Lord, live in such a way that Christ's sheep may be fed by your example. As the Lord says: *Let your works so shine*

before men and women that they may glorify your Father who is in heaven.†

†Mt 5:16

‡To preserve silence in the monastery, the Cistercians, like other monks, used a sign language which had been developed by monks over the centuries to communicate with each other in most daily affairs. It was a very limited vehicle of communication and was to be used only for necessary communications. Aelred refers here to the distracting abuse of sign language.

†1 Co 8:12

13. In each and every holy soul our Lord also possess certain sheep—that is, virtues—which should be fed by anyone who loves Christ. These sheep are charity, humility, spiritual joy, and such like. We feed these sheep when we perform the kind of deeds that will make such virtues grow in us. Each one of us ought also to feed these virtues in the other. This we do if we behave before our brothers in such a way that our example enlarges their charity, their joy, their humility and patience. 14. For how do I feed humility in my brother if I am proud in his presence, if I speak proudly, if I answer proudly and strut proudly? How do I feed obedience in my brother if he sees me contrary and disobedient? How do I feed his patience if I murmur or lose my temper or speak harshly or make signs in his presence?‡ Someone who behaves like this in his brother's presence does not feed Christ's sheep in him, but to the best of his ability destroys and slaughters them because he scandalizes them. Someone who scandalizes his brother, however, sins against his brother. Yet someone who sins against his brother, as the Apostle says, sins *against Christ*.† But someone who sins against Christ does not love Christ. Therefore, if you love Christ, feed Christ's sheep and you will belong to this pillar which was made firm by the love of Christ.

15. After this firming up, Saint Peter was made firm again when the Holy Spirit was sent. Then this pillar was made so strong that strokes and stones and threats and in the end death itself could not move it from its place. Also, that other

pillar was without doubt at first infirm. For sins are an infirmity of the soul. And hear how infirm he was: *At first I was a blasphemer and persecutor and a man of violence.*† Again, when he was hurled to the ground and blinded and in that state led into the city, when Ananias came to him and instructed him, then he was infirm.† 16. But hear how strong he afterwards became: *I am convinced,* he said, *that neither death nor life, neither angel nor any other creature can separate me from the charity of God.*† Therefore, brothers, all strength is in charity, as it is written: *Love is as strong as death.*† What does death do to a person? It extinguishes all his vices and all his evil passions, it closes the eyes and renders the body senseless, so that only the spirit lives. Love, too, does this. 17. It extinguishes lust, takes away anger, overpowers pride, and drives out all vices. It shuts the eyes so that they are not curious and it so extinguishes all the physical senses that someone can say with Paul: *I live, yet not I, but Christ lives in me.*† He himself does not live, because charity puts to death in him whatever was his own. But Christ lives in him because only the love of Christ has any force in him. Therefore, brothers, let us imitate this fortitude of these pillars.

†1 Tm 1:13

†Ac 9:10ff

†Rm 8:38f

†Sg 8:6

†Gal 2:20

18. But now, concerning the holiness of these Fathers, what can we say? All holiness is in purity of heart and the testimony of a good conscience. Contempt† of the world brings about purity of heart. All impurity of heart then comes from love of the world. Love of the world contaminates the heart and therefore when a person perfectly despises the world he has no contamination in his heart The good *testimony of a conscience* is born of two things: good action and a right intention.

†Aelred follows *contemptus mundi* here with a series of phrases using *contemnere.* To avoid the somewhat stilted 'contemn' in English, we have continued to translate this verb as 'despise'.

For someone who does not act well cannot have a good conscience. Again, if someone does praiseworthy deeds and does not do them from a right intention but either from love of praise or to gain some temporal advantage, he cannot have a good conscience. 19. Who despised the world more perfectly than the man who spoke so confidently to the Lord, saying: *We have left everything.*[†Mt 19:27] What a *testimony* he had from his own *conscience* who said: *You know, Lord, that I love you.*[†Jn 21:15ff] Again, how perfectly Paul despised the world, he who counted everything of the flesh as so much dung for the sake of gaining Christ.[†Ph 3:8] Again, concerning his own deeds, he said: *I have worked harder than all of them.*[†1 Co 15:10] And again: *I have fought a good fight, I have finished the course, I have kept the faith.*[†2 Tm 4:7] Concerning the testimony of his conscience he says: *This is our glory, the testimony of our conscience.*[†2 Co 1:12]

20. Therefore, brothers, let us imitate these holy Fathers of ours. Let us strive to do good, to despise the world, to have a good conscience, so that we may come to share their companionship. But since it is of no advantage to begin all these if we do not strive to persevere in them, it is then essential that we imitate the perseverance of these holy Fathers.

21. Perseverance is recognized only in death. For although someone may begin early to serve God it is of no advantage to him if just a little while before his death he abandons the good he began. And although a person may live long in evil, if in his old age he turns to God, no matter how short a time he may live, nevertheless he will have persevered. Therefore, it seems to me, to persevere is nothing other than to end one's life

praiseworthily. 22. Therefore, brothers, as long as we live, no one can be confident, no one can presume on himself. For if, as they said, praise is sung only at the end, our salvation consists in perseverance alone. Yet before his death no one can be confident of this perseverance. Therefore it is better to listen to the Apostle say: *Work out your salvation in trembling and fear.*† We ought to realize, however, that the more tribulations and sorrows a person suffers in the Lord's service, the more praiseworthy is that person's perseverance.

†. Ph 2:12; Eph 6:5

23. Accordingly, these holy Fathers of ours are preeminently praiseworthy. They put up with so very much for Christ and nonetheless persevered perfectly. It is no great thing to persevere with Christ in joy, in prosperity, in peace; but it is a great thing indeed to be stoned, scourged, buffeted for Christ and through it all to persevere with Christ. It is a great thing with Paul to be cursed and to bless, to suffer *persecution* and bear up, to be reviled and to pray, to be *as it were the rubbish of this world* and to glory in that.†

†1 Co 4:12f

24. How praiseworthy is Paul's perseverance, one which persevered in the midst of such things? He was nearly always either *in prisons* or *in chains, hungry, cold* or *naked.*† And through them all he persevered with Christ without murmuring or lamenting. Rather he was content when he had such trials to endure, as he says: *I find contentment in my infirmities, in insults, in tribulations, in hardships for Christ.*† To the very end, today, he consummately commended his own perseverance by not hesitating to endure death for Christ.

†2 Co 6:5; 11:23ff; Ph 1:7; Phm 10:13

†2 Co 12:10

25. What shall I say of Peter's perseverance? If he had borne nothing else for Christ it would

be enough that today he was crucified for Christ. How praiseworthy, too, is the fact that he refused to be crucified in the same way as our Lord, but chose to have his feet up and his head down. He well knew where the One was whom he loved, for whom he longed, for whom he sighed. Where, but in heaven? Why then did he want his feet to be turned upwards if not to show openly that by his suffering he would go to the Lord? That cross was, as it were, a pathway.

26. And truly, brothers, the cross of Christ is the pathway to heaven. And there is no other pathway. Therefore, brothers, let us set before our eyes the life and the death of these saints and their reward. And let us ponder that if here we imitate their sufferings as far as we are able, we shall without any doubt come to share their companionship. Through their merits may our Lord Jesus grant us this,
who lives and reigns
with the Father and Holy Spirit
through all the ages of ages.
Amen.

Sermon Nineteen
For the Assumption of Saint Mary

1. *JESUS CAME INTO A CERTAIN VILLAGE and a certain woman named Martha received him into her home. She had a sister whose name was Mary.*† You have heard in the Gospel of the great good fortune of the two women. Truly great, brothers, was the good fortune of Martha, who welcomed such a guest, who served him, who was occupied with her ministrations. Great was the good fortune of Mary, who recognized the preeminence of this guest, who listened to his wisdom, who tasted his sweetness. 2. For so the Evangelist tells us that our Lord Jesus Christ *came into* this *village* and that *a certain woman* who was called *Martha* welcomed him *into her home* and served him. She had a sister who was called Mary who, as soon as Jesus came in, hastened to his feet and sat there, listening to his sweet words. So absorbed was she in the Lord's words that she paid no heed to what was going on in the house, what people were saying, even how hard her sister was working.

†Lk 10:38–39

3. Which one of you, if our Lord were physically on earth and chose to come to you, would not be wondrously, unspeakably happy? What shall we say then, brothers? Since he is not now on earth physically, since we cannot welcome him physically, must we therefore despair of his

coming? Not at all. Let us prepare our homes and without doubt he will come to us better than if he were to come physically. There is no doubt that these women were blest because they welcomed him in the flesh but they were far more blest because they received him in spirit. 4. For at that time there were many who welcomed him in the flesh and ate and drank with him but because they did not welcome him in spirit, they remained in their misery. Who was unhappier than Judas? And yet he served the Lord physically. I will go further. The blessed Virgin Mary herself, whose glorious assumption we are celebrating today, was beyond doubt blest because she welcomed the Son of God in body but she was more blest because she had welcomed him in spirit. I would be a liar if the Lord himself had not said this.

5. Yesterday[†] it was read out how *a certain woman said to our Lord: Blessed is the womb that bore you and the breasts you suckled.* And the Lord said to her: *Rather blessed are those who hear the word of God and keep it.*[†] Therefore, brothers, let us make ready a spiritual castle[†] and our Lord shall come to us. I dare say that if the Blessed Mary had not prepared this castle within herself, the Lord Jesus would not have entered her womb or her spirit, nor would this Gospel be read on her feast today. 6. Let us then make ready this castle. Three things make a castle strong: a moat, a wall, and a tower. First the moat, then the wall rising above the moat, and finally the tower, which is stronger and more significant than the other two. The wall and the moat protect one another, since if the moat were not in the way people would be able to devise a way of approaching the wall and undermining it. And if the wall did not rise above the moat they could approach the moat and fill

[†] In the Gospel of the vigil Mass.

[†] Lk 11:27–28

[†] *castellum*. The latin word can mean both village and castle. The Gospel of the day uses it in the former sense, but here Bernard uses it in the latter sense to develop his spiritual teaching. The analogy was widely used by later writers, the best known of whom is Teresa of Avila.

it in. The tower, on the other hand, protects the whole because it is higher than all the other parts.

7. Let us now enter into our soul and let us see how all this ought to be realized in us spiritually. What is a moat but deep ground? Therefore, let us hollow out[†] our heart so that it may be very low ground. Let us take away the earth which is inside and heave it up, for that is how a moat is made. The earth that we should take and mound up is our earthly fragility. Let this not lie hidden within but let it always be before our eyes, so that in our heart there may be a moat—that is, low-lying[†] and deep ground. This moat, brothers, is humility.[†] 8. Remember what the vinedresser in the Gospel said about the tree which the owner of the vineyard wanted to cut down because on it *he found no fruit: Leave it, Lord, this one year while I dig around it and manure it.*[†] He wanted to make a moat there—that is, to teach humility. In this way, then, brothers, let us begin to build this castle. For unless this moat—that is, true humility—is first established in our heart, we shall only be able to build something that will fall in ruins about our head. 9. How well the blessed Mary had made this moat for herself! Truly she was mindful more of her own fragility than of all her dignity and holiness. She knew full well that the fact that she was fragile came from herself, that the fact that she was holy, that she was the Mother of God, that she was lady of the angels and the temple of the Holy Spirit, came only by God's grace. Therefore, what she was of herself she humbly confessed, saying: *Behold the handmaid of the Lord. Be it done unto me according to your word.*[†] And again: *He has looked upon the humility of his maidservant.*[†]

[†] The correspondence between 'moat' (*fossatum*) and 'hollow out' or 'dig' (*fodio*) cannot be reproduced in English.
[†] *Humilis.*
[†] *Humilitas.* The wordplay with *humilis* cannot be reproduced in English.
[†] Lk 13:6–8
[†] Lk 1:38
[†] Lk 1:48.

10. After the moat we must make the wall. This spiritual wall is chastity: a wall that is utterly strong and preserves the flesh intact and undefiled. It is the wall that preserves the moat of which we spoke, so it cannot be filled in by the enemy. For if someone loses chastity, the whole heart is immediately filled with dirt and filth, with the result that humility—that is, one's spiritual moat—utterly ceases to exist in the heart. But just as this moat is protected by the wall, so it is essential that the wall be protected by the moat. For someone who loses humility will not be able to preserve chastity of the flesh. Thus it comes about that a virginity which is preserved from infancy itself right up to old age is sometime lost because when the soul is defiled by pride the flesh too is defiled by wantonness. 11. Holy Mary had this wall within herself more perfectly than anyone else. For she is the holy and untouched virgin. Her virginity, like the stoutest of walls, could never be penetrated by any projectile or by any other instrument—that is, by any temptation of the devil. She was a virgin before giving birth, a virgin in giving birth, and a virgin after giving birth. Yet, even if you are already imitating the most blessed Mary and have this moat of humility and the wall of chastity, it is essential that you build the tower of charity.

12. A great tower is charity, my brothers. As the tower is usually higher than every other structure in the castle, so charity is above all the other virtues that form part of the soul's spiritual structure. This is why the Apostle says: *Now I will show you a far more excellent way.*[†] He said this of charity, because it is the more excellent *way that leads to life.*[†] No one who is in this tower has any

[†] 1 Co 13:1

[†] Mt 7:14

fear of his enemies, because *perfect charity casts our fear.*† Without this tower the spiritual castle we are describing is weak. 13. For someone who has the strong, stout wall of chastity, yet either despises or passes judgement on his brother instead of showing him the charity he ought to show, because he does not have a tower, his enemy scales the wall and kills his soul. Similarly, if he seems humble in his garb, in his food, and in his attitudes, and yet entertains bitter feelings towards his superiors and his brethren, that moat of humility cannot defend him from his enemies. 14. Who can say how perfectly the most blessed Mary had this tower? If Peter loved his Lord, how much did the Blessed Mary love her Lord and her Son! How much she loves her neighbors— that is, [all] men and women—is demonstrated by the many miracles and the many visions by which the Lord has deigned to show that she prays in a special way to her Son for the whole human race. Brothers, it would be superfluous for me to try to show even the beginnings of her charity. So great is it that no mind is up to conceiving of it.

†1 Jn 4:18

15. This is without a doubt the castle which Jesus deigns to enter. And without a doubt those who receive him spiritually in such a castle are more fortunate than many who then welcomed him physically into their homes. But why is it that the Evangelist does not mention the name of the village and only says that *Jesus entered a certain village?*† *Certain* indicates something unique and therefore refers properly to our most blessed Lady. For she is a unique castle, since in no other human being is there such humility, in none other such perfect chastity, in none other such surpassing charity. A unique castle, without a

†Lk 10:38

doubt; one which the Father fashioned, which Holy Spirit sanctified, and which the Son entered, one which the whole Trinity uniquely chose for themselves as a lodging.

16. This is the *castle* which *Jesus entered.* He entered with the gate shut and with the gate shut he exited, as the holy Ezekiel had foretold: *He brought me round to the gate that faced eastward and it was shut.*† The east gate is Mary most holy. For the gate which faces east generally receives the brightness of the sun first. So Mary most blessed, who always looked to the east, to the brightness of God, first received within herself the ray, indeed, the whole fullness of the brightness of the true sun—the Son of God, of whom Zachary said: *The Rising Sun visited us from on high.*† 17. *The gate was closed and* well *secured.*† The enemy could find no entrance, absolutely no opening. It was closed and sealed with the seal of chastity which was not broken but rather made more solid and firmer by the entrance of the Lord. For he who gives the gift of virginity did not take virginity away by his presence but rather confirmed it. Therefore, *into this castle Jesus entered.*† And we, brothers, if we have within us this spiritual castle of which we speak, without a doubt Jesus will spiritually enter into us. But he entered into the Blessed Mary not only spiritually but also physically because in her and from her he took a physical body.

18. *And a certain woman named Martha received him into her home. She had a sister whose name was Mary.*† If therefore, brothers, our soul, as we have said, becomes this castle, it is important that two women dwell in it: one who sits *at the feet of Jesus and listens to his word;*† the other who serves Jesus

†Ezk 44:1; cfr. 47:2

†Lk 1:78
†Ez 44:1–2; Jos 6:1

†Lk 10:38

†Lk 10:38–39

†Cf. Lk 10:39–40

and feeds him. Notice, brothers! If Mary alone were in this home, there would be no one to feed the Lord; if Martha alone, there would be no one delighting in the words and presence of the Lord. 19. Therefore, brothers, Martha symbolizes that activity whereby a person works for Christ; Mary, however, that rest by which a person is at leisure from physical work and delights in the sweetness of God—whether through *lectio*[1] or through prayer or through contemplation. So it is, brothers, that as long as Christ is poor and walks by foot on the earth and is hungry and thirsty and tempted, it is essential that both these women be in the one house—that is, both these activities be in each soul.

20. As long as you are on earth, and I and anyone else—provided that we are [Christ's] members—he himself is on earth. As long as those who are his members go hungry and thirsty and are tempted, Christ is hungry and thirsty and tempted. This is why he will say on the day of judgement: *As long as you did it for one of these the least of mine, you did it for me.*[†] Accordingly, brothers, in this wretched and toilsome life, it is essential that Martha be present in our house— that is to say, that our soul attend to physical activities. For as long as we have a need to eat and drink, we have a need to labor. As long as we are tempted by physical delights, we have a need

[†] Mt 25:40

---

1. As above (p. 150), we have left this word in Latin to retain its rich meaning in the monastic tradition. *Lectio* conveys a whole process: *lectio, meditatio, oratio, contemplatio,* (reading, meditation, prayer, contemplation). Aelred goes on to speak of all four stages here. *Lectio* perceives God's presence, by preference in the Holy Scriptures but in all that is written and created, and listens to and receives what God has to say, carrying it until it forms the heart through *meditatio* and calls forth the particular response of *oratio* or the total response of contemplation.

to subdue the flesh with vigils, fasts, and manual labor. This is Martha's part. 21. Yet Mary ought to be present in our soul—that is, spiritual activity. For we should not always be intent on physical pursuits but sometimes we should be at leisure and see *how good and how sweet the Lord is*,† [we should] *sit at Jesus' feet and listen to his word*.‡ By no means should you neglect Mary for the sake of Martha, nor again Martha for the sake of Mary. For if you neglect Martha, who will feed Jesus? If you neglect Mary, what benefit will it be to you that Jesus entered your house since you will have tasted nothing of his sweetness?

†Ps 45:11 [46:10]; 33:9 [34:8]; 1 P 2:3
‡Lk 10:39

22. Realize, brothers, that never in this life should these two women be separated. When the time comes when Jesus is no longer poor or hungry or thirsty or able to be tempted, then Mary alone—that is, spiritual activity—will occupy the whole of this house—that is, our soul. Saint Benedict saw this, or rather the Holy Spirit in Saint Benedict. That is why he did not say and decree that we be intent only on *lectio*, like Mary, and lay aside work, like Martha, but he commended both to us, allotting certain times to Martha's work and certain times to Mary's work.

23. These two activities were perfectly present in the Blessed Mary, our Lady. The fact that she clothed our Lord, that she fed him, that she carried him and fled with him into Egypt—all this pertains to physical activity. But that *she treasured all these words, pondering them in her heart*,† that she meditated on his divinity, contemplated his power, and savored his sweetness—all this pertains to Mary. Accordingly, the Evangelist beautifully says: *Mary, sitting at the feet of Jesus, listened*

†Lk 2:19

to his word.† 24. In the role of Martha, Blessed Mary did not sit *at Jesus' feet*. Instead, I should think, the Lord Jesus himself sat at the feet of his dearest mother. For, as the Evangelist says: *He was subject to them*†—that is, to Mary and Joseph. But in that she saw and recognized his divinity, beyond doubt she sat at his feet, for she humbled herself before him and reckoned herself as his handmaid. In the role of Martha, she tended him as someone weak and small, hungry and thirsty; she grieved at his sufferings and at the outrages which the Jews heaped on him. This is why she is told: *Martha, Martha, you are troubled and anxious about many things.*† In the role of Mary, she entreated him as Lord, worshiped him as Lord, and yearned with all her might for his spiritual sweetness.

†Lk 10:39

†Lk 2:51

†Lk 10:41

25. Therefore, my brothers, *as long as we are in this body*, in this exile, in this place of penitence, let us realize that what is most proper and most natural for us is what the Lord said to Adam: *You shall gain your bread by the sweat of your brow.*† This pertains to Martha. Whatever we taste of spiritual sweetness is only, I might say, a certain pittance by which God sustains our weakness. Let us then, dearest brothers, do Martha's tasks punctiliously and let us exercise ourselves with all fear and care at Mary's tasks, and let us not abandon the one role for the sake of the other. It will sometimes happen that Martha will want to have Mary [with her] at her work, but this must not be granted her. *Lord,* she said, *do you not care that my sister has left me to get on with the work alone? Tell her to help me.*† This is a temptation. 26. Notice, therefore, brothers, that when, during the time we should be at leisure for *lectio* and prayers, the thought occurs to us that we ought

†Gen 3:19

†Lk 10:40

to go to this or that job, as if it were necessary, then, as it were, Martha is calling Mary to help her. But the Lord judges well and justly. He does not order Martha to sit down with Mary, nor does he order Mary to get up and serve with Martha. Mary's role is certainly better and more pleasant and more delightful. Yet he does not want Martha's task to be left undone on account of it. Martha's role is more laborious, yet he does not want Mary's repose to be disturbed. What he desires therefore is that both should do their own parts.

27. Yet those who understand this to mean that there are some who should do nothing in this life but follow Martha's part and others again who should give all their attention to Mary's part, are indubitably mistaken and do not understand. Both of these women are in the one castle, both in the one house, both pleasing and acceptable to the Lord, both loved by the Lord, as the Evangelist says: *Now Jesus loved Mary, Martha, and Lazarus.*[†] Or let them tell us which of the holy Fathers ever came to perfection without both of these activities?

[†Jn 11:5]

28. Since, however, each of us must practise both these roles, we must surely do Martha's task *at certain times* and *at certain times* Mary's task,[†] unless there intervenes some necessity, which knows no law. Therefore we must punctiliously keep to those times which Holy Spirit has determined for us: at the time of *lectio* we must stay still and quiet, not yielding to idleness or drowsiness, not departing from Jesus' feet, but sitting there and *listening to his word.* But when it is time for work we should be alert and ready and on no

[†Cf. RB 48.1]

account should we neglect the ministry of love in order to obtain quiet. 29. We should never mix the one activity up with the other unless obedience alone—to which we ought never to prefer quiet or work, action or contemplation, or any other thing—compels us to leave, as we might say, the very *feet of Jesus*. For certainly, although Mary considered it a greater pleasure to sit at Jesus' feet, if the Lord had told her to do so she would have got up and served with her sister without the slightest hesitation. But the Lord did not tell her, and this was so that he might thereby commend both activities and that we might discharge both roles punctiliously, if no other command is given us, and not abandon one for the sake of the other.

30. We must also reflect on what it was the Lord said: *Mary has chosen the best part which shall not be taken away from her.*† The Lord has given us great consolation in these words. Martha's part *will be taken away* from us, but Mary's part *will not be taken away*. Who would not grow weary of these labors and miseries if they were to be always with us? That is why the Lord consoles us. Let us then act manfully. Let us manfully put up with these labors and miseries, knowing that they will have an end. Again, who would care much for these spiritual consolations if they did not last longer than this life lasts? But Mary's part *will not be taken away* from us; indeed it will be increased. 31. What here we begin to taste in some tiny droplets, after this life we will drink to the point of a kind of certain spiritual drunkenness. As the prophet says: *They will be drunk with the rich plenty of your house and you will let them drink from the flowing stream of your delights.*† Let us not then be vanquished by these labors for they will be taken

†Lk 10:42

†Ps 35:9 [36:8]

away from us. Let us yearn hungrily for a taste of the divine sweetness, for here indeed it begins but after this life it will reach its perfection in us and remain with us for all eternity. May blessed Mary aid us in attaining this happiness before her Son, our Lord,
who lives and reigns
with the Father and Holy Spirit,
God, through all the ages of ages.
Amen.

Sermon Twenty
For the Assumption of Saint Mary

OUR LORD DOES NOT WILL to put up with our having any spiritual boredom. Consequently, he visits us, sometimes by himself, sometimes by the sacred Scriptures, sometimes through our sermons in which we express aloud something about him, sometimes even by the sweetness of good things which happen to us through him, sometimes by what happens to us through his followers. These are our dishes with which he feeds our soul so that we neither suffer hunger nor in eating have to put up with boredom.[†]

[†] Cf. Sermon 26.1

2. Now, among all those who are his, she who tastes his goodness more intimately and more delicately is of greater excellence, more blessed, and more attractive. She is to him not only a creature, a handmaid, a friend, and a daughter, but also a mother. So then it is only right that we welcome her feast with greater delight and gladness and in its celebration allow ourselves a more abundant spiritual banquet. Indeed, brothers, we ought always to praise and honor her and with complete devotion recall her sweetness. But today even more should we rejoice with her because today her joy was completely fulfilled. 3. Great was her joy when the angel greeted her. Great was her joy when she felt the coming of Holy Spirit, when

that marvelous fusion of the Son of God with her flesh took place in her womb, so that he, one and the same, was the Son of God and her Son. Great was her joy when she held such a Son in her arms, when she kissed him, when she took care of him, when she listened to his words, when she saw his miracles. And because her sorrow was so great at the passion, she took wondrous joy again in his resurrection and greater still in his ascension. But all these joys were surpassed by the joy which she receives today.†

†Section 2 is repeated in Aelred's Sermon 45.6–7

4. You well know, my brothers, that in our Lord Jesus <Christ> there are two natures: the divine and the human. These two natures are so perfect in him that the divine nature was not diminished on account of the human nor the human reduced to nothing on account of the divine. That is why he is at once equal to the Father and less than the Father: equal on account of his divinity and less on account of his humanity. Certainly, brothers, it is a great good and a great joy to know our Lord Jesus Christ in his humanity, in his humanity to love him and to reflect on him and, as it were, to see in one's heart his birth, his passion, his wounds, his death, and his resurrection. But a much greater joy has someone who can say with the Apostle: *Even if we knew Christ in the flesh, now we no longer know him* in this way.† A great joy it is to see how our Lord lay in the manger, but a much greater joy it is to see how the Lord reigns in heaven. A great joy it is to see how he suckles at the breast but a much greater <joy> to see how he feeds all things. A great joy it is to see him in the arms of a maiden but a <much> greater joy to see how he himself contains all things in heaven and on earth.

†2 Co 5:16

Sermon 20.3–7

5. Up to this day, brothers, Mary, the blessed mother[†] of God, knew her dearest Son in the flesh. Although she fastened all her desires and all her love there, where he was, after her dearest Son and Lord ascended into heaven, so long as she remained in this corruptible flesh, what she had seen of him in the flesh could not fade from her memory. For his deeds and his words were always coming to her mind and above all there lingered in her heart the features of his exquisite face.[†] Today, however, she passed from this world and went up *to the heavenly kingdom*.[‡] There she began to contemplate his brightness, power, and divinity, and her joy and her longing were fulfilled. So with good reason could she say: *I have found him whom my soul loves*.[†] She holds him and she does not let him go.[†]

[†]*Dei genitrix*

[†]Cf. Sermon 20.5 with Sermon 45.6

[‡]Cf. antiphon *Exaltata es* for the Assumption (Hesbert 3:2762)

[†]Sg 3:4
[†]Cf. Sermon 45.9

6. Previously she had found him whom her flesh loved, since the flesh still appreciated flesh, a human being [another] human nature. She held him but she let him go. She held him—but in the flesh—and therefore through death she lost him to some extent—but in the flesh. Today she found *him whom* her *soul loves*[†] because, although it may be—as some believe—that she was taken up into heaven with her body, that body had, however, been made spiritual, so that all the love with which she loves her Lord, her Son, is not according to the flesh but according to the spirit. Today she has found *him whom* her *soul loves*,[†] she has found him in spirit, she loves him in spirit, she holds him in spirit and therefore she will never again lose him.

[†]Sg 3:4

[†]Sg 3:4

7. Today she has found [him] because today the shadow of night has retreated and the Light of

light has risen on her. During the night she sought him but she did not find him. Therefore she says: *On my bed night after night I sought him whom my soul loves. I sought him but I did not find him.*[†Sg 3:1] As long as she lived in this life it was night. And yet during this night she did not cease seeking him. And therefore when the night was over she found him. *On my bed*, she said, *I sought him whom my soul loves.*[†Sg 3:1] What is this bed? Who can say what this bed was like? If this bed were an ordinary, material[†*Corporalis*—usually translated as 'physical'] bed, there would be no need to seek for long.

8. I think this is the same bed of which she says elsewhere: *Our bed is covered with flowers.*[†Sg 1:15] And what was this bed but her heart, where there were the flowers of all the virtues? Well [may it be called] a bed because of the wonderful rest and tranquility which she had <in her heart>. For there was there none of the uproar of empty thoughts, there were there no desires for the things of this world, there were there no physical passions or desires. Where these exist is not a bed, since no one can have rest and tranquility who has these uproars going on within the heart. 9. Many make themselves a bed,[†Aelred switches here from *lectulus*, 'little bed', the word used in the *Song of Songs*, to *lectus*, simply 'bed'.] not in their heart but in their flesh, for in their heart they have no rest because of a bad conscience. They stretch out on their lower nature—that is, *in the desires of the flesh*—and there take their rest as in a bed. To such as these the Apostle says: *Awake, you who sleep, arise from the dead and Christ will shine upon you.*[†Eph 5:14] But the blessed Mary took her rest, not in the flesh, but in the mind and in a good conscience. There she rested—and did not rest. She rested from all the cares of the world, from all the uproar of the vices, from all the turmoil of

empty thoughts. And yet she did not rest, because she yearned and sighed and sought with moaning and tears him whom she loved. *In my bed night after night I sought him whom my soul loves.*† Let us see when she began to seek.

†Sg 3:1

10. First, before the coming of the Lord, she sought him and longed for him. She sought, that he might come to earth as he had promised, that he might redeem the world, that he might set her, together with others, free from their miserable captivity. She sought him, not in public or in the marketplace, but *in* her *bed,* in the secret chamber of her heart. This is the bed in which Abishag the Shunamite warmed King David.†

†1 K 1:1–4; 2:16–23

11. We read in the Book of Kings that because of his great age King David had grown so cold that nothing could warm him. Clothes were heaped upon him, Scripture tells us, but he did not feel warm. Then the king's *servants said* to him: *Let us look for a maiden for your majesty, a beautiful virgin, to wait upon you and sleep in your arms and warm your majesty. They found a virgin, whose name was Abishag of Shunam, and she stayed with the king, serving him and warming him. The king never knew her, however.*†

†1 K 1:1–4

12. You know well that King David signifies our Lord, Jesus Christ, who was born of his seed. He had spiritually an infancy and childhood, a youth and an old age. It was his infancy, as it were, when he was first born in the hearts of the holy Fathers who lived before his coming. He was born in their hearts in two ways: by knowledge and by love. 13. He began to be born in Abraham's heart when [Abraham] was told how there was to be born

of his seed One in whom all nations would be blessed. We now see that fulfilled, for in our Lord Jesus Christ, who was born of Abraham's seed, *all nations* are now blessed.† Similarly he began to be born in Isaac's heart, as it were, when his coming was first made known to Isaac—and in the same way [he was born] in Jacob and the other patriarchs. 14. But this was still, as it were, his infancy. Infancy is the age at which a child cannot yet speak. Then, knowledge about our Lord was, as it were, born but not yet speaking, since the holy Fathers Abraham, Isaac, and Jacob did not openly proclaim his coming to all. But, although they did not speak of him openly, they still warmed him—because they embraced him with ardent love.

†Cf. Gen 22:18; 26:4

15. Afterwards came, as it were, his childhood, when the Law was given, when knowledge about him already began speaking to all by the various provisions and sacrifices which existed in the Old Law. In all of these Christ without a doubt spoke and made himself known to them, but spoke somehow in the language of childhood—that is, through carnal observances and ceremonies.

16. Afterwards he began to display his youth, when much more openly he began to display his strength—which in humans is usually superior in youth—the strength by which he was to vanquish the devil, despoil hell, redeem the world, rise from the dead, condemn the wicked on the day of judgement, and crown the saints. Of all this our Lord himself spoke through his prophets. All this we could show you plainly in the writings of the prophets, but we would be making too long a digression. 17. The spiritual feats of strength that our Lord Jesus Christ did were foreshadowed by

David's feats of strength, the battles and victories he won in his youth. For no doubt anyone who could examine those battles and victories of David and evaluate them spiritually, would find that there are no empty fables or simple narratives in holy Scripture. Everything would be seen to be full of mysterious significance.[†] During this—as it were, his youth—our David was the warmer the more there were who recognized, loved, and longed for him.

[†]*plena magnis sacramentis*

18. Afterwards, holy David began, as it were, to feel cold. For iniquity spread far and wide and *the charity of many* grew chill,[†] so much so that when the coming of the Lord was drawing near, the prophet exclaimed about the large number of evil-doers: *All have gone astray, all alike have become worthless. There is no one who does good, not a single one.*[†] Then it was that our David was covered with clothes without being warmed. Like clothes to him must have been the high priests, the priests, and in general all the Jews, whom Our Lord had spiritually brought into close contact with himself as he would clothes. 19. Already before his coming he was, as it were, covered with these clothes. For the Jews went frequently to the temple. The high priests and the priests offered sacrifices. They celebrated their festivals, sabbaths, new moons and such like. But none of these brought any warmth to our Lord because the warmth of true love was not in their hearts. All these things they did all, not out of love, but through hypocrisy, as our Lord demonstrated quite plainly. It was necessary therefore that a young virgin maiden be provided in whose arms this true David might rest, in whose bosom he might sleep, who would warm him in his bed now that he was growing old and feeling cold.

[†]Mt 24:12

[†]Ps 13 [14]:3

20. This virgin—purer than all other virgins, holier than all women, stronger than all men, fairer than the sun, more intense than fire—our David provided for himself. He knew her, indeed it was for himself that he prepared her like this, and yet he chose to seek her out through his servants. Solomon sought her when he said: *Who shall find a strong woman?*[†Pr 31:10] Isaiah sought her and he found her. This is why he says: *Behold a virgin shall conceive and give birth to a son and his name will be called Emmanuel.*[†Is 7:14] Jeremiah sought her and found her. And in his admiration for her he declared: *The Lord has created something new on the earth: a woman shall encompass a man.*[†Jer 31:22] 21. Finally, holy Gabriel sought her, found her, knew her, greeted her, and invited her into the embrace of the true David. She alone it was in whose bosom the true David could rest quite intimately. Her embrace would quite gently warm him. With her he would sleep quite quietly in his bed. This is Our Lady, Saint Mary, in whose most sacred breast the flame of love had not died down. She loved him more than anyone else did, so she yearned for him more than anyone else did, and therefore sought him more persistently. But him whom until now her flesh loved, now her *soul loves*.

22. This is why she says: *In my bed I sought him whom my soul loves.*[†Sg 3:1] She does not say *whom my soul loved* but *whom my soul loves*. For then, so to speak, it was her flesh that loved. Although the force of divine love wholly possessed her most holy soul, so that she could rightly be called a Shunamite—for Shunamite means 'scarlet'[†Jerome, Letter 52:3 (CSEL 54:419,10–11)] and scarlet is the color of fire—she was on fire with the flame of charity, red with the fire of divine love. Therefore, although she *loved God*

with her whole soul, nonetheless because she was still concerned about her own salvation and that of the whole world which he had still to work out—indeed by means of his flesh—she therefore longed for his humanity. She still thought of him in the flesh. She sought him in the flesh. And her soul loved him in the flesh. Indeed, she sought him whom her soul loved, but to some extent in the flesh, not wholly in the spirit.

23. *In my bed*, she said, *night after night I sought him whom my soul loves.*† During this first quest of hers it was doubtless nighttime, since the night of unbelief was then in possession of the whole world. *I sought him*, she says, *but I did not find him.*† What are we to say? Did she really not find him? Did this Shunamite of ours really not embrace the true David, not only in the bed of her heart but also in the bed of her flesh? What then is the meaning of *I sought him but did not find him?*† Ponder therefore whether these words apply to her, not at the time when she cherished the Son of God in the flesh, but today, when she ascends into heaven. This is why she tells of it in the past tense: *In my bed I sought him whom my soul loves.*†

24. And notice how subtly she places her search in the past tense: *In my bed*, she says, I sought him; but her love she places in the present tense. It is as if she said: Then *I sought him whom* now *my soul loves.* And she adds: *I sought him but I did not find him.* But how is it that she did not find him— she who conceived him in her womb, brought him forth from her chaste body, fed him at her breast, and caressed in her sacred arms Him *whom a virgin conceived*, to whom *a virgin gave birth*, and *whom after his birth a virgin* nutured?† It is aptly said of Abishag the Shunamite: *The King did not know her.*‡

†Sg 3:1

†Sg 3:1

†Sg 3:1

†Sg 3:1

†Cf. the response *Adorna* from the liturgy of the Feast of the Purification of the Blessed Virgin Mary. (Hesbert 4:6051)
‡1 K 1:4

25. Nowhere do we read of Abishag as anything but a virgin. Now Adonijah, the brother of Solomon, who had the effrontery to seek an incestuous liaison with her, was sentenced to death.† Abishag then was a virgin before the king's embrace, a virgin during the king's embrace, and a virgin after the king's embrace. Do you see then how transparently the virginity of the most blessed Mary is commended in this holiest of virgins? [Mary] was a virgin before she conceived the king—when in an embrace of marvelous unity the Son of God took to himself flesh from her virginal flesh. She remained a virgin, neither losing at conception nor unsealing at birth the seal of virginity. And after the birth she preserved it in its full integrity. 26. Would you like to hear further what Solomon, wisest of men, felt about the outstanding qualities of Abishag the Shunamite? When Bathsheba asked that Abishag be given to Adonijah, Solomon answered: *Why do you request Abishag the Shunamite for Adonijah? You might as well request the kingdom for him.*† O wonderfully outstanding virgin! To be found worthy of her embrace is to be found worthy of the kingdom. Why? Because for this Shunamite of ours, only a king's embrace was worthy. It was for him that her utterly chaste womb was reserved and her mind prepared by the work of Holy Spirit. How then can it be that our Abishag did not find him whom she sought in the bed of her heart and received in the bed of her flesh?

27. Notice, brothers, and, if you can, conceive and conjecture how she felt about her dearest Son today, to what glory she attained, how perfectly the love and knowledge of his divinity absorbed her. This is why she says that up to this time she did not find him, even though she gave birth to

him from her own womb. This we have said of her first quest. She sought him again through his passion, after his death. This was a quest full of sorrow, full of anxiety. Then was fulfilled in her what holy Simeon had prophesied: *And your soul a sword shall pierce.*† A sword of pain, a sword of grief, a sword of compassion.

†Lk 2:35

28. What streams of tears burst from her chaste eyes then, when she saw her Son—and such a Son—hanging on the cross, drinking gall and being mocked by wicked men. With what pain did she hear [him say]: *Woman, behold your son,*† [telling her] to receive the disciple in the place of the Son, the servant in the place of the Lord! Then indeed a sword of pain *pierced her soul, plunging* nearly *to the very place where soul* and body *divide.* Then without a doubt she sought him whom now her soul loves. She sought him with attachment, sought him with yearning, so hard that she did not avoid the Apostle's lament: *The flesh lusts against the spirit and the spirit against the flesh.*† As far as her natural attachment was concerned I have no doubt that she then wanted to set her Son free from that death, to check the Jews' mockery, or even, if possible, to undergo death herself. Then, too, it was night, for extreme distress overclouded all her joy, extreme grief almost deprived her mind of reason. Therefore she sought him then but did not find him, because her natural desire, her will that her Son not suffer, was not granted so that through the death of her Son her eternal salvation might be fully accomplished. For the third time she began to seek him after his ascension.

†Jn 19:26

†Gal 5:17

30. She sought, I believe, in two ways. There still lived on in her memory what she had seen of him

physically. She thought about his delightful way of life, his gentle comments, his attractive appearance, his always touching sense of compassion. And because she still was living in the body, she often sought his physical presence as well. At times, however, she gave herself to loftier thoughts and meditated on the heavenly way of life. Then she would tire of all the things earthly and sigh from the depths of her being for the things of heaven. Remaining on earth *in body alone*,[†] in her heart she was dwelling there, where she reflected on her Son reigning over all things. 31. Then, surely, this absence of her Son was night to her, that cloister of the body which held her bound as if by chains so that she could not rest wholly in her Son's embraces. During these nights, then—first before his coming, then during his passion, and again after his ascension—she sought *him whom her soul loves. I sought him*, she says, *and I did not find him*.[†] And she adds: *I will rise up and go the rounds of the city, through the streets and the squares; I will seek him whom my soul loves.*[†]

[† Cf. the Responsory *Iste sanctus* used in the liturgy for feasts of confessors of the faith (Hesbert 4:7009)]

[† Sg 3:1]

[† Sg 3:2]

32. The city I take to be here *the heavenly Jerusalem*. Its *streets*, according to the Prophet, are *paved with pure gold. And along its thoroughfares Alleluia is sung.*[†] But what does she mean: *I will rise and go the rounds of the city?*[‡] If I dared, I would say that the ever blessed Mother of God, Mary, first left the body and then in the same body rose to eternal life. But although I dare not assert this, because I have no way of convincing possible opponents, I still hazard the opinion, and I dare assert unhesitatingly that today the Blessed Virgin, *either with her body or without it, I know not, God knows*,[†] went up into heaven and went round the whole of that heavenly city in the full natural

[† Cf. the response from the liturgy of the day, *Plateae* (Hesbert 4:7390); and Tb 13:22; Rv 21:21.]
[‡ Sg 3:2]

[† 2 Co 12:3]

vigor of her mind. 33. Today, she entered that heavenly court, <she saw> the white robes of the virgins, the ruddy crowns of the martyrs, the thrones of the apostles, and in the midst of them all she found her Son reigning. Why then does she still say: *I sought him but I did not find him?*[†] Recall, brothers, what I said a little while ago. In that first quest of hers, in which she sought <him she did find> him, but on this day she found him so perfectly, so blissfully, that she duly confesses that previously she had not found him. So it is here. For ascending higher than the very highest of the saints she has arrived at such knowledge of the divinity that she then glories in having found him for the first time.

[†]Sg 3:2

34. This is why she says: *The watchmen who guard the city found me.*[†] The 'watchmen' are the angels who guard the city of God—that is, the holy Church—and protect it against the snares and assaults of the devil. And indeed, brothers, it is certain that the whole host of angels came today to meet the most blessed Mary. *They found her* in the world and they bore her from the world. But she, although she saw the brightness of the angels and their glory and blessedness, she was still not satisfied with that. Instead, she longed to see him whom alone she loved above everything. And therefore she says, *Have you seen him whom my soul loves?*[†]

[†]Sg 3:3

[†]Sg 3:3

35. And she adds: *Scarcely had I left them behind when I met him whom my soul loves.*[†] O blessed soul, who left behind not only the patriarchs and prophets, the apostles, martyrs, confessors, and virgins, but also the angels, thrones, and dominations, the cherubim and seraphim and all

[†]Sg 3:4

heaven's array, and so reached her dearest Son. Then she utterly found *him whom* now *her soul loves* utterly. She found him and she held him. *I held him*, she says, *and I will not let him go*.[†] She held him and she holds him and she will never let him go. She holds him in the embraces of an utterly perfect love and she can never lose him because she can never love him any less.

36. Let us lift up our hearts therefore, brothers, to Our Lady, our Advocate.[‡] Let us reflect on how much hope we can have in her.[†] Just as she surpasses every creature in excellence, so also she is more merciful and kinder than any creature.[†] Let us then confidently entreat her who can by her excellence assist us and by her mercy chooses to do so, that she may implore her Son for us so that as he deigned to be born of her for us,[†] he may through her deign to have mercy on us,

who lives and reigns
with the Father and Holy Spirit
through all ages of ages.
Amen.

[†]Sg 3:4
[‡]These closing lines seem to reflect the hymn to Mary with which the Cistercians traditionally ended their day, the *Salve Regina*.
[†]Cf. Sermon 45.43

[†]Cf. Sermon 45.41

[†]Cf. Sermon 45.43

Sermon Twenty-one
For the Assumption of Saint Mary

KING SOLOMON DESCRIBED for us— or rather Holy Spirit through Solomon —a certain *woman: strong,*[†] wise, an excellent worker, so far as I can estimate, in comparison to that unwise and weak woman in paradise who was *seduced* by the devil because of her lack of wisdom,[†] overcome *by her own concupiscence because of* her own self-willed *weakness,*[†] and therefore thrown out into this exile to [suffer] her penalty. *Who shall find a strong woman?*[†] 2. This is the woman about whose strength the Lord warned the serpent: *I will place enmity,* he said, *between you and the woman and your seed and her seed; she*[‡] *will trample on your head.*[*] This is that wife of the new Adam who was brought into being by him from his own side when he was sleeping on the cross. His wife, his spouse—indeed his holy Church—is so strong that she triumphs over the world, so wise that she triumphs over the devil, so good a worker that she earns heaven. *Who shall find a strong woman?*[†] Who? Only him who left *the ninety-nine sheep in the desert,* who went out to seek the one who had wandered off.[†]

3. Because in a certain sense this prophecy characterizes the holy Church, this truth has frequently and by many been expounded[‡]—and, especially because an exposition of the moral

[†] Pr 31:10

[†] Bar 3:28
[†] Heb 7:18

[†] Pr 31:10
[‡] Following the commonly received text of his time, Aelred has a feminine pronoun here. Today Scripture scholars commonly agree that the pronoun here should be masculine.
[*] Gen 3:15
[†] Pr 31:10

[†] Mt 18:12; Lk 15:4
[‡] For example, Augustine, Sermon 37 (CCSL 41:446–473); Bede, *On the Proverbs of Salomon* 3 (CCSL 119B:149–163)

sense is usually more profitable and more pleasing to fairly simple people. But since we are responsible to both the wise and the simple, we are going to speak—in so far as we can—about how this prophecy characterizes the perfect soul. It is appropriate enough that the perfection which characterizes the mother spiritually should also be attributed to the daughter, in that the daughter, having regarded the perfection of the mother, may choose to imitate it.

4. Therefore, it seems to me, this prophetic comment depicts for us a certain model of the finest life under the guise of the woman and describes in a mystic comment what each and every soul growing [towards perfection] should rely. Solomon, reflecting on how prone the human soul is to evil, how liable to sin, how weak against the devil after that first original sin, turned his mental musings to the grace of the Gospel and in admiration of how powerfully it operated in the human soul, said: *Who can find a strong woman?*[†]

[†Pr 31:10. Cf. these lines with Bede, *On Proverbs* 3.31.10 (CCSL 119B:150, 82–87)]

[†Gal 5:16]

5. Since the woman in Paradise proved to be so weak, who in this place of misery will be able to find a strong woman? Brothers, strong is that soul who leaves the world, who tramples on the desires of the flesh,[†] who spurns the glory of the world. Someone like this, [Solomon] asks, who can find her? Not Moses, not Joshua, not David, not Solomon himself, but he who said: *If you will be perfect, go and sell all you have and give to the poor and come, follow me.*[†] He found such a soul, so strong [a soul], because first of all he taught this strength.

[†Mt 19:21; Lk 18:22]

6. This strength shone forth exceptionally in the ever blessed Mary, Mother of God, who *without*

any previous *example*[†] despised the delights of this world, abhorred the lewdness of the flesh and—something no one before her had done—chose the purity of virginity. He who foresaw before the world was made[†] that she would become his mother, found this *strong woman*. This strength, brothers, imitate; this purity, emulate! But this is already a fact. Thanks be to God! 7. For how great your strength is, you who have despised the world, who submit to this poverty and this arduous way of life, who have completely cut yourselves off from the attachment of fathers, mothers, brothers and friends. Solomon, in spirit seeing this strength, wondered at it and, because this ought to be brought about not by any human virtue but solely by God's grace, exclaimed: *Who can find a strong woman?*[†] Not because no one [could find such a woman] but because no one but God alone [could].[†]

8. This strength is evident in you, but there seems yet something to be sought. You have done great things, you have acted with strength, but for what reward, with what intention, for what end? What reward have you hoped will be given to you for this strength? Indeed foolish persons who have been called the wise of this world—*for the wisdom of this world is folly before God*[†]—certain fools like Socrates and Diogenes despised riches and for the most part cut themselves off from the delights of the world. What then is the difference between you and them? 9. I see a *strong woman*— a strong soul, that is—in Paul, who is stoned, who is beaten with rods, who is afflicted with *hunger, thirst and cold*.[†] How many thieves have suffered the same things without flinching! Wherein lies the difference, then? Certainly, in the reason—that is,

[†]Antiphon *Beata Dei Genitrix* for the Feast of the Assumption (Hesbert 3:1563)
[†]Eph 1:4; 1 P 1:20

[†]Pr 31:10

[†]Lk 18:19. Cf. Augustine, Sermon 37.2 (CCSL 41:448, 49–50)

[†]1 Co 3:19

[†]2 Co 11:25ff

in the intention, in the reward that they expect. So, let us heed the worth[1] of this strong woman: *Far beyond*, he says, *the farthest ends is her worth.*† Great is the strength of philosophers, great is the strength of thieves, but little their worth.

†Pr 31:10

10. Why is it little? Because they expect the glory of this world, the favor of the public, the admiration of the crowd. They hope for money or clothes or a horse or something like that. It is a cheap reward, for it is close at hand. Yet *far beyond the farthest ends is the worth* of this woman. If you think of gold, it is not *far beyond*; or of silver, neither is it *far beyond*; if you think of the honors of the world, of temporal dignities, neither are these *far beyond* because they are passing things. The worth of this woman is *far beyond*. 11. Utterly *far beyond*, because it is not perceived by the eyes, nor detected by the ear, nor tasted by the throat, nor smelt by the nose, nor handled by the hands. What is [this worth], this *reward*? *What no eye has seen nor ear heard nor has it entered into the human heart.*† This is *far beyond*. As *far beyond* as heaven is from earth, as death is from life, as misery is from happiness, as light is from blindness. This woman is in darkness but *her reward* is light; she is in death but *her reward* is life; in misery but *her reward* is happiness; on earth but *her reward* is heaven; she is a human being, but *her reward* is God.

†1 Co 2:9

12. Therefore *far beyond the farthest ends is her worth.*† But why *the farthest ends*? There are indeed

†Pr 31:10

---

1. The same latin word, *pretium*, can be taken as reward, worth, or price and so it has been translated variously according to context; yet it is this single word of Scripture that Aelred uses here to weave this part of the sermon together and the diverse translations in the English can cause us to fail to appreciate this thread.

two ends: one [end] for the good and the other for the wicked. And both have limits, both a primal and an ultimate. Each person comes to an end when he dies. But the death of the wicked is one thing, the death of the just another, because *the death of sinners is despicable*† but *precious in the sight of the Lord is the death of his saints*.† These are the primal ends. Although the holy soul who has gone forth from his body receives no small share of blessedness, nonetheless *far beyond the farthest ends is her reward*.† 13. What are the ultimate ends? When *all indeed shall rise but not all will be changed*,† when all molestations are ended, then in flesh incorruptible, shall the strong woman hear from the Lord: *Come, blessed of my Father, receive the kingdom that has been prepared for you from the beginning of the world*.† The impious, on the other hand, will hear: *Depart from me, accursed, into eternal fire*.†

†Ps 33:22
†Ps 115:15

†Pr 31:10

†1 Co 15:51

†Mt 25:34

†Mt 25:41

14. It is from these ends that this woman expects her reward. For this reward she now sells herself as a handmaid and, looking forward to this reward, she sweats, works, goes wherever she is commanded, willingly suffers whatever is imposed upon her. Place this reward before your eyes, brothers. In view of this reward endure labors, vigils and the other molestations. If human beings sustain such bitter labors to acquire money, what ought you to do to whom heaven is promised.

15. Therefore, to put it briefly, Solomon, musing on the soul that despises the world completely and hopes for nothing except the things to come, says: *Who can find a strong woman? Far beyond the farthest ends is her worth*.† And he added: *The heart*

†Pr 31:10

of her man trusts in her and she will have no need of spoils.†2 Who the man of this strong woman is I do not need to reveal to your charity. For he is the One of whom the Apostle says: *For I have espoused you to one man, show yourself a chaste virgin to Christ.*† So *the heart of her man trusts in her.* The comparison is drawn from human experience. 16. The man knowing his wife to be chaste, sober, modest, and accommodating, *trusts in her.* Confidently he goes out and confidently he returns, knowing that whether he is absent or present, she will not let in any adulterers, listen to any debauchers, attend to any deceivers.† For she fears chastely, she loves perfectly; she loves her husband not for his possessions but for his very self. She fears, not being beaten, but being left even for a little while. Thus is this soul described. If there is such a soul—that is, so chaste, so sober, so perfectly loving, so chastely fearing—*the heart of her man trusts in her.*

†Pr 31:11.

†2 Co 11:2

†Cf. the lines between notes 30 and 32 with Bede, *On Proverbs* 3.31.2 (CCSL 119B:150–151, 111–119)

17. Confidently he is absent, confidently he is present. Confidently he commits his goods to her for they will not be wasted with adulterers or shared with fornicators. But this spiritual man, how does he come and how does he go? He is everywhere and he is never absent, because he is always and totally and everywhere present. But when we are worn down by various adversities, it is as though he takes leave. When we are consoled by prosperity, it is as though he returns. When he visits our mind with his grace, it is as though he were present; when that grace is withdrawn,

2. Translators usually render the subject of *non indigebit* (have no need) in the masculine, taking it to refer to the man (*vir*); Aelred however interprets the text to mean that the woman (*mulier*) is the one who will not need spoils. The latin text is open to either interpretation.

he seems to be far beyond us. 18. Happy is the mind in which God, confidently as it were, does all these things. Truly, *the heart of her man trusts in her.* Happy the mind which is not broken by adversity nor made dissolute by prosperity, which does not murmur in adversity nor grow proud in prosperity. Indeed, *the heart of her man trusts in her.* Happy is the mind which does not despair when grace is withdrawn, which does not exalt itself above others when grace is present. Truly, *the heart of her man trusts in her.*

19. Brothers, I want you to be careful here. For many, when they are neither undergoing temptation nor torn by adversity nor afflicted by some molestations, exult and dance about and set themselves above others as if they acquired this by their own merits. If on the contrary all these things befall them, they are saddened, feel overwhelmed, murmur, and despair. Of such a soul is not said: *the heart of her man trusts in her.* 20. Well, brother, whoever you are who yesterday wept, prayed, experienced a great sweetness from God, know he is your man because he was present. What then did you promise your man? *I will not be moved forever.*[†] Today, on the contrary, things are changed. Meditation is insignificant, prayer abhorrent, *lectio* contemptible; moreover lust attacks, the flesh burns, the mind is stirred up as if by the furies. Your man is absent. 21. Now let us see if it can be said of you: *The heart of her man trusts in her.* He is absent. You be faithful! What if, as if despairing the return of your man, you look to adulterers, to unclean spirits who urge you to immoderate sadness or an inappropriate joy in vain and superfluous things? Because now you do not experience that sweetness of your

[†] Ps 29:7 [30:6]

man, you turn back to the despicable sweetness of the flesh. It will not be said of you: *The heart of her man trusts in her.*

22. I want, brothers, to give you some little instruction against this despicable temptation. If it does happen that you are visited by God's grace, infused with some heavenly sweetness, watered by a river of tears, diligently watch yourself lest pride creep in, lest some inattentiveness insert itself into your other activities, lest you be remiss in abstinence, tepid in obedience, and, above all, lest you judge to be inferior to yourself someone whom you see not receiving a similar grace. For because of these inattentivenesses, grace is usually taken away and a certain deterioration or tepidness comes to birth. 23. Yet, when grace is withdrawn, if you remember that you have done any of these, never murmur against God but, humbly accusing yourself instead, manfully gird yourself to repair what has been damaged. True, if you are not conscious of having been remiss in these, never be unreasonably saddened by the withdrawal of grace but, as if you were about to receive the same grace again, be consoled by a sure hope. For the Lord teaches you insofar as you have humility in prosperity and patience in adversity.

24. Again, the man having a woman in whom *he trusts* confidently entrusts his goods to her, either to disburse or to preserve. None of his goods does the woman pilfer for herself, none does she hand over to adulterers or seducers. So let every soul see how faithfully she can conserve her man's goods. If she has knowledge, if she has wisdom, if she has an understanding of the Scriptures, all

these she has received from her man not only to preserve but also to disburse. If she has the grace for work, for vigils, for psalmody, all of these she has received to disburse. If she has the grace for compunction, for prayer, for spiritual affection, for contemplation, these she has received not to disburse but to preserve.

25. Let each soul now look to see whether she is faithful to her man and whether <of her> it ought to be said: *The heart of her man trusts in her*. First of all it is essential that in all these things she not be proud and she not impute to herself anything which belongs to her man. Then let her take care that nothing of what she has received to disburse be grudgingly hidden or arrogantly disbursed. Finally, that she not impudently squander anything she has received only to preserve. 26. To express myself more plainly, the soul who does not puff with pride over the grace given her does not usurp for herself anything of her man's substance. But if she does not begrudgingly hide what can profit others but speaks humbly in praise of her man, she faithfully disburses her man's things. If she does not inanely brag about the hidden grace that she received—for example, compunction, devotion, prayer, contemplation—, she prudently conserves the goods of her man. Of such a soul can it be said: *The heart of her man trusts in her*.

27. Concentrate for a little on this perfection which shone in the most blessed Mary. Her humble response to the angel bears witness that she was not at all puffed up with pride about the grace given to her: *Behold the handmaid of the Lord.*[†] That she did not place herself above others because of it is made clear by that humble

[†] Lk 1:38

visitation which she, carrying God in her womb, undertook to greet a handmaid.[†Lk 1:39f] With what great reverence she preserved the goods of her man the words of the Gospel proclaim, saying: *Mary kept all these words, pondering them in her heart.*[†Lk 2:19] How faithfully she spoke what was not to be kept silent; that mellifluous hymn proclaims: *My soul magnifies the Lord.*[†Lk 1:46] Deservedly, *the heart of her man trusts in her.*

28. *Of spoils,* it says, *she will have no need.*[†Pr 31:11] Who is this soul so decorated with ornaments that she has no need of extraneous *spoils*? This is not said of those foolish virgins who, having kept no oil for themselves, were obliged to beg it of others.[†Mt 25:3ff] Ornaments or garments—usually those which are taken from others—are called spoils. And there are many who, having nothing of holiness in themselves and nonetheless unhappily envying others, cover their vices—like some naked disgrace—with what they have taken from others; they fancy they are well covered if they can take from others the garments of a good reputation. 29. And there are those <who>, having nothing of good in their own consciences, in order to appear religious to others, promote their reputation by doing some good outwardly. So on the day of judgement, because they are empty and naked in themselves, they will need the commendation of others as a sort of extraneous spoils. Hence the cry of the foolish virgins: *Give us some of your oil because our lamps have gone out.*[†Mt 25:8] This wise woman, then, *will have no need of spoils* because, adorned with *the glory* of her own *conscience*,[†2 Co 1:12] she will go forth confidently to meet her spouse.[†Mt 25:1ff] That *she will have no need of spoils* can be straightforwardly understood because she abounds in the ornaments of the virtues.

30. [The text] continues: *She gave back to him*—that is, to her man—*good and not evil all the days of her life.*[†] That [the text] is to be taken in this way is manifest in another translation which has: *For her man she will do good and not evil.*[†] If, rightly, this woman's man is understood to be Christ, it is perfectly correct that whatever good any soul tenders in his service is given back rather than given. 31. If pure humility, sweet charity, true obedience, perfect patience are offered to him, where do they come from, if not from him? If zeal at work, purity in watching, abstemiousness in food, a humble silence [are offered to him], where do they come from, if not from him from whom *is every wonderful endowment and every perfect gift.*[†] Therefore the holy soul, because she first received these goods from God, rightly returns them. *She gives him back good and not evil.* This is a great commendation, brothers.

[†]Pr 31:12

[†]Augustine, Sermon 37.5. (CCSL 41:451, 137)

[†]Jm 1:17

For many do otherwise. 32. They receive good things and give back evil. They receive riches and then dissipate more in lust. If [they receive] honors they get miserably overblown; if knowledge, they exalt themselves above others. They receive physical beauty and, to the degree they are more beautiful, they act more disgracefully because they abuse [what they have received]. What shall I say? That they receive this commonplace light, air, bread from God and then abuse them all, and offend him? It is not of this sort that it is said: *She gives back to him good and not evil.*

33. Brothers, it is a great, an utterly great, perfection not to abuse any gift of God. As to spiritual gifts, what shall I say? If we make progress in the knowledge of God, if we penetrate a little more subtly into the inner meanings of the Scriptures,

if we abound in tears, if we are serious in our comments, mature in our deportment, and if we take pride in all this, it will not be said of us: *She gives back to him good and not evil.* Oftentimes the Lord visits us so that we sense something of his sweetness. If that sweetness is then taken away and we are pounded by some temptation, if then, as if forgetting that sweetness, we are dejected, surely we are giving back not good for good but evil for good.

34. Therefore, brothers, the soul who does not abuse any gift of God is not undeservedly held worthy of that praise: *She gives back good and not evil.* And because the reward is not promised to beginners but given to those who persevere, the prophetic comment is added: *all the days of her life.*[†] He said earlier that *she will have no need of spoils* because she has an abundance of her own ornaments. Where she got these ornaments is manifest when he adds: *She sought wool and flax and worked them with the skill of her hands.*[†] Deservedly *she will have no need of spoils.* 35. For she did not laze about in idleness, she did not loll in pointless sleep. *She sought wool and flax and worked them with the skill of her hands* because she was aware that someone *who yields to idleness is filled with want.*[†] Therefore, eager to work, energetic to get things done, *she sought wool and flax.* Why, if not to make clothes, keep out the chill, cover nakedness. Our clothes are those very works of justice by which our nakedness is covered and the chill of eternal damnation is avoided. Any soul without good works stands naked before the eyes of God and chilled through and through by being separated from the love of God.

[†] Cf. Bede, *On Proverbs* 3.31.12 (CCSL 119B: 151, 143–147)

[†] Pr 31:13

[†] Pr 28:19

36. But there are clothes made of hair, there are woollen, there are linen and there are purple ones. Hair cloth scratches, but woollen dispels the chill, linen is quite soft, and purple [signifies] great honor. To apply this to the spiritual realm, therefore: it seems to me that hair cloth belongs to penitents, wool to those undertaking good works, linen to those making progress, and purple to the perfect. The soul who has up to now been demeaned by vices needs to be scratched by the great bitterness of penitence so that the contagion of the iniquities will be rubbed off by the roughness. 37. This woman need not be concerned about this cloth because she has already passed beyond the level of penitents. In the following verses the Scriptures make mention of the purple cloth but first it speaks of wool and linen[3]—for it is not enough to repent past evils without girding oneself manfully for good works: *She sought wool and flax and worked them.* Let us— if it is all right with you—look at the difference between woollen and linen cloth and, if we can, draw out something spiritual from that.

38. Woollen cloth is rougher, linen softer. Wool keeps out the chill, linen does not sufficiently protect us against winter's harm. Therefore, someone who wears only wool suffers some roughness, someone who wears only linen enjoys little warmth. It is better then to wear both so that the wool can keep out the coldness and the

---

3. Once again, a single Latin word, *linum*, which Aelred uses to weave his thoughts together, is capable of more than one understanding. It can mean, as it does in the Scripture text, flax. But it also signifies the cloth made out of flax, namely linen. And this meaning is at times more appropriate to the sense of the text, and is thus used in the translation, even though something of Aelred's obvious weaving becomes less obvious.

linen temper the roughness. The clothes of this woman—that is, of any member of the Church—we called good works. And not without merit. With these one is clothed, by these adorned, by these, if perhaps one has disgracefully suffered from association with the flesh, concealed from the eyes of God. Lacking this clothing, a soul will appear naked on the day of judgement; there will be no way of concealing his shame. Therefore he will very likely be cast into eternal fire.[†Cf Mt 18:8; 25:41] 39. Yet all our good works consist in two things: that is, in the active life and in the contemplative. The active life is like woollen cloth; the contemplative, like linen. The active life is rougher, the contemplative more delicate; the active more on the outside, the contemplative more on the inside. The active life can protect us well enough from the chill of damnation, can wipe away the disgrace of our sins; without it not even the contemplative life, in this mortal state at least, can lead anyone to perfection.

40. *Let no one deceive himself,*[†Col 2:4] my brothers. They are wholly deluded, brothers, deluded—in fact, I think, they are not only deluded but strive to delude others—those who shroud their idleness and curiosity with the veil of contemplation. They are *erring and leading others into error*[†1 Tm 3:13] while they know *neither what they are saying nor that which they are asserting*[†1 Tm 1:7] because they are idle and indolent, *doing nothing but indulging their curiosity.*[†2 Th 3:11] They say: What is the point of working? What is the object of whacking a tree with an ax or a stone with a mallet? *Mary has chosen the best part.*[†Lk 10:42]

41. These Paul, writing to the Thessalonians, openly contradicted: *We have heard that some of*

you walk about restlessly, doing nothing but indulging your curiosity. We denounce them in the name of our Lord, Jesus Christ. *Let workers eat their own bread in silence.*[†] Therefore let them contend with Paul and say: Who are you to order us to work? *Mary has chosen the best part.* And it is true, brothers. *Mary has chosen the best part.* Truth has said it. On this feast of Saint Mary we had a reading about these two sisters, Martha and Mary. 42. Not without cause is it read on this feast, because in the blessed Virgin herself both of these lives, the active and the contemplative, were perfectly undertaken. Certainly, *Mary has chosen the best part.* But we must realize that in that one house Martha worked and Mary was at leisure, because in the soul in which Christ is received both lives are undertaken, each in its own time, its own place, its own order. Therefore this strong woman works not only with wool but also with flax. *She sought wool and flax and worked them.* Why, if not to have a twofold cloth, wool and linen.

[†] 2 Th 3:11f

43. Yet because we have spoken of these clothes, then of wool and linen, let us now look at how these clothes are made. It seems to me, indeed it seems to the very blessed Augustine,[†] that by 'wool' is to be understood the corporal works by which the active life is brought to perfection; by 'linen' the spiritual [works] which make up the contemplative life. I call vigils, labor, and fasting corporal works; prayer, readings, meditations, and compunction, spiritual. 44. There are many who wear themselves out in corporal works but never rise far towards the spiritual. Others flatter themselves at doing only spiritual [exercises], as it were [having only] linen cloth, and freeze out

[†] Augustine, Sermon 37.6 (CCSL 41:452, 148–150)

all spiritual fervor. They would not freeze if they stayed with the spiritual exercises with fervor and constancy. But although spiritual practices cannot be exercised without some intermingling of the corporal, while these people get bored of one they are totally lethargic about the other. Both of these types are then drawn away from imitating the wisdom of this woman who *sought* both *wool and flax and worked them.*

45. But where did *she seek?* How did *she seek?* Certainly a soul eager for salvation and zealous for perfection goes into the life, practices, and teaching of the holy Fathers. In one Father she seeks enterprisingness in work, in another attentiveness to vigils. She explores the abstinence of this one, investigates the obedience of another. From this one she learns, I might say, certain veins of prayer, from that one she takes up a method of meditation. And gathering all this together in her lap she works it *with the skill of her hands.*† 46. Why *with the skill of her hands?* What is this *skill of the hands?* It is obvious that a person is fed with his own hands, defended with hands. The hands arrange the rest of the members in order, the hands raise themselves to ward off blows. Therefore let us reflect on that body of which the Apostle says: *Although one body, we are many.*† All of us who are in this community are one body. Some function as feet, others as hands, others as eyes. 47. It seems to me, therefore, brothers, that by the term 'hands' the superiors can be understood, those who feed the others by teaching and defend them by prayers. They also arrange the other, as it were, members in order and they rise up to ward off the blows of exterior cares. Consequently, brothers, if you seek for

†Pr 31:13

†1 Co 10:17

yourselves wool and linen—that is, physical and spiritual exercises—act, not according to your own counsel, but according to *the skill of your hands*, that all of your works may depend on the judgement of your superiors.

48. I had thought, brothers, that I could cover in one sermon all that is said here concerning this woman, but I see that I have a very wordy sermon and I have covered barely four verses. And maybe this has something to do with the flax of this woman.[†] For when flax is perceived on the spindle, how long a thread can be made from it is unknown. Therefore, what is in the following verses we will keep for another sermon or, if we cannot manage that, for other sermons.[4]

[†]Cf. Augustine, Sermon 37.13 (CCSL 41:458, 287–291)

---

4. The continuing sermon or sermons, if they were ever composed, have not come down to us.

Sermon Twenty-two
For the Nativity of Holy Mary

CROSS OVER TO ME, all you who crave me and be filled with the fruit of my begetting. For my Spirit is sweeter than honey and my inheritance than honey and the honeycomb. My memory [lasts] to endless generations.† The words I have just quoted are written in a book [which puts them] in the mouth of Wisdom. Wisdom calls us and says: *Cross over to me.*†2 Yet you know, brothers, that our Lord Jesus Christ is the Power of God and the Wisdom of God.† Therefore these words are Christ's, calling us to himself and saying: *Cross over to me.*† Notice, brothers. He stands as if on a high mountain and, seeing us down in the valley, says: *Cross over.*† 2. Between us and him there is a wall or a sea or something of this sort that we must cross over in order to come to him. And I am of the opinion that between us and him are both—the sea and the wall—and also a cloud. For this is what a certain holy man says to the Lord: *You have interposed a cloud to prevent prayer from crossing over to you.*† If we would come to Jesus, we must cross over all these things—that is, the wall, the sea, and the cloud. Yet we ought to know the differing qualities of these things and then the way of passing over them. Now the sea we can cross over only by ship, the wall only by an iron tool, and the cloud only by light.

†Si 24:26–28 (Vulgate) [NJB Si 24:19–20]

†Si 24:26

†1 Co 1:24

†Si 24:26

†Si 24:26

†Lam 3:44

3. Let us be aware then, brothers, that this sea which is between us and God is the present world, of which the Psalmist spoke: *This vast and uncharted sea.*† Unless we cross this sea we shall never be able to come to him who says: *Cross over to me.*† Some sink in this sea, others cross over it. Those who sink down are those who are on this sea without a boat or who leave the boat or are cast out by some storm. This boat, without which no one can pass through this world, is the profession [of faith] in Christ's cross. Without this board no one can cross the sea. But some people have a better and stronger boat than others.

†Ps 103 [104]:25

†Si 24:26

4. Like a boat is marriage contracted in faith in Jesus Christ. But this boat is flimsy and rickety and ships great quantities of water in its hold; and unless it is bailed out all the time it quickly sinks. For there are many worldly preoccupations in this profession of faith. They very often involve sins— even if not always damnable, then certainly still many. Unless these are bailed by almsgiving and generous works of mercy, they sink the boat so it cannot reach port. Yet the profession [of faith] in Christ's cross during this life is a boat and by this boat a person can cross over to Christ. Anyone, however, who, after professing marriage, falls into adultery or other damnable sins, leaves the ship and then sinks. No one can cross the sea unless he returns to his boat through repentance.

5. There is another boat: renunciation of this world. Someone who has forsaken the world and has given himself to a holy community to be under a rule and the sway of another has gone on board ship in order to cross over the world.

But anyone who after entering some community comes out again and returns to the world has left the ship and will sink under the sea unless he returns again to the ship. The storm which tosses a person out of the boat is temptation. Therefore I warn you, dearest brothers, you who have chosen this way of life for yourselves as the strongest and best boat, cling to it and do not to allow yourself to be cast away by any sweet talk or impulse. For *your enemy the devil prowls around*[†] this boat and sometimes sweet talks you and sometimes frightens you to cast you away.

6. He sweet talks, when he presents to you the amusements of the world, the glory of the world, when he promises you long life and points out to you the great breadth of God's mercy and things like that. He frightens when he presents to you the harshness of this way of life, speaking to you, as it were, in the depth of your heart, saying: How will you be able always to put up with these things? You have a long life before you and you will forever be in this wretchedness, forever struggling against your flesh, against your thoughts. You will never be without fear and after thirty or forty years by one sin you can forfeit all these labors. These are his fabrications and lies. Let us not listen to them. Let us stay in this boat. Let us cling to Jesus' cross so that we may come to him who calls us and says: *Cross over to me.*[†]

7. There is still another wall between us and God. This is the wall that we ourselves have built out of various vices and sins, like so many stones, and about which the prophet says: *Your sins separate you and God.*[†] It is a wall that we cannot break down and destroy except by an iron tool, and it must be sharp. This tool is penitence.

[†1 P 5:8]

[†Si 24:26]

[†Is 59:2]

Therefore if anyone wants to shatter and destroy his sins, which are without doubt like a wall between us and God, it is essential that he give himself to works of penitence. 8. With the tool of abstinence let him destroy lust, with the tool of poverty let him destroy avarice, with the tool of silence let him destroy wranglings. By disregard for honor and dignity—as if with the sharpest tool of all—let him destroy envy. By mortifying his own will let him destroy the wantonness of the mind. By each of these practices, which are like extremely sharp implements, let him pound and crush the vices, one by one, like very hard stones, and let him constantly cross over to him who says: *Cross over to me.*† †Si 24:26

9. But the cloud still impedes us. The cloud is the ignorance by which we are often blinded, so that in many cases we do not know what we ought to do, what we ought to seek. Accordingly, the Apostle says: *We do not know how to pray as we ought.*† Lest this cloud impede us, we need to turn †Rm 8:26 our eyes to that lamp of which the Prophet says: *Your word is a lamp for my steps and a light upon my paths.*† The Word of God, sacred Scripture: †Ps 118 [119]:105 this is the light and the lamp to which we must unremittingly look if the cloud of ignorance are not to hinder us, and if we are to carry out these exercises and the other things which are to be done, not according to our own will but in accordance with the rule of sacred Scripture and the teaching of those who minister the Word of God to us.

10. Therefore, brothers, since you are in the boat by which you can cross this *vast and uncharted sea*—that is, the world—because you have the

best and sharpest of implements by which you can shatter the wall that separates *you from God,* because you have a lamp with which you can penetrate the cloud of ignorance: do not stand still but cross over to him who is calling you and saying: *Cross over to me.*† But to whom does he say this? Who is it he is calling? Listen: *Cross over to me, all you who crave me.*† 11. Clearly it is only those who crave him who can cross over to him. Not, therefore, those who crave gold or silver or the wealth of this world or honors; they cannot cross over to Christ. Therefore, brothers, crave Christ and in doing so cross over to him.

But what does crossing over to Christ mean? There are three crossings to Christ: one in this life; another after death; a third on the day of judgement after the resurrection. In this life, to cross over to Christ is to imitate him; after this life, to rest with him; and on the day of judgement, to reign with him.

12. The ever blessed Mary listened to this invitation, she listened to it and she followed. She crossed perfectly over this sea of which we have been speaking, and over the wall and through the cloud. Therefore she arrived perfectly at that Wisdom which cries out and says: *Cross over to me, all you who crave me.*† This is why these words are read especially on her solemnity. She craved Christ; therefore she passed over to Christ. She craved him perfectly; from infancy itself she despised the world for love of him, cut away the longings of the flesh and made nothing of all the glory of the world. 13. Do not be astonished that I have said that she craved Christ from her infancy, when he had not yet been born. After all, the

Apostle says of Moses: *He considered the reproach attaching to Christ greater wealth than the treasures of Egypt.*† Moses lived long before the birth of Christ and yet with a view to Christ's sufferings he chose to undergo suffering rather than to rule in Egypt. So it was with the ever blessed Mary; because she knew that Christ was to be born she began to imitate his way of life, although this way of life had not yet been seen on earth, just as Moses already imitated his passion although that passion had not taken place.

†Heb 11:26

14. No one therefore so perfectly crossed over this sea of which we have been speaking as did blessed Mary. She so perfectly crossed over to Christ in her heart that Christ also crossed over to her and remained with her even in her body. This is what it means that Aaron's sister, who is named Mary, led the sons of Israel when they crossed over the Red Sea and led them with a tambourine.† Without doubt the ever blessed Mary—the true Mary, that is—whom the other Mary foreshadowed, leads all who have crossed over this sea—that is, the present world. She leads the way in dignity, she leads in holiness, she leads in purity, and she also leads in mortification of the flesh—that is, with a tambourine. 15. She led in this as well, that she was the first of all of us to cross over. For she was the first of the whole human race who escaped the curse of our first parents. Therefore she deserved to hear from the angel: *Blessed are you among women*†—that is, while all women are under a curse, you alone among them deserve this astounding blessing. Therefore, dearest brothers, let us imitate, in so far as we can, our most blessed Lady. Let us crave Wisdom, let us cross over to Wisdom, who cries

†Ex 15:20

†Lk 1:42

out and says: *Cross over to me, all you who crave me and be filled with the fruit of my begettings.*[Si 24:26]

16. What is the fruit of Wisdom's begettings? It can be taken in two sense: the begettings by which she is begotten in us or the begettings which she herself begets in us. Today there was read at the Gospel: *The book of the generations of Jesus Christ.*[Mt 1:1] As the Evangelist goes on to say: *From Abraham to David fourteen generations were begotten*[Mt 1:17] and so on, until he reaches Christ. These are the generations by which Christ was begotten and if Christ, therefore Wisdom. These are the begettings by which Wisdom herself is begotten in us, but according to the body. 17. Perhaps, however, according to these begettings Wisdom is born in us spiritually as well. Therefore we can understand *and be filled with the fruit of my begettings*[Si 24:26–28] to mean that we should have in us spiritually Abraham, Isaac, and Jacob, Judah and the other holy Fathers by whom the begettings of Wisdom—that is, of Christ—are recorded, for without doubt it is from them that Wisdom is born. If then you choose to have Christ born in you, fill yourself with the begettings of Wisdom—that is, of Christ. How? Have in yourself Abraham, Isaac, and Jacob and the others in whom the begettings of Christ are described.

18. Abraham was first and was proved perfect in faith. Isaac was the son [born in fulfilment] of promise. Jacob saw the Lord *face to face.*[Gen 32:30] Have within yourselves, therefore, perfect faith and you will have Abraham spiritually. Hope for the promises of things to come [and] scorn present delights and you will have Isaac. Hasten as fast as you can to the vision of God and you will have Jacob. If you are *fervent in spirit*, you will have

Abraham; if you *rejoice in hope*, Isaac; if you are *patient in tribulation*, Jacob.[†Rm 12:11–12] 19. Now, Abraham was so fervent in spirit that he was willing to sacrifice his only son to God. The name Isaac means 'laugh'[†Interpretatio 7 (CCSL 72:67, 15) et passim] and therefore denotes the joy which we should have in hope. Jacob was patient in toil, as he himself told Laban: *By day the heat consumed me and the frost by night, and so I have served you for twenty years.*[†Gen 31: 40–41] If we have within us spiritually in this way all the Fathers of whom the Gospel speaks today, the bidding of Wisdom will be carried out: *Be filled with the fruit of my begettings.*[†Si 24:26]

20. But if you want to understand these begettings as those which Wisdom herself begets in us, ponder that Wisdom is the mother and teacher of all virtues. For, as it is written of her: *She teaches sobriety and prudence and justice and might.*[†Ws 8:7] These are the first of Wisdom's begettings—that is to say, they are the four primary virtues that even pagan philosophers, with reason to teach them, were able to recognize: temperance—which here is called sobriety—, prudence, justice, and fortitude—which is here given the name 'might'. 21. From these begettings others are born and from them others again, and with all of them Wisdom would have us filled, saying: *Be filled with the fruit of my begettings.*[†Si 24:26] By temperance we are chaste, by prudence we choose the good and reject the evil, by justice we love God and neighbor, by fortitude we persevere in all these good things. Cross over then to Wisdom and *be filled with the fruit of* her *begettings.*[†Si 24:26]

22. *For my Spirit*, she says, *is sweeter than honey and my inheritance is sweeter than honey and the*

honeycomb.[†Si 24:27] To the palate of flesh nothing tastes sweeter than honey, to the palate of the heart nothing tastes sweeter than the Spirit of God. But two things have been mentioned here: [Wisdom's] Spirit and its inheritance. And more seems to be attributed to the inheritance than to her Spirit: *For my Spirit is sweeter than honey and my inheritance is sweeter than honey and the honeycomb.*[†Si 24:27] But what is sweeter than the Spirit of God, since that Spirit of God is God? What could be more excellent, what sweeter, what more delectable than God? 23. But we here ought to understand [this to mean] the Holy Spirit in so far as we now receive her in ourselves, as the Apostle says: *God, who has shaped us for this very end, has a pledge of it given us the Spirit.*[†2 Co 5:5] These are the spiritual visitations and consolations by which we are delighted for the time being, as if by some sort of pledge, until we arrive at full possession of the inheritance. This inheritance is in the Kingdom of Heaven. And this spiritual sweetness, the one with which we are refreshed at present, is appropriately compared to honey.

24. The bee, whose task it is to make honey, is an extremely chaste animal—for bees do not propagate by physical intercourse. Therefore the bee signifies the chaste and sober mind, the sort which Wisdom gladly indwells. The chaste soul accordingly—like a bee—wings her way through the field of the Scriptures by assiduous meditation. There, from the sayings and examples of the saints, she gathers spiritual flowers and from these produces in her heart a wondrous delight and a great sweetness, one of heavenly delicacy. Thus it experiences that *the Spirit* of the Lord *is sweeter than honey.* 25. *And my inheritance*, it says,

is sweeter than honey and the honeycomb.† An apt comparison. Do the cells which you always see in a honeycomb not display some likeness to the inheritance of which the Lord says: *There are many dwelling places in my Father's house?*† Therefore he adds honey to the honeycomb because in those eternal dwelling places there is an everlasting and inexpressible sweetness. Notice: although crossing over to Wisdom may seem quite laborious, the fruit [it yields] is great. You should not let fear of hard work outweigh the attractiveness of the fruit. †Si 24:27

†Jn 14:2

26. It is indeed hard work to cross over the waves and storms of this world, to trample on all its amusements and pleasures, to despise physical relaxation and repose. But this is the crossing-way to Wisdom whose *Spirit is sweeter than honey and* whose *inheritance is sweeter than honey and the honeycomb.*† On the other hand, it seems to be easy and pleasant to love the honors of the world, to follow one's own will, and to lead a life of pleasure and amusements, but the fruit is bitter. 27. The Apostle distinguishes between these fruits when he says: *The wages of sin are death but the grace of God is life eternal.*† Eternal death is a bitter fruit, eternal life a sweet fruit. To the one leads sin; to the other, not our desserts, but God's grace. Why? Because we should ascribe everything about our crossing over to Wisdom to God's grace which gives us the strength to make the crossing. †Si 24:27

†Rm 6:23

28. *My memory lasts to endless generations.*† If you had a memory of gold and silver and riches, how far could that memory stretch? At most, a hundred years. For who lives longer than that in †Si 24:28

this day and age? If you think of Christ, if you think of Wisdom, that *memory* can be extended *to endless generations*—that is, to eternity. For Wisdom will always be, and you can always be with Wisdom, because, as it is written, *Wisdom is immortal.*† 29. Anyone can be rich perhaps for as long as he lives and therefore the memory of his riches can last that long. But if someone has a memory of lust and the physical pleasures, how quickly it ends, how short a time it lasts. In one moment that whole delectation passes away. What about the delights of the stomach? When a rich man has gorged on ten or twelve courses, does all the delectation given by that very rich food not vanish? 30. Finally, to be brief, no memory of temporal things can be extended any longer than a person lives, for no one can think of possessing these temporal things for any longer than he lives in a life time. But if someone thinks of the Kingdom of heaven, of the glory of the angels, of the blessedness there is in the vision of God, in incorruption and immortality: this *memory* can be extended *to endless generations*—that is, to eternity, because all these things will endure for eternity. Accordingly, Wisdom says: *My memory lasts to endless generations.*†

†Ws 1:15

†Si 24:28

31. Therefore, brothers, to conclude our sermon at last, let us cross over these earthly and perishable things that we may come to Wisdom and to be filled with [the fruit of] her begettings—that is, with the virtues by which she may be begotten in us. Let us experience, in so far as we can, that her *Spirit is sweeter than honey and her inheritance than honey and the honeycomb.*† Let us, as far as we can, detach our memory from this world and fix our heart on eternal things, so that—by the

†Si 24:27

intercession of our most blessed Lady, holy Mary, whose feast we are celebrating today—we may at length arrive at those things that are eternal, by the gift of our Lord Jesus Christ,
> who with the Father and Holy Spirit
> lives and reigns, God,
> through all the ages of ages.
> Amen.

Sermon Twenty-three
For the Nativity of Holy Mary

WONDROUS IS THE MERCY of our Lord Jesus Christ. He is our judge and he knows that we are wretched and when he judges us have no good case on our own. He is merciful and wants to show us mercy but he cannot judge other than justly. How then has he provided for us? He teaches us to live well, and we on the contrary live badly. Right at the start he has remitted all our sins through baptism and we have fallen right back into them. We have often promised to mend our ways and yet we are always sinning. He gives us opportunity for repentance and we pay no attention. And yet for all of this he spares us. And because we are unworthy and not the sort he should listen to, he sets before us his friends so that we may appeal to them and through them may approach him and be reconciled with him.

2. You know that men of the world do this very thing. When their master is angry with them, they seek out his intimate companions—sometimes his sons, very often even his wife—so that, if it happens they are not to blame, their master may more readily hear their case when it is presented by those [sons or wife] whom the lord dearly loves. And if they are to blame, he may forgive them through the prayers of these

[loved ones]. We discover that a certain holy king rejoiced when anyone appealed to him on behalf of someone whom by the law he was forced to punish, because then he could have a just cause for pardoning him. This king, without a doubt, was imitating our Lord, who, so that he can still justly pardon us, wills that his intimate companions pray for us.

3. Let each person now reflect on himself. Let him see what sort of cause he has [to present] before the Lord. How have we lived in his sight? Certainly we are people; he is God. We are servants; he is Lord. We are creatures; he is Creator. We have not worshipped our God as we ought to have done; we have not obeyed our Lord as we ought to have done; we have not loved our Creator as we ought to have done. Therefore, brothers, if we really reflect about ourselves, we will not be able, as the Scriptures say, *to answer him one question in a thousand.*† 4. What then shall we do? We can hide nothing from him.† For, as the Apostle says, *Everything lies naked and open to his eyes.*† Let us offer him our prayers. Let us say to him: *Do not enter into judgment with your* servants.† It is too little however to offer only our own prayers. Let us seek the help of someone whose prayers he will never despise. Let us therefore approach his Bride. Let us approach his Mother. Let us approach his greatest Handmaid. The blessed Mary is all of these.

†Jb 9:3
†Jb 13:9
†Heb 4:13

†Ps 142 [143]:2

5. Therefore *let us with gladness celebrate the birthday of the blessed Mary, that she may intercede for us to the Lord our God.*† If by God's grace we have done any good, he will not scorn it if she presents it to her Son. Without any doubt she

†Antiphon for the Feast of the Assumption (Hesbert 3:2016)

will obtain lenience for the wrong we have done. What is utterly necessary for us then is so to bear ourselves in her presence that she will be willing to accept our case. But what shall we do for her? What sort of gifts shall we offer her? Would that we could at least bestow on her what in strict justice we owe her. We owe her honor, we owe her service, we owe her love, we owe her praise.

6. We owe her honor because she is the mother of Our Lord. For anyone who denies honor to the mother clearly dishonors the son. As Scripture says: *Honor your father and mother.*† What then shall we say, brothers? Is she not our mother? Assuredly, brothers, she is truly our mother. For through her we were born, through her we are nourished, through her we grow. Through her we were born, not to the world, but to God. Through her we are nourished, not with physical milk, but with that of which the Apostle says: *I gave you milk to drink instead of solid food.*† Through her we grow, not in physical bulk, but in spiritual might. Now let us see what sort of birth this is, what sort of milk this is, what sort of growth this is.

†Dt 5:16

†1 Co 3:2

7. We were all—as you believe and as you know—[ensnared] in death, in old age, in darkness, and in misery. In death, because we had lost the Lord; in old age, because we were corrupt; in darkness, because we had forfeited the light of wisdom and so had utterly perished. But through blessed Mary we were born in a much better way than through Eve, because in that Christ was born of her, we have recovered newness of life in place of old age; incorruption in place of corruption; light in place of darkness. She is our mother, the mother of our life, the mother of our incorruption, the

mother of our light. 8. The Apostle says of Our Lord: *God made him our wisdom, our justice, our sanctification, and our redemption.*[†] She, therefore, who is the mother of Christ is the mother of our wisdom, the mother of our justice, the mother of our sanctification, the mother of our redemption. So she is more a mother to us than the mother of our flesh. Our birth from her is therefore better because from her comes our newness of life, our holiness, our wisdom, our justice, our sanctification, and our redemption. Therefore *let us with gladness celebrate the birthday*[†] of her from whom we have been so well born.

[†]1 Co 1:30

[†]Antiphon for the Nativity BVM (Hesbert 3:2016)

9. Now let us see what sort of milk we have received from her. The Word of God, the Son of God, the Wisdom of God, is *bread* and he is *solid food*. Accordingly, only those who were strong—that is, the angels—ate of him.[†] We who were little were not able to taste this food because it was *solid*. We who were on earth were not able to get up to this bread, because it was in heaven. What happened then? This *bread* entered into the womb of the Blessed Virgin and there it became milk. What kind of milk? The kind we are able to suck. 10. Reflect now on the Son of God on the Virgin's lap, in the Virgin's arms, at the Virgin's breast. All this is milk; suck it in. This is the milk that our good Mother provides for us. Now too reflect on her chastity, her charity, her humility; and by her example grow in purity, grow in charity, grow in humility, and in this way follow your mother. Notice! This is how she is our mother. Therefore we owe her honor. For this, as we said, is the Lord's commandment: *Honor your father and mother.*[†]

[†]Cf. Ps 77 [78]:25

[†]Dt 5:2

11. We also owe her service because she is our Lady. The bride of our Lord is our Lady; the bride of our king is our queen. Therefore let us serve her. For the Apostle bids us: *Servants be subject to your lords with all fear.*† And if someone who does not serve physical lords violates the prescription of the Lord, without doubt those who do not serve their heavenly Lady are utterly reprehensible. But how should we serve her? 12. Brothers, no service pleases her so much as when we humble ourselves to her Son with entire attachment and love, because all the praise and all the service that we show to her Son she reckons as all paid to herself. Let no one say: Although I do this or that against the Lord, I do not much care; I will serve Saint Mary and I shall be safe. That is not so. The instant someone offends the Son, then without a doubt he also offends the Mother. But when we want to be reconciled to our Lord after our sins, then it is essential that we must seek her out and entrust our cause to her.

†1 P 2:18

13. Again, we owe her love. *For* she is of our *flesh* and she is our sister.† Do not let what I say seem overbold to you. The Son of God himself, because he is the Son of Man, is our brother. But he [derives] his humanness only from his mother; she derives hers from both father and mother. Notice now how bold we may be with her because she is our sister. Let us love her for she does indeed love us. We ought to love this sister whose holiness, whose kindness, whose purity has been of advantage not only to herself but to all of us.

†Cf. Gen 37:27

14. Again, we owe her praise. For Scripture says: *Praise the Lord in his saints.*† If our Lord is

†Ps 150:1

to be praised *in* the *saints* through whom he works wondrous deeds, how much more is he to be praised in her in whom he made himself a wonder surpassing all wonders! If those who set out to preserve their chastity are to be praised, how is she to be praised who, without any example, chose to preserve her virginity and yet together with virginity obtained fruitfulness! If those through whom God raises the dead are to be praised, how is she to be praised through whose holiness he raised the whole world from everlasting death! 15. Therefore, brothers, let us praise her and *let us with gladness celebrate the birthday of the blessed Mary, that she may intercede for us to the Lord our God.*[†] But if we praise her with our voice, let us not insult her by our behavior. Consequently, let us then not praise her in travesty but in very truth. To be unwilling to imitate to the best of our ability that which we praise is to offer false praise. Truly to praise the humility of Saint Mary is strive for humility as hard as possible. Truly to praise her chastity is to detest and scorn all taint and lust. Truly to praise her charity is to direct all our thoughts and energies to loving God and neighbor perfectly.

[†]Antiphon for the Nativity BVM (Hesbert 3:2016)

16. Consequently, brothers, if we would praise Mary worthily, we must strive for these three things in particular: good thoughts, holy words, and upright deeds. For anyone who has these in so far as possible and aims at having them perfectly is imitating Saint Mary. These three things the Holy Spirit commends in her [when] she says through Solomon: *Your lips are a dripping honeycomb, honey and milk are under your tongue and the fragrance of your robes is like the smell of incense.*[†]

[†]Sg 4:11

17. By 'lips' we should understand words, since we speak through the lips. A honeycomb is wax which has honey in it. *A dripping honeycomb* is <wax> which has such an abundance of honey in it that it is beginning to overflow. Aptly then can the words of the blessed Mary be compared to a overflowing honeycomb because all her words were sweet and full, not of physical, but of spiritual sweetness. There are many who have honey in their mouths but not a dripping honeycomb because many have sweet words but they do not come from an abundance of inner sweetness. 18. In some respects they resemble the bee, which possesses sweetness and a sting. On the one hand they posses honey, because they speak sweetly, they flatter everyone, they fall in with everyone's wishes. But this is all outward [show]. For in secret, or perhaps in their hearts, the very people they bedaub with honey outwardly, they sting inwardly with unfounded rumors and judgements. These people do not possess a *dripping honeycomb* because this sweetness of utterance does not come, as we have said, from an abundance of inner sweetness. Not so with the blessed Mary. *Your lips are a dripping honeycomb*,† it says— that is, your words are sweet by reason of an abundance of interior sweetness.

†Sg 4:11

19. To let us know the source of this sweetness in utterances, the text immediately adds: *honey and milk are under your tongue.*† Those who would possess in their words a holy sweetness such as will please God must have two qualities in their thoughts and in their heart—that is, holiness for themselves and compassion for their neighbors. When they possess these two [qualities] in their hearts and in both of them keep

†Sg 4:11

their thoughts, their comments will always be full of spiritual sweetness. As honey is made from various flowers, so all holiness consists in many virtues. Accordingly, by 'honey' we can understand 'holiness'.

20. Since milk is the sign of motherly charity and nourishes little ones and causes a mother to bend over her infant, by 'milk' we understand 'compassion'. Nothing more impels a person to speak with another caringly and kindly and sweetly than compassion. But compassion without holiness is indulgence. Notice therefore what is said: *Your lips are a dripping honeycomb, honey and milk are under your tongue.*† As if it would say: Your comments are full of spiritual sweetness because they come from inner holiness and compassion. Things *under the tongue* have not yet come on to the tongue. Therefore *under your tongue* is as much as saying 'in your thoughts'.

†Sg 4:11

21. There follows: *The fragrance of your robes is like the smell of incense.*† The 'robes' we should take to mean our good works, because our sins—as it were our disgrace—are covered by our good works. They are also our adornments before God. By 'incense' we can reflect on two [elements]: a good odor and a divine sacrifice. Saint Mary's robes are compared to incense therefore because they both pleased God and they offered human beings the odor of a good reputation. There are many whose robes have a nice odor, but it is not the odor of incense. For many exude the reputation of religion and their deeds seem to people to be holy, but it is not the odor of incense because their deeds are not offered to God in sacrifice.

†Sg 4:11

22. Therefore, dearest brothers, let us imitate the ever blessed Mary as much as we can. Let us practice holy meditation and kindly compassion towards our neighbor, like *milk and honey*. Let our *lips* be like a *dripping honeycomb* so that all our words may flow from the sweetness of charity. If we correct [someone], let it be with charity, if we are corrected by another, let us listen with charity, so that, according to the Apostle: *All that we do may be done in charity.*[†] By our deeds let us offer sacrifice to God with a good conscience. Let us by them waft a good odor so that others may benefit by our example. In this way let us have gladness, not from the flesh, nor from feasting nor jesting nor worldly pomp. Instead, let us *with* complete spiritual *gladness celebrate today the birthday of the blessed Mary, that she may intercede for us with our Lord Jesus Christ,*[†]

who with the Father and Holy Spirit,
lives and reigns through all the ages of ages.
Amen.

[†] 1 Co 16:14

[†] Antiphon for the Nativity BVM (Hesbert 3:2016)

Sermon Twenty-four
For the Nativity of Holy Mary

YOU KNOW, DEAREST BROTHERS, that today we are celebrating the birth of our Lady, the holy Mary, and that it is therefore right that we rejoice in the Lord and call to mind what great joy came to us through her birth; for it was at her birth all our joy began to appear. Therefore it is right that we rouse ourselves on this feast to praise our Lord. Yet even though you have this night been roused by songs, readings, psalms and the other things appropriate to the feast, in order that you may lack nothing we wish also, so far as we can, to rouse you by our sermon. I do hope, however, that even if our sermon does not increase the burning ardor of your devotion, it will nonetheless not lessen it.

2. It seems to me that nothing ought to rouse you more to the love and praise of our Lord and to spiritual joy than for us to remind you of what our Lord began to show us today. For it was today that he began <to show> us that marvelous mercy of his, his wondrous kindness which so many years earlier he had promised to Abraham—namely, that *in his seed all nations* would be blessed. *In your seed*, he said, *all nations will be blessed.*[†] Today was born that seed from which *arose the Sun of Justice*,

[†]Gen 22:18; 26:4

Christ our God,[†] in whom without doubt is blessed not merely one nation but indeed *all nations*. For the faith of Christ and his blessing is [spread] through all nations. 3. This seed, brothers, is the blessed Mary, who today was born of the seed of Abraham, she who received so wonderful a *blessing* from the Lord that it took away the *curse* [which lay] on the world.[†] Now, as the Gospel that is read today narrates, it is utterly certain that she is of the seed of Abraham. For we read there: *The book of the generation of Jesus Christ, son of David, son of Abraham.*[†] From this we know that our Lord, who did not have a father on earth, could not rightly be called the son of Abraham and the son of David unless his mother was of their seed. Again, that we might be certain that he is the one of whom God spoke to Abraham, the evangelist Matthew chose to narrate for us the whole lineage of our Lord from Abraham down to blessed Mary, *from whom arose the Sun of Justice, Christ our God.*[†]

4. We ought, moreover, to reflect that the Evangelist aimed not only at this—simply showing us the fathers from whom Christ was born and letting us know his human lineage—but also that we might derive spiritual fruit from his physical ancestry. Because if the Evangelist had intended nothing more, why should he make these three groupings[†] and in each group place fourteen generations— that is, fourteen names? 5. For he says this: *From Abraham to David there are fourteen generations, from David to the deportation to Babylon there are fourteen generations, and from the deportation to Babylon to Christ there are fourteen generations.*[†] And because he did not want to exceed this number but to preserve these groupings, he omitted

---

[†] From the antiphon, *Nativitas tua*, for the Nativity BVM (Hesbert 3:3852)

[†] Cf. the antiphon *Nativitas gloriosae* for this feast (Hesbert 3:3850)

[†] Mt 1:1

[†] Antiphon *Nativitas tua*; cf Mt 1:16

[†] *Distinctiones*

[†] Mt 1:17

from his enumeration some fathers and sons who belong to this lineage and passed directly from father to great-grandson. And therefore by these fathers through whom Christ descended to us we ought to understand something spiritual and to mark certain steps by which we are to ascend to him.

6. Let us see then how he sets forth this lineage. He begins from Abraham and by descending he arrives at our Lord. As it seems to me, by this descent by which our Lord came down[†] to us he wanted to show us some sort of ascent by which we are to go up to him. For he descended that we might ascend. He became poor for us that we might become rich.[†] The Evangelist, however, begins this descent from Abraham. 7. Now 'Abraham' means *father on high*,[†] which can signify him who is truly the Father on high—that is God, the Father of our Lord Jesus Christ.[‡] It was from there—that is, from the bosom of the Father on high—that our Lord came down to come to us. By this he came to us: by becoming a human being among us. And by the fact he is a human being, he is indeed the Son of Mary. Therefore at the end of this descent the Evangelist says, *Jacob begot Joseph, the husband of Mary who gave birth to Jesus who is called Christ.*[†]

[†]*Come down* and *go up* are also, as one would expect, *descendere* and *ascendere*.

[†]2 Co 8:9

[†]*Interpretatio* 2, where Abram, rather than Abraham, is explained (CCSL 72:61, 28–29)
[‡]Rm 15:6; 2 Co 1:3, 11:31; etc.

[†]Mt 1:16

8. Therefore, dearest brothers, if we wish to ascend to that place from which he descended to us—that is, to the Father on high—let us begin our ascent here. Where? From the Son of Mary—that is, from the humanity of Christ. And so let us ascend to his divinity. For he himself is the way, as he says: *I am the way.*[†] Apart from this way no one can succeed in coming to the Father

[†]Jn 14:6

on high. This is why he says, *No one comes to the Father except through me.*† For no one can begin anything good unless he begins from Christ. He is the *foundation* of all that is good. As the Apostle says, *No one can lay any other foundation than that which is already laid, which is Christ Jesus.*† 9. But because we are in the depths while he to whom we are supposed to ascend is exceedingly high, we can get there only by certain steps. These spiritual steps by which we are to go up, we can, as we have said, mark in the fathers through whom our Lord descended to us so that we might ascend to him. Therefore, as he descended to us from Abraham—that is, from God the Father—through these fathers according to the flesh, let us ascend to the same God the Father also through these fathers understood spiritually. And first let us see the meaning of the three groups which the Evangelist constructs.

†Jn 14:6

†1 Co 3:11

10. I think we should take these three groupings as three states in which are all those who want to ascend by these steps to the place from which Christ descended to us. The first state is our conversion; the second our purification; the third our anticipation. This is how everyone is to advance. For first a person is converted to the Lord from the vanity of this world. Afterwards he is purified from the vices which he contracted through bad habit. Then, after he has been purified from vices—in so far as human frailty allows—he ought to anticipate his release with great desire, that moment when he is to go forth from this body and come to Christ and confidently receive his reward. But if a person wants to ascend to this highest step, he must first be perfected in the first and then in the second and so ascend to the third.

11. Accordingly, it is necessary that anyone who is converted to the Lord be not timid or lukewarm in converting. To be timid and lukewarm in converting to the Lord is to be unwilling perfectly to abandon all one has when one leaves the world but, contrary to the Lord's command, to be anxious about the morrow and to keep something back for oneself and from one's own belongings to build some new and novel[†] dwelling. It is to fear one cannot endure that strictness which goes with being underneath another's rule and to begin to live independently and to take care of oneself and to be a master before one has been a disciple.
12. To be lukewarm in converting to God is—although having left everything one had and put oneself under another's authority—nonetheless to choose a place and install oneself there, where one may have all the pleasures one would have had in the world, or even more. And to be lukewarm in converting to God is, in whatever house one should be, as much as one can, always to seek repose and the amusements of the flesh and to care for nothing but remaining by any means possible in the house to which one has come.

[†]*Nouellam habitationem*: new and novel are both intended.

13. Again, there must be a certain perfection in our purification, so that we are not content with relinquishing the abominable things we did in the world while the eye of our heart is still stained with anger, envy, rumor mongering, murmuring, and even hidden impurities. And in our anticipation there must also be a certain perfection—that is, perseverance *right to the end*[†] and a desire always fervent. We can understand the three groups of fourteen[‡] as representing these perfections.[†]

[†]Mt 10:22; 24:13
[‡]*Tessarescedacades*
[†]Jerome, *On Matthew* 1 (CCSL 77:8, 34)

14. But why did [the Evangelist] allot this number —that is, fourteen—to each grouping? This number signifies perfection. For ten and four stand for the Law and the Gospel, in which all perfection exists. Ten signifies the perfection of the Law, because of the ten commandments which were in the Law. Four signifies the perfection of the Gospel, because of the four books of the evangelists. Accordingly, the Evangelist selected this number, which signifies perfection because in each state a human being ought to be perfect. 15. Surely our conversion ought to be perfect. Now, if we were not perfect in this state by no means can we come to that other state. For unless we are willing to be converted perfectly from this world to the Lord, we shall never be able to be purified from our vices. And unless we have been perfectly purified from our vices, we can by no means confidently expect the heavenly reward. But since a person can succeed in coming all at once neither to the first perfection—which lies in conversion—nor from there to the others, he ought on that account to ascend, as it were, step by step until he arrives at the place from which our Lord descended to us. 16. Here and now, then, brothers, let us ascend. And let us begin from Christ and let us arrive at Christ. Let us begin from Christ as a human being and let us arrive at Christ where he is one with the Father on high.[†]

†Jn 10:30

And if we want to take these fathers whom the Gospel mentions to mean those spiritual steps by which we ought to ascend, we ought to begin from Joseph and go up *as far as the deportation to Babylon*.[†] For these are the steps which pertain to the first state.

†Mt 1:17

17. 'Joseph' means *increase*.[†] We ought to know that the Lord created the rational creature to

†*Interpretatio* 7 (CCSL 72:67, 20) et passim

share his own blessedness, with the result that nothing else can be adequate [to bring him] happiness save God alone. Thus the whole perfection of the rational creature and his entire *good is to cling to God.*† And so, withdrawing from that, he tends toward nothing. By this means, by withdrawing from God., came about all the harm that befell humankind Therefore when a person converts to God his *increase* begins. 18. And therefore if we wish to ascend to him the first thing to do is to be converted to him. In this way begins our *increase*, which we can understand [to be represented] by Joseph, whose name means *increase*.† Our Lord Jesus Christ, *since he was in the form of God did not think it wrong to make himself equal to God but he emptied himself*† and descended to our weakness. But because *the weakness of God is stronger than human strength,*† therefore, where he came down to our deficit, there our *increase* began. †Ps 72 [73]:28

†*Interpretatio* 7 (CCSL 72:67, 20)
†Ph 2:6f

†I Co 1:25

19. Yet from that great brightness we fell into this darkness. From that great repose which the first human being had in Paradise we fell into *this great and immeasurable sea*† where the winds of temptation and the waves of persecution teem and into this night in which all the *wild beasts of the forest* roam†—and in this sea there are also *reptiles without number,*† malign spirits who are bent on deceiving us. Amid all these evils and dangers we must ascend to the place from which we fell. In this night and. from this sea we ought to ascend. It is essential that we have some light which enlightens us, by which we can ascend these steps.

†Ps 103 [104]:25

†Ps 10 [104]3:20
†Ps 103 [104]:25

20. Therefore a certain *star* has risen for us today:† our Lady Saint Mary [whose name] means *star* †Nb 24:17

of the sea;† without doubt the *star of* this *sea*—that is, the world. Accordingly, we ought to lift up our eyes to this star which has appeared on earth today so that she may lead us, so that she may enlighten us, so that she may show us these steps so we may recognize them, so that she may encourage us lest we fall back on the ascent, so that she may aid us in being capable of ascending. And therefore it is a beautiful thing that Mary is placed in this stairway of which we are speaking, there where we have to begin to climb. As the Evangelist says, *Jacob begot Joseph, the husband of Mary*,† so immediately at our very first conversion she appears to us and receives us into her care and enlightens us by her light and accompanies us along this laborious path.

21. Therefore, with her enlightening and teaching us in everything, let us who have begun to convert to God bring our conversion to perfection. And let us begin from Joseph where our *increase* begins. Let us advance and ascend until we pass through the *deportation to Babylon*, so that we who, because of our vices and sins, had been prisoners subject to the power of Nebuchadnezzar in Babylon†—that is, in *confusion*‡—may be set free through the grace of Christ to whom we have converted. Having thus come back from Babylon by perfect conversion to God, let us pass on to the second stage. And beginning there to purify ourselves, let us ascend step by step until we come to Solomon, [whose name] means *peacemaker*,† so that, purified from evil passions, we may come to possess a certain peace and tranquillity. And thus we enter the third stage, which begins at David—*whose name means desirable*†—so that we too may desire and burn to see that

object of our longing, the face of our Creator. And in this longing of ours let us come at last to Abraham—to the Father on high—and let us look upon *the God of gods in Sion.*† †Ps 83:8 [84:7]

22. But since it would take a long time if we wanted to work through all these names and look for the steps in each of them, let us look at what perfection we should reach in each of the three states. And first of all, let us look to it that the foundation is laid—that is, faith in Christ. For *without faith it is impossible to please God.*† Next, †Heb 11:6 let us carefully reflect on always keeping before our eyes this star which today appeared on earth, lest we falter on account of the darkness of the night in which we are. And let us begin to ascend to the first state in such a way that our conversion may be perfect.

23. This stage begins with Joseph. Joseph, as we have said, means *increase*. What does this *increase* mean? The Lord says in the Gospel, *Who, wanting to build a tower, would not first sit down and calculate to see whether he can afford to finish it?*† This tower †Lk 14:28 is the perfection to which we ought to ascend. Anyone who is going to want to build this tower spiritually must increase his resources [to have the wherewithal] to finish it and so to be in this first state—that is, *increase*. But what are these resources? We would hesitate to say if the Lord himself had not previously told [us]. For when he told us we must calculate the *cost* for this spiritual building, immediately—at the end of this Gospel which speaks of the costs—he shows us saying, *None of you can be my disciple who does not renounce all his possessions.*† 24. What a wondrous †Lk 14:33 thing! Persons of this world, if they wish to

build something great, not only keep what they possess but also gather up and acquire more. But someone who would undertake spiritual building ought not only to refrain from seeking what he does not possess but also to part with what he does possess. What then to them seems to be a loss is our *increase*. For the more these material riches are diminished for Christ's sake the greater the increase in spiritual [wealth]. Therefore, we who long to ascend and to build a spiritual tower first have set before us Joseph—that is, *increase*—so that we may reject earthly riches and so have our spiritual riches increased.

25. We ought to realize, however, that temporal wealth and worldly occupations are like a chain by which the devil holds persons bound so they cannot be free to ascend God's stairway. This is why a certain *rich man* who was told by the Lord, *Go, sell all you have and give to the poor and come, follow me, went away sad.*[†Mt 19:22] Why he *went away sad* the Evangelist tells us when he says, *For he was a man of great wealth.*[†Mt 19:21f; Lk 18:22f] The devil held him bound with worldly occupations as if with chains. Therefore he was *sad*. He saw what he ought to do, but because he was bound with these chains he could not extricate himself without great sadness.

26. Someone who casts away the riches of this world out of fear and for love of God can easily ascend God's stairway and overturn the devil. For there is no easier way for a person to be able to overturn the devil than by [using] the fear of God as if it were a sharp file[†Ps 51:4] to cut off these chains by which the devil holds him shackled. But when a person begins to convert from his sins to God, excessive fear sometimes seeks to drive him to

despair; so let him ascend and look to him who is truly merciful. Let him place all his hope in him and love him above all, for without any doubt he pardons all the sins of all those who turn to him.

27. Solomon says in the Book of Proverbs, *My son, when you enter the service of God, stand in justice and fear and prepare your soul for temptation.*† The devil does not trouble to tempt a person whom he has in his power. When someone obeys his own unruly appetites in everything and satisfies the desires of his flesh,† the devil does not trouble to approach him. But if someone begins to reject those unruly appetites and struggle against the desires of his flesh, then the devil is grieved and assails him in a fiercer conflict. Let the person whom the devil assails not grow faint but ascend higher and scorn the devil and all his arguments. Let him say, *My God is my helper and I will hope in him.*† For *if God is for us who is against us?*‡ 28. The riches of the world which the person rejected the devil puts before his eyes and wants him to *return to his vomit.*† But let him with utter confidence say, *My God is my helper and I will hope in him.*† Let him reflect that if earthly and fleeting things are delightful, beyond doubt he is yet more delightful who made not only these earthly things but all things good and beautiful, both those of heaven and those of earth. For love of Him let him despise everything and say, My God, my riches, my honor, my treasure, and all my good. At this stage all riches are now perfectly despised. For when a human being considers the beauty of his Creator, whatever he left in the world seems slight to him.

†Pr 2:1

†Gal 5:16

†Ps 17:3 [18:2]
‡Rm 8:31

†Pr 26:11
†Ps 17:3 [18:2]

29. But now, once wealth has been trampled underfoot, since it cannot hinder his conversion to God, physical attachments begin to assault

him: love of father and mother, relatives and friends. This is a very dangerous place. For when a person chooses to leave the world and convert to God, all these stand in his way, hold him back and cry, 'Are you leaving us? Who will support your father in his old age? Who will comfort your mother when she is a *desolate widow?*† Who will help your brothers, sisters, the youngsters who all look to you? 30. Even if these things are not spoken outwardly, that physical attachment or the devil still utters them in the heart. On the other hand, those close to him—friends and companions with whom he has enjoyed very pleasant experiences—flock to him and say, 'Are you leaving us like this? Are we to be separated like this?' But someone who is ascending this spiritual stairway and wants to sing the canticle of the steps must say, *Lord, deliver my soul from evil lips and from the deceitful tongue.*† And again, *The wicked tell me tales but not in accordance with your law, Lord.*†

†Bar 4:12; 1 Tm 5:5

†Ps 119 [120]:2

†Ps 118 [119]:85

31. Certainly these attachments, rather like clouds, darken the soul and attempt to obscure all spiritual joy. But here especially we ought to reflect on that Star of ours† that she may shine upon us in this night, in this darkness. We ought to reflect on the Beam that has issued from this Star, who has in a way been darkened for our sakes in order to free us from this darkness. Let us set him against all physical attachments and let us reflect on him as father, mother, brother,† friend.‡ As father, because he instructs us; as mother, because he comforts us and nourishes us with the milk of his sweetness; as brother, because he has taken flesh from our flesh; as friend, because he has shed his blood for us.†

†*Stella nostra*, that is, Mary, *Stella maris*.

†Mt 12:50
‡Jn 15:15

†Lk 22:20

32. This is the direct way.† But here we have to beware of robbers who lie in hiding and often ambush the heedless.† The lion, too, is accustomed to lie in wait here, *the lion that prowls around looking for someone to devour.*† When it is unable to wound a person with its sword, it assails him with the person's own arms. Its weapons are the vices with which it attacks us openly. Our arms are the virtues by which we resist it. Accordingly, when it cannot destroy us through the obvious vices which are its weapons, it tries to kill us with our own arms. 33. For it endeavors to persuade our state of mind to preen ourselves as though we renounced wealth our own virtue and by our own virtue had scorned all attachments. In response to this pest we should ascend, so that each of us, in so far as he has made progress, remembers that he was helped by the Lord and has not arrived, and could not arrive, at any good by his own virtue; and so glory not in himself but in the Lord.† For *it is he who works in us both to will and to act for his good will.*‡ That is why the Apostle says, *What have you that you have not received? If you have received it, why do you glory as if you had not received it?*†

†Jn 14:6

†Lk 10:30

†1 P 5:8; Ps 9:29f

†1 Co 1:31; 2 Co 10:17
‡Ph 2:13

†1 Co 4:7

34. Therefore, let someone who wants perfectly to convert to the Lord ascend like this from step to step until he reaches the *deportation to Babylon.*† But as in the descent the deportation is understood to be that which took place from Jerusalem to Babylon, so in the ascent we ought to understand it as the migration we must make from Babylon to Jerusalem. This is the perfection of our conversion, to leave Babylon completely. Babylon signifies *confusion.*† 35. As long as a person sets his heart either on the riches of this world or on

†Mt 1:17

†*Interpretatio* 3 (CCSL 72:62, 18) *et passim*

amusements or on the physical love of parents and friends, or on his own will, he is indeed in Babylon—that is, in *confusion*. For in the heart where these things exist there is without doubt great confusion and little peace. Therefore, that our conversion may be perfect, let us cast out all these things and leave Babylon wholly behind us. Let us not only leave Babylon behind, but let us become Babylon's master.

36. For it is a great thing, my brothers, to be a master of Babylon. I ask you, look into this great mystery. All the sons of Israel who were in Jerusalem were led captive to Babylon. Yet among those captives there was a division: some served the Babylonians while others became masters in Babylon itself and ruled over the Babylonians. Daniel, Ananias, Azarias, and Misael[†] were appointed princes over all the satraps of the king of Babylon.[‡] All were nonetheless captives. *All these things were done symbolically for us*, the Apostle tells us.[†] 37. For all of us, my brothers, absolutely all of us, are held captive in Babylon—that is, in *confusion*. Who will declare himself free of this captivity when Paul says, *I see in my members another law, fighting against the law of my mind and making me a prisoner under the law of sin?*[†] Behold this miserable captivity. Everyone—who does not rejoice in it like a lunatic—groans under it. The Babylonians by whom we are held captives are our unruly appetites. It is good, my brothers, to rule these Babylonians. It is miserable indeed to live among them but most miserable of all to serve them. But many serve, few rule.

38. They serve the Babylonians in Babylon in this wretched captivity of which we spoke, those who

[†]Shadrach, Meschach, and Abed-Nego in the Hebrew
[‡]Dan 6:1ff
[†]1 Co 10:6

[†]Rm 7:23

obey unruly appetites, the desires of the flesh; they present their members to sin as implements of evil.† They rule who check their unruly appetites, who govern their members so well that *sin does not reign* in their *mortal body*,† and they are masters of their own *confusion* and not servants. Since, however, no one manages to achieve this by his own strength, let us cry with the Apostle, *Who will set us free from this body doomed to death?*† Thus let our cry always be to God, *our eyes always on the Lord*.† And so let us enter into another stage.

†Rm 6:12; Gal 5:16
†Rm 6:12

†Rm 7:24

†Ps 24 [25]:15; 122 [123]:2

39. Now, although we have done these things perfectly, and we have rejected wealth and pleasures and all physical attachments and our own will, nonetheless our vices still assault us: anger, impatience, pride, self-indulgence, and all the rest of them. Therefore let us enter into another stage and let us begin to purify ourselves of our vices by work, by vigils, by fasting, by prayer, by compunction, by reading, by meditation. 40. But because nothing avails as much for our perfection as assiduous prayer to God, at the head of this division is set Jeconiah, a name which means *the Lord's preparation*.† This is so that we may know and commit to memory [the fact] that of ourselves we are not capable of preparing or purifying ourselves but that our conversion to God by renouncing this world and our purification as we make progress has to be the preparation of the Lord preparing us† to be made worthy of seeing him when all temptation has come to an end.

†*Interpretatio* 54 (CCSL 72:127, 18). See also 1 Ch 3:16, Jer 24:1, 27:20, 28:4.

†Ps 28 [29]:9

41. We must indeed realize that as long as any [hint] of earthly covetousness lingers in our heart we shall never be able to hunger for that true and delightful good. Yet whether someone who

does not hunger for justice here will ever be able to take his fill of it, I do not know. Although we may have abandoned the world, although we may have subjected ourselves to another's will, although we may resist our former vices and, not relying overboldly on ourselves in anything, be intent in prayer, even so some covetousness arising from our weakness which has not yet been perfectly healed may darken the eye of the heart and prevent it from seeing the purity of the true light for which it should yearn.

42. We must make it our business then and strive with all our might to lessen this covetousness, heal this weakness, and increase our charity by which we may love more fervently, desire more intently, and taste more sweetly the one sole sweet and truly delightful good. Here a vast amount of hard work faces us but we must not despair, for we put our hope not in ourselves but in the Lord. From the Lord let us hope for salvation, so that weakness may not overwhelm us nor covetousness vanquish us and so that charity may be nurtured. Therefore let us pray to him continually that he may prepare us and purify us and make us *vessels held in honor* and not *in shame*.[†] 43. From this hard work let us not cease but ascend step by step until we come <to Solomon>, or rather until we ourselves become Solomon, who is the last step in the second grouping. Solomon means *Peacemaker*.[†] This long therefore are we obliged to purify ourselves from vice: until such time as we have peace in ourselves and the vices have been laid to rest, unable to lift their head against us or to wage any war against us. For this is the perfection of the second stage, that we be so purified from our vices that

[†] 2 Tm 2:20; Rm 9:12

[†] *Interpretatio* 63 (CCSL 72:138,5)

we begin even in this world to taste some first fruits of that peace which will be ours at our resurrection when we shall say, *Where is your victory, death? Death, where is your sting?*† †1 Co 15:55

44. If, however, we have reached perfection at this stage, what remains but to desire the presence of Christ, to sigh for that blessed vision, so that *our tears are our bread by day and by night.*† With all the affection of our heart let us exclaim, *When shall I come and appear before the face of God?*† Now this stage begins with David—that is, with holy desires. 'David' means *desirable.*† And who is more desirable than the one of whom the Prophet says, *And then will come the desired of all the nations?*‡ *Desired*, plainly, and to be desired. 45. So that this desire may be perfect however, it should not end until we come to Abraham—that is, to the Father on high, so that we may see *the God of gods in Sion.*† This is the perfection to which we should ascend. This is the reward that we expect: the vision of God—that is, the Father on high. O what a reward! How great! How good! The just shall look upon him; the wicked will look upon him. But the wicked in one way, the just in another. The wicked *shall look upon him whom they have pierced.*† And again, *Let the wicked be taken away lest he look upon the glory of God.*† The righteous shall look upon him but *as he is;*† as John says: *Now we are the sons of God, but it has not appeared yet what we shall be. But we know that when he has appeared we shall be like him because we shall see him as he is.*† The being of God is never unlike Being.

†Ps 41:4 [42:3]

†Ps 41:3 [42:2]

†*Interpretatio* 74 (CCSL 72:152, 3] *et passim*
‡Hg 2:8

†Ps 83:8 [84:7]

†Jn 19:37; Zch 12:10
†Is 26:10
†1 Jn 3:2

†1 Jn 3:2

46. Therefore *we shall see him as he is,*† because then we shall contemplate him in the very substance of his godhead, something never granted

†1 Jn 3:2

to any of the elect in this life, not even to Moses, who was accustomed to contemplating him in angelic form. The Lord told him, *You will not be able to see my face, for no human being can see my face and live.*† Yet on account of his great holiness God told him, *I will show you all good.*† Then we shall see him *who surpasses all the sons of men in beauty,*† *him upon whom the angels long to look.*† For, as someone has said, *Insofar as we are able to know, God is a spiritual substance of such inconceivable beauty, of such inexpressible sweetness, that the angels, who are seven times more beautiful than the sun, yearn continually and insatiably to gaze upon him.*† 47. Then we shall see him whose *Spirit is sweeter than honey, whose heritage surpasses honey dripping from the comb.*† With spiritual arms we shall embrace him and kiss him with wondrous sweetness. Then we shall see and sense how good and how sweet it will be in that blessed life to enjoy the sight of our Creator, to share the company of the angels, to be endowed with the immortality of eternity. Then we shall look upon him who came down from *the bosom of the Father*† into the lap of a mother, so that we—beginning as we have said, from his humanity which he assumed from his mother—may come to his divinity which he forever had with the Father.

†Ex 33:20
†Ex 33:19
†Ps 44:3 [45:2]
†1 P 1:12

†Source unknown

†Ws 24:27

†Jn 1:18

48. This, our entire good, began with this feast on which was born his blessed Mother, who by her grace leads us to such heavenly heights. And therefore, at the beginning of this ascent is set Jesus himself, and Mary is also set, so that under Mercy himself, under the utterly kind Mother of Mercy himself, no one may despair, no one may hesitate to ascend. Instead, placing in them all one's hope and delight, one may ascend,

confident, fearless. For anyone who has such helpers to assist him will never be able to fail.

49. Let us then lift our gaze to Christ himself, imploring him by the merits of his ever sweet Mother, to cause us to choose, to aid us as we ascend, to receive us when we arrive:
>who lives and reigns
>with the Father and Holy Spirit
>through all the ages of ages.
>Amen.

Sermon Twenty-five
FOR THE FEAST OF ALL SAINTS

MY BROTHERS, if we are not qualified to speak of one of God's saints and proclaim her glory, how qualified are we give a sermon on all of the saints? It is all the more necessary then that we bear ourselves in a way enabling us to come to share their glory. What then must we do? How can we attain these heights? Accordingly, brothers, let us listen to some wholesome advice. For whom should we be more ready to believe than someone who has already attained that glory? He certainly knows the way by which he went up. Let us listen then to one of the great friends of Jesus telling us: *Humble yourselves under God's mighty hand that he may raise you up.*†

† 1 P 5:6

2. You know how today throughout the entire world everyone is praising God's saints—the angels and archangels, the apostles, the martyrs, confessors, virgins. [In their honor] today in our holy Church there are canticles, hymns, torches and all the rest that goes with a feast. The canticles connote the everlasting celebration in which the saints live because of the inexpressible joy which is theirs in God. The hymns connote the inexpressible praise by which they are always praising God. So it is the Psalmist says: *Blessed are*

those who dwell in your house, Lord; they will praise you through ages of ages.† The torches connote the everlasting light in which God's saints live. This is why this past night you sang: *Around you, Lord, is a light that will never fail where the souls of the saints find rest.*† 3. Now, brothers, ponder, if you can, how exalted in heaven are those who can be exalted and honored this way on earth. Surely, brothers, if we could behold all the glory of the world and all the praise of the world and all the joy of the world all at the same time, in comparison with their joy it is nothing but absolute misery.

†Ps 83:5 [84:4]

†Antiphon for the Feast of All Saints (Hesbert 3:3208)

4. Therefore, brothers, you ought to know that we celebrate these feasts with torches, canticles and so on for only two reasons. (These things do not profit God's saints. They take no delight from this earthly singing, nor do they glory in this earthly torchlight and trifles. Their praise is Christ and he is their light, *who enlightens every human coming into this world.*†) The first [reason for these things is] that by these reminders we may rouse ourselves to greater devotion; then [the second] because of the connotations of which we have already spoken. We ought, then, to do as much as is adequate to these two [reasons]. 5. They do not celebrate these feasts well—or reasonably, it seems to me—who by excessive pomp and ceremony pursue these external glories and splendors—with the result that the outer self becomes so intent on the canticles, the ornaments, the torches and such lovely trappings that the mind is scarcely able to conceive of anything but what it sees with the eyes, hears with the ears, or perceives with the other senses.

†Jn 1:9

6. As for us, brothers, who do not see these things—even though we know that they are common practice—let us ponder and delight in that true loveliness in which the saints live free of corruption; in those spiritual ornaments that the saints possess in righteousness and holiness: in the hymns and praises with which they praise God without weariness; and in that light which they see in the face of God. And let us keep our feasts in such a way that our mind is not turned back to those earthly and perishable delights but rather is roused to those that are spiritual and eternal.[†] And so let us reflect on their glory and exaltation. 7. To enable us to reach this exaltation, let us listen to the advice of the Apostle: *Humble yourselves beneath God's mighty hand.*[†] The Apostle was very well aware of the reason why we are cast down, why we have lost that exaltation in which we were created, why we were driven out into this unhappiness. What is this reason, brothers, if not pride? Therefore, to counteract this pride he taught humility. *Humble yourselves,*[†] he says. But because he knew that not all those who humble themselves humble themselves wisely, he therefore added: *under God's mighty hand.*[†]

8. Some are humbled under God's glorious hand, others under his strong hand, others under this generous hand, others *under God's mighty hand.*[†] There are good angels and there are bad angels; there are good human beings and there are bad human beings. As the Apostle says: *In the name of our Lord Jesus Christ let every knee be bent, in heaven, on earth and in the depths.*[†] 9. But notice that everyone is humbled before our Lord and everyone is subject to him. Everyone, assuredly, both good and bad, for *no one can resist his will*[†] and

†Cf. RB 2.33

†1 P 5:6

†1 P 5:6

†1 P 5:6

†1 P 5:6

†Ph 2:10

†Est 13:9; Rm 9:19

everyone serves his will, willingly or unwillingly. Therefore it is wholesome advice the Apostle gives us to humble ourselves before him—that is, to submit our will to him—for then we shall have merit. If we refuse to submit to him of our own will, we shall be subjected to him unwillingly and we shall incur eternal punishment.

10. Now let us notice who they are who are humbled beneath the glorious hand of God. They are the good angels who, after the blessed Mary Mother of God, are the focus of this feast. They doubtless humble themselves beneath the glorious hand of God for they look for nothing from his hand but his glory in which they are happy without end, each one according to the rank in which he was created.

11. But the bad angels are those who are humbled beneath God's strong hand, for the strength of God weighs down on them and makes them, willingly or unwilling, serve his will. This is why the psalm speaks of *this dragon whom you have fashioned to make sport of.*† Does our Lord not wisely make sport of him, when everything that he does to wreak the destruction of the elect, the Lord turns to their advantage, and when whatever he does to lessen Christ's glory only increases that glory? I think, my brothers, that today [the dragon] regards himself as made sport of. 12. He reflects today on the glory of the apostles, the martyrs, and all God's saints and he sees that by his malice that glory has been increased. For why is their glory so great if not because, as the Apostle says: *They had to face jeers and flogging, even fetters and prisons. They were stoned, they were sawn in two, they were tempted, they were put to the*

†Ps 103 [104]:26

sword for Christ.† All this was inflicted on them through the devil's malice. For he influenced the hearts of the unbelievers and the godless who tortured them so. And see, all these torments have been turned into glory and a crown for them.

†Heb 11:36–37

13. In the same way, my brothers, although we do not suffer the bodily torments which they suffered, even so the devil is mocked by us as well. For he tempts and he torments, but because the strength of God's hand weighs upon him, preventing him from tempting us *beyond what we are able to endure*,† all these temptations work to our glory and his reproach. Likewise bad human beings are humbled beneath God's strong hand because the Lord allows them to practice their cruelty only to the extent that he sees will be expedient for [those who are] his own.

†1 Co 10:13

14. Others are humbled beneath God's generous hand, yet not all in the same way. Some, seeing that it is he *who gives food to all flesh*† and firmly believing that all riches and honors are *in his hand* and that he gives them to whomsoever he wills, begin to serve him either in order to acquire these earthly things or in order not to lose them. 15. Others, better than these, reflecting on the generous hand of him *who makes his sun rise upon good and bad alike and sends rain on the just and the unjust*,† who bestows temporal blessings in abundance on good and bad alike, stop to think about how marvelous, how inexpressible are the blessings that he keeps exclusively for those who are his own. And desiring that blessedness that *eye has not seen nor ear heard nor has even entered into the human heart*,† they humble themselves and serve him.

†Ps 135 [136]:25

†Mt 5:45

†1 Co 2:9

16. Again, there are others who are humbled beneath God's mighty hand.† These are those who, reflecting on his *power* with which he humbles the proud and raises up the humble, with which he damns whom he will and saves whom he will, are smitten with a wholesome fear and humbled. To this humility the Lord invites us when he says: *Do not fear those who kill the body* but can do nothing more. *But fear someone who is able to destroy both body and soul in hell.*† 17. This is the first reason for us to humble ourselves: fear of the Lord. But there is a higher step: when a person reflects, not on the power with which He condemns the wicked, but on that by which He mightily defends his own in this life and on the day of judgement welcomes them into the kingdom of heaven. It is to this level that the Apostle invites us when he says: *Humble yourselves beneath God's mighty hand*, not for fear of punishment, but *that he may raise you up at the time of his visitation.*†

†1 P 5:6

†Mt 10:28

†1 P 5:6

18. The time *of his visitation* is the day of judgement. First he visited the world in his mercy; afterwards he will visit it in judgement. He visited us mercifully when he shed his blood for us; he will visit us by judgement when he *gives to each according to each one's deeds.*† There are countless other visitations by which the Lord visits here not only the elect but also the reprobate. 19. He visits us by prosperity; he visits us by adversity. He visits us when we are tempted; he visits us when we are consoled. He visits us in hidden inspiration; he visits us by outward comments. He visits us through the Scriptures; he visits us through the sacraments. All these things take place for salvation to the good and perdition to the bad. If, however, we would be raised up in all these

†Mt 16:27

visitations, let us humble ourselves *under God's mighty hand.*†

†1 P 5:6, cf. RB 7.69

20. What are these feasts we celebrate but visitations of his? But in these visitations some are lifted up while others are cast down. Notice, today we are celebrating the Feast of All Saints. And we are not the only ones celebrating it. For what Christian is there who is not celebrating this feast today? But many do so *in wantonness, in reveling, in drunkenness, in impurity*† and pollutions of this sort. They are not lifted up by this visitation but rather cast down. 21. Yet someone who begins to reflect upon the saints of our Lord, the glory of the angels, the teaching of the apostles, the patience of the martyrs, the constancy of the confessors, and the modesty of the virgins, and in all this longs even now for the glory which they have attained, burns now to follow along the way by which they have gone ahead. He is so smitten by compunction, sorrow, and lamentation for his past negligences and sins that he resolves to serve God more fervently in order to win the glory of the angels, to endure all hardships more patiently in order to arrive at the crown of the martyrs, to guard his heart and his flesh with greater purity now in order to enjoy the company of the virgins.

†Rm 13:13; 1 P 4:3

22. But who are they who do these things? Not the proud, not the high and mighty, not the contentious, not the grumblers. But who? Surely those who humble themselves *beneath God's mighty hand.*† Those who keep *the fear of God always before their eyes,*† who are always reflecting on the divine power, who keep *the thought of death ever before their eyes.*† Therefore, brothers, let us humble ourselves *beneath God's mighty hand that*

†1 P 5:6
†RB 7.10

†RB 4.47

he may lift us up at the time of his visitation.† 23. At these visitations may he lift us up through good deeds and through holy desires, so that when he comes at that great visitation when he will demand from everyone an account of what they have done in this life so as to *give to each according to the deeds of each,*† he may lift us up totally and we may hear that endearing voice saying: *Come, you blessed by my Father. Receive the kingdom that has been prepared for you from the beginning of the world.*† This will be our true up-lifting, when we enjoy in heaven the company of those whose feast we are celebrating today on earth. Through their merits may our Lord Jesus Christ deign to grant us this,

†I P 5:6, cf. RB 7.69

†Mt 16:27

†Mt 25:34

who with the Father and Holy Spirit
lives and reigns through all the ages of ages.
Amen.

Sermon Twenty-six
For the Feast of All Saints

BLESSED BE OUR EMPEROR, who does not cease to visit his poor family. Sometimes, dearest brothers, he visits us through one of his servants, sometimes through several of them, sometimes through his dearest mother, and sometimes, which is yet greater, in his own person. For what are these feasts of the saints we celebrate so often but visitations through which our Lord visits and reassures us?[†]

[†Cf. Sermon 20.1]

2. Because it was expedient for us always to be mindful of his benefits which he bestowed on us by his physical presence, and because he knew that our memory was impaired by forgetfulness, our understanding by error, and our attentiveness by covetousness, he made provision for us in his kindness. His benefits are not only recounted for us in the Scriptures but are also made present again to us by certain spiritual actions. That is why when he handed down to his disciples the sacrament of his Body and Blood he told them: *Do this in remembrance of me.*[†]

[†Lk 22:19]

3. For this reason, brothers, these feasts have been established in the Church, so that by representing now his birth, now his passion, now his resurrection, now his ascension, there may always be fresh in our memory the wonderful loving-kindness, the wonderful gentleness, the

wonderful charity that he showed towards us by all of these. From them all our faith, too, should derive the greatest profit, when we both hear with our ears and, as it were, see right under our eyes what Christ endured for us, what he gives us even in this life, what he promises us after this life. He endured death for us, at present he gives us forgiveness of sins, after this life he promises eternal happiness.† †Cf. Sermon 9.1–2

4. We should recall to memory, dearest brothers, this our liberation, this our hope, this our happiness† when we celebrate one of his feasts. But why do we celebrate these feasts of his faithful if not in order to reflect more attentively on their glory, bestowed on them by God's mercy, so that by this reflection we may long for it and love it more ardently? Then too, from hearing about their life, their sufferings, and the toil by which they came to such glory, we should draw great consolation and great hope. And the more we see ourselves *in the toils* and *the difficulties* of this life,† the more confidently we can hope for the glory and happiness to which they have preceded us. †Cf. Sermon 9.3

†Cf. 2 Cor 6:4–5

5. Dearest, let no one delude you, no thought nor any cajolery of the enemy delude you. True indeed, brothers, is that Scripture which says, *To enter the kingdom of God we must pass through many hardships.*† My brothers, may anyone, although it be *an angel*, who tells you otherwise be *anathema*.† We often celebrate the feasts of the apostles, often those of martyrs, sometimes those of confessors, and sometimes those of virgins. Who is there among all of them who did not pass through the sorrows and hardships of this life? 6. Behold, today the King himself, our †Ac 14:21

†Cf Gal 1:8

Emperor himself, visits us with his entire army. Let us reflect, to the best of our ability, on all its ranks; how beautiful they are, how well arrayed. Let us long to be in their company, but first let us not shrink from the toil that was theirs. The battle is indeed hard but the crown should delight us. We do not lack help in this battle. Around us are the angels and archangels of whom the Apostle says: *What are they all but ministering spirits, sent out to serve for the sake of those who are to inherit salvation?*† †Heb 1:14

7. Let us look then at our Emperor in the very vanguard. Let us hear how he exhorts his soldiers. *In this world*, he says, *you will have distress.*† †Jn 16:33
Brothers, Truth cannot lie. Listen, therefore, to what he has promised. There are two worlds: the present and the future. Our Lord has foretold to us how we ought to fare in both of them. *In this world*, he says, *you shall have distress*. Again, he himself has told us how his own will fare in the other [world]: *The righteous will shine as the sun in the kingdom of my Father.*† †Mt 13:43; 6:29 And again: *They will be like angels of God in heaven.*† †Mt 22:30 8. Accordingly, brothers, perhaps that rich man who the Gospel tells us was tormented in hell and *saw Lazarus in Abraham's bosom*, had done many evil things. And perhaps the poor man Lazarus had many good qualities in him. Even so, the only reason Abraham mentioned for the rich man's damnation was that he had received good things in his lifetime. And the only reason he gave for Lazarus' salvation was that he similarly had received evil while he was alive. So he says: *Remember, child, that you received good things while you were alive, and Lazarus evil.*† †Lk 16:23–25

9. Accordingly, brothers, to the extent that any of you sees himself [caught up] in the distresses of

this life for Christ's sake, let him know for certain that his glory in that other life increases. And to the extent that he sees himself enjoying the good things and the amusements of this life, let him fear that his glory will be diminished in the next life. Therefore, brothers, we should keep these two things in our memories: how we ought to be in this life and how we ought to be in heaven with the Lord. And to these two lives we should always give some thought. 10. To this life belongs toil, to that life rest; to this life belongs temptation, to that life security; to this life poverty, to that life wealth; to this life struggle, to that life consolation; to this life hunger and thirst, to that life repletion. This, my brothers, is what the Lord says in the Gospel: *Blessed are the poor, for yours is the kingdom of God. Blessed are you who <now> weep, for you shall laugh. Blessed are you who now hunger, for you shall eat your fill.*† And again: *Alas for you who are rich; you have had your consolation!*† And again: *Alas for you who laugh now, for you shall mourn and weep.*† †Lk 6:20–21
†Lk 6:24
†Lk 6:25

11. But now notice what I have said: it is necessary that we keep these two in our memory: that is, how we ought to be here and how we shall be there. For if we attend only to what concerns this life, we shall not be able to bear up. Who, without danger of murmuring or despair, can without some consolation always be in the midst of distress, unhappiness, and temptations? Who is there, brothers, in this life, who does not experience this unhappiness, unless he be wholly destitute of feeling? Because of this unhappiness everyone seeks to have some consolation. 12. The worldly and those who love this world seek their consolation in riches and honors, in a host of idle speculations, in the desires of the flesh and its pleasures. They are unhappy when

they are afflicted but much unhappier when they are consoled this way. *But you, a chosen race, a royal priesthood, a holy nation, and a redeemed people,*[†] should not have the sadness they have nor the consolation they have.

[†1 P 2:9]

13. Reflect on our Emperor's entire family, which today he shows us, and in it notice these two things: the sadness that they did have and the joy that they have received. This is the family of Christ, the Bride of Christ, who says in the Song of Songs: *I am black but comelyl.*[†] Note, brothers, the two things of which we have spoken. Blackness belongs to this life, comeliness to that in which we shall—God willing—be after this. 14. Whatever the saints had of this life was black, but together with the blackness they had great beauty. The distress, the difficulties, and the temptations that they endured in this world were blackness. As the Apostle says of them, *they went about dressed in sheep skins or goat skins, needy, harassed, and afflicted. The world was not worthy of them.*[†] They had as well that certain beauty [that consists] in faith, in chastity, in purity, and in charity.

[†Sg 1:4]

[†Heb 11:37–38]

15. Let us reflect first on those leaders of our army. Let us listen to what one of them says about them: *Notice your calling, brothers*, he says. *Not many of you were wise according to the flesh, not many noble. But to confound the wise God has chosen what the world counts folly and what the world counts weak and contemptible and mere nothings.*[†] And again he says: *We are made to be as the scum of the earth, the very dregs.*[†] This is the blackness of which we have spoken. But where was their beauty? Listen: *Our glory is this, the witness of our conscience.*[†] Their beauty was inside, not outside.

[†1 Co 1:26–28]

[†1 Co 4:13]

[†2 Co 1:12]

16. What about the holy martyrs? Was <blackness> not evident in them when they were dragged into prisons, when they were led off fettered with chains in front of everybody, when they were stoned, when they were flogged, and when they were subjected to all manner of outrage and torture? Their voice it is [we hear] in the psalm: *Have mercy on us, Lord, have mercy on us, for we are overwhelmed with insults. Our soul has drunk its full. We are mocked by the rich, we are scorned by the proud.*† But all this blackness, outward as it was, did not diminish but increased the beauty that was within. 17. What of the other saints who did not live during these persecutions—such as the confessors, the many holy virgins, and the holy monks and hermits? Did not they have this blackness? The Apostle says of all of them alike: *All those who choose to live a devout life in Christ will endure persecution.*† To live a devout life is to be able truthfully to say: *Who is weak and I am not weak? Who is scandalized and I do not blaze with indignation?*† This is grave persecution, brothers, as we ourselves often experience, we who know the weaknesses, the sorrows, and the burdens of many.

†Ps 122 [123]:3–4

†2 Tm 3:12

†2 Co 11:29

18. It is a grave persecution to have everyone's care, to bear everyone's sorrow, to be saddened when someone is sad, to be afraid when someone is tempted. Again, what an intolerable persecution it is that sometimes befalls us when one of those whom we nurture and care for and love as our own flesh and blood is so overwhelmed by the devil that he even departs from us or lives so perversely and prodigally that we have no choice but to expel him from our midst.† 19. Brothers, if you feel sorrow and great sadness when such

†Cf. Walter Daniel's *Life of Aelred*, chapters 15, 22, 28 (CF 57:107–108,112–113, 116–117).

things happen, you who are the brothers of those concerned, what sadness do you think we feel who are both brothers and fathers and guardians, who have undertaken to *render an account* for them?† Surely, brothers, you should have great compassion for us and gladden us by your upright way of life, for so many other things cause us sadness. Yet blessed is someone who suffers this blackness for Christ.

†Cf. RB 65.22; 2.37–38.

20. This blackness makes him not unseemly but beautiful. For it does not come from the flame of covetousness but from the fire of charity. Such a soul can say that *the sun has scorched me*.† The sun, that is, of charity which shines on and burns in his heart. The more he loves, the more often he grieves and is saddened for those whom he loves. There is still another blackness which you have often experienced. It is one which none of the saints has ever been able to avoid. This blackness, brothers, is temptation, whether from the enemy or from the flesh or from this world. 21. Paul himself had this blackness, as he himself says: *A thorn in my flesh was given to me as Satan's messenger who buffeted me*.† About temptation of the flesh he says: *I perceive that there is in my [bodily] members a different law, fighting against the law of my mind and leading me captive under the law of sin*.† This blackness the whole company of God's saints has experienced, so it is able to say: *I am black but comely*.† This can be said as well by every holy soul so long as it lives in this flesh. For what saint is free from temptation, when Job says: *Human life on earth is temptation?*† *I am black but comely*.† Is not the soul of each and every one of us able to say this?

†Sg 1:5

†2 Co 12:7

†Rm 7:23

†Sg 1:4

†Jb 7:1
†Sg 1:4

22. *I am black but comely.*† *Comely* beyond doubt is the soul that preserves the beauty of chastity, but she is nonetheless black, because the heat of lust still assaults her. *Comely* is the soul that despises the world, but she is still black because in her heart she often dwells on and thinks of the world. *Comely* is the soul that loves God as best she can, but she is still black because she often feels within herself the love of carnal things. *Comely* is the soul that, as best she can, does what she knows to be profitable for others for the sake of charity, but she is still black because she often feels within herself anger, impatience, and the other obstacles to charity. Comely, finally, is the soul that does not consent to any vice, but she is still black because she is aware of those vices.

†Sg 1:4

23. Is it surprising, brothers, if the saints pass through this blackness when the Lord himself chose to live in this world with a certain amount of blackness? He, too, even he, brothers, could say: *I am black but comely.*† Therefore his bride— that is, the whole company of the saints or each holy soul—has no shame in confessing herself: *I am black but comely.*† But listen in what way: *Like the tents of Kedar, like the skins of Solomon.*† 24. This is what I said: that our Lord himself chose to display a certain blackness in himself but beneath that blackness he had great beauty. Would you like to hear about both the blackness and the beauty? Of his blackness Isaiah says: *We looked on him and there was no attractiveness in him, and we desired him; disfigured and the lowest of men.*† Of his beauty David says: *He was handsome beyond all the children of the human race.*† But he did indeed suffer

†Sg 1:4

†Sg 1:4
†Sg 1:4

†Is 53:2–3

†Ps 44:3 [45:2]

temptations, as the Apostle says: *He has been tempted in every way like we are, yet without sin.*[†Heb 4:15]

25. Therefore all his saints have followed *in his footsteps* and *his example*, so that each holy soul can say: *I am black but comely, daughters of Jerusalem, like the tents of Kedar, like the skins of Solomon.*[†Sg 1:4] Who is this Kedar? Who is this Solomon? I think it is our Lord Jesus. He is himself in one sense Kedar and in another sense Solomon. For Kedar means 'darkness'[†35 *Interpretatio* 4 (CCSL 72: 63, 6–7) et passim] and Solomon 'peacemaker'.[‡*Interpretatio* 63 (CCSL 72:138, 5)] 26. To see how these two names fit our Lord Jesus Christ let us heed what he says in the Gospel: *It is for judgement that I have come into this world, that the blind may see and that those who do see may become blind.*[†Jn 9:39] Many were blinded by his presence and many were enlightened. For, as Simeon said, he was set *for the ruin and the resurrection of many in Israel.*[†Lk 2:34] To those who chose not to believe in him but were blinded by their malice in his presence, he was Kedar.

27. Did they not regard him as Kedar, those who said: *Is this not the carpenter's son?*[†Mt 13:55] They saw him poor and not seeking but rather fleeing the glory of the world. They saw him hungry and thirsty. And therefore they despised him. They thought he was Kedar—that is, darksome and lacking the light of divinity, like other human beings. But why did they think this? How were they offended by him? Because of his tent,[†*Tabernaculum*, translated in an earlier context as 'tabernacle'] surely. They despised it. They considered his tent—that is, his flesh in which, as in a tent, the godhead dwelt—vile and darksome. 28. In this tent our Lord was black: he suffered hunger, thirst, reproach; and at the end they spat on him, buffeted, scourged him and so they crucified him. But the whole of that

blackness was in the tent—that is, in his flesh. It was outward, not inward, for inwardly *he was handsome beyond all the children of men in beauty.*† Inwardly he was such that *the angels longed to look upon him.*† And therefore, brothers, all that blackness was more ours than his. We bear sinful flesh. What he bore was not sinful flesh but its likeness.

†Ps 44:3 [45:2]

†I P 1:12

29. Call to mind that Jacob who, in order to acquire a blessing, hid his own likeness within and outwardly assumed the likeness of someone else. You have often heard that story, brothers: how Rebecca clad her son in goatskins to be like Esau, the hairy [son]. What does 'hairy Esau' stand for, if not the children of those who with tunics of skin were expelled from Paradise. All the children of Adam are hairy and black because of their sins and iniquities. The Son of God did not have these hairs. 30. For how should he have any sin who was one with the Father, perfect and almighty God? Nor was there in his divine nature the likeness of any sin or corruption. Brothers, if he did not take upon himself the likeness of our skin, the likeness of our hairs, we would never have been able to free ourselves from our hairs. That is why he deigned to put on *the likeness of sinful flesh* in which outwardly he showed weakness and a certain blackness. Inwardly, however, he preserved this marvelous and indescribable beauty.

31. Now picture Jacob to yourselves, clad in goatskins. Could he not say truthfully: *I am black but comely?*† Black on account of the tents of Kedar and the goats' black skin, but on account of his own likeness inwardly comely. In the same way pay attention to the true Jacob, our Lord

†Sg 1:4

Jesus Christ, *black because of the likeness of sinful flesh,* beautiful because he had no sin. 32. But by that blackness he won for us a blessing. Not for himself, for he had no need of it, but for us who needed a blessing because we were under a curse. For without any doubt we were meant in the blessing which Isaac gave his son and so by this meaning we were blessed. Listen to what he said: *Behold, the scent of my son is like the scent of a bounteous field that the Lord has blessed. <May God give you of the dew of heaven and of the fatness of the earth, an abundance of grain, wine and oil.>*[†]

[†Gen 27:27–28; Ps 4:8 [7]]

33. This is the field, brothers, which we should especially reflect on today. This field is full of every delicacy, every sweetness, every embellishment. For, as you sang a short while ago: *Its flowers lack neither roses nor lilies.*[†] Here are the sweetest fruits of the apostles. Here are the roses of the martyrs. Here are the lilies of the virgins. Here is each and every one of the saints, like fruitful trees in the Lord's field. Yes indeed, brothers, and may we belong to that bounteous field *which the Lord has blessed.*[†] To this field the Lord has granted *the dew of heaven and of the fatness of the earth, an abundance of grain, wine and oil.*[†] 34. The *dew of heaven* is spiritual grace, which this field usually receives in [the form of] compunction, in meditation, in psalmody, in *lectio*. The *fatness of the earth*—what is that? Our earth is our flesh. Happy the someone who can receive fatness from this earth. This fatness, brothers, is good works, which to be sure we only perform by our body. Those who know how to work this earth well and wisely and discreetly know by experience that vigils and toil and fasting are wonderful sort of fatness.

[†Responsory *Beata es, mater Ecclesia* for the Feast of All Saints (Hesbert 4:6170)]

[†Gen 27:27]

[†Gen 27:27–28; Ps 4:8 [7]]

35. It is then from these two things, from the dew of heaven and the fatness of the earth—that is, to speak more plainly, from bodily and spiritual exercises—that this field—namely, the whole fellowship of the saints—has its *abundance of grain, wine and oil*: the grain of wisdom, the wine of contemplation and the oil of charity. So Paul was an excellent tree in this field, toiling as he did with his hands night and day—this pertains to *the fatness of the earth*,—and praying uninterruptedly—which belongs to *the dew of heaven*. By these means he acquired that grain, wine, and oil. 36. For he used to speak *wisdom among the perfect*,[†] allocating his grain among them. He was rapt in contemplation *up to the third heaven*[†] and intoxicated with that wine which *gladdens the heart of man*.[†] This is why he says: *If we are beside ourselves, it is for God; if we are in our right mind, it is for you*.[†] He says that he was sober when he was accommodating himself to the condition of the weak, and doubtless wanted to call that ecstasy of mind which he declared to be for God alone, a certain spiritual intoxication. As for charity, there is no need to assert its existence in Paul.

[†] 1 Co 2:6
[†] 1 Co 12:2
[†] Cf. Ps 103 [104]:15
[†] 2 Co 5:13

37. You see, brothers, what a blessing the Lord won for this bounteously full field, full without a doubt of all the virtues, full of all perfection. Not surprising, when in this field there are all the saints from the beginning of the world and each has his own place, his own beauty, his own virtue in the field. Brothers, our Jacob acquired this blessing for you by becoming black, by putting on a covering of skins. These skins are the tents of Kedar—that is, his flesh, his humanity. Following his example all the saints chose to be black in this

life so that afterwards they might be comely *like the skins of Solomon.*

38. What are these *skins of Solomon?* There were some skins which covered the sanctuary which the ancient Jewish people had—that is, the ark of which you have often heard, and the altar of incense and the rest of those things. The blessed apostle Paul shows clearly what they stand for: *Christ has entered not the sanctuary made by human hands which is only a symbol of the reality but heaven itself.*† Therefore *the skins of Solomon* are the heavens. And they are beautiful skins. For in these skins is not Kedar but Solomon. 39. In them he displays his beauty, his gentleness, and his light. He appears to everyone not as darksome but as *peacemaker,* for *he is the peace* and tranquillity of the angels, who are the heavens in which God dwells. You see now what and of what sort is this beauty in which the holy Church, the fellowship of the saints, glories. The beauty of Solomon's skins is the beauty of the heavens, the beauty of the angels. It is the beauty which Our Lord promises when he says: *They shall be like the angels of God.*†

†Heb 9:24

†Mt 22:30

40. Happy is someone who can say: *I am black but comely, like the tents of Kedar, like the skins of Solomon.*† These two, dearest brothers, must go together in this life—that is, the blackness of the tent and the beauty of the skins. Yet this beauty can be only in the soul in this life, but after the day of judgement it will be in both soul and body. Where in this life, brothers, shall we find any emulation of the angels, of the beauty of those who are in eternal bliss with the Lord? 41. Where shall we find those who emulate the ardor of that love of God which is possessed

†Sg 1:4

by the order of angels who, on account of the exceeding great love with which they love God, are called seraphim?† Where shall we find those who emulate the knowledge of those who, on account of the wonderful knowledge which they possess, are called cherubim—that is, the *fullness of knowledge*?† And since it would take too long to go through all nine orders of angels, where shall we find those who emulate that chastity, that purity, that unity and charity possessed by the angels?

†*Interpretatio* 50 (CCSL 72:121–122, 24–25)

†Augustine, *On the Psalms* 79.2, 98.4 (CCSL 39:1112, 17; 1381, 7–8)

42. Blessed is the soul that can truthfully glory in saying: I am *comely like the skins of Solomon*. But look, brothers, at what ought to bring you great consolation and much rejoicing. I think I discern here one soul who can truthfully say both: *I am black like the tents of Kedar*, [and] *comely like the skin of Solomon*. First of all, look at who this soul is.

43. Each and every one of you, before you came here, had one soul which was his alone. You converted to God and, behold, the Holy Spirit, that heavenly fire which our Lord sent to earth and willed to burn, inflamed your hearts, set your souls aflame. And from all your hearts and all your souls made one heart and one soul. This is the soul which can truly say: *I am black like the tents of Kedar, comely like the skin of Solomon*. 44. It has a certain blackness like the tents of Kedar because it imitates the sufferings of Christ in hard work, in vigils, in fasting, in mortification of the flesh. It also has a certain blackness from its own tent on account of the temptations it suffers and the unruly appetites of the flesh that are not yet perfectly subdued. Yet it is still *comely like the skins of Solomon*. For what virtue do the angels possess

which this soul does not possess, even if it does not possess them as perfectly as the angels do?

45. The angels have chastity and it is surely that which reigns in this holy community. The angels have charity which can without doubt be found very perfectly in this holy fellowship. They have perfect humility by which they humble themselves *beneath the hand of God*. They have obedience by which they carry out his commands and bring his messages to us. They have such unity and concord among themselves that, although some are inferior and others superior, nonetheless through their unity and concord whatever belongs to each is the common property of all and whatever belongs to all the property of each. All this is found in this fellowship, although, on account of the tents of Kedar, not as perfectly.

46. Accordingly, brothers, let those who may be sickly and weak and therefore cannot do as much as others, not be saddened or despair. Only let each person beware of consciously withholding—through laziness or inattention—anything of what he is able to do. Let him fear what the prophet says: *A curse on the person who does the work of the Lord inattentively.*† For someone who consciously and injudiciously shirks anything that he is able to do is guilty of fraud, for his potency and his strength belong not only to himself but also to the whole community. 47. Again, let those who can do more not vaunt themselves over the others, for the grace they have received they have received not for themselves alone but for the sake of those who cannot do as much. If then there is true unity and charity among you, without a doubt whatever each does will belong to all and whatever all do

†Jer 48:10

will belong to each. Thus the soul of each one of you will be able to say: *I am comely like the skins of Solomon.* The only one who cannot say this is the one who departs from this fellowship or who cuts himself off through discord, envy, or some culpable sin.

48. We could go on talking about this blackness and this beauty, but the hour is getting late and it is not only in this way but in another way as well that we must praise the Lord and proclaim him wonderful *in his saints.* Into their fellowship may our Lord Jesus Christ bring us,
>he who lives and reigns with
>the Father and Holy Spirit
>through all the ages of ages.
>>Amen.

Sermon Twenty-seven
For the Feast of All Saints

OUR LORD JESUS CHRIST when he was on the mount took care to provide food not only for the body but also for the spirit.[1] He showed us quite clearly that we should raise our hearts—along with all our attachments and all our longings—to that mountain of which Isaiah says: *In the last days the mountain of the Lord's house shall be set at the summit of the mountains.*† †Is 2:2

This is that *fat mountain*†[2] from which heavenly fatness does not cease flowing to us. This is the *curdling mountain*†[3] from which spiritual milk has long been distilled for us. This is that high ground of which Moses sang: *He established him on high ground so that he might eat the fruit of the fields, so that he might suck honey from the rock and oil from the hardest rock.*† †Ps 67[68]:16 †Ps 67 [68]:16 †Dt 32:13

2. Appropriately then the Evangelist says: *When Jesus saw the crowds he went up onto the mountain.*† [He did this] that he might show himself to be a mountain, that he might proclaim the excellence of his precepts. *Come* then, *let us go up the* †Mt 5:1

---

1. This sermon takes its theme from the Gospel of the day, Matthew's account of the beginning of the Sermon on the Mount, in which Jesus proclaims the beatitudes.
2. 'Fat' in earlier times meant 'rich', 'fertile', 'abundant'. Modern translations from the Hebrew have 'the mountain of Bashan, a haughty mountain'.
3. Milk which 'curdles' or coagulates becomes cheese, a staple food source.

mountain of the Lord and to the house of the God of Jacob and he will teach us his ways.† *For opening his mouth he taught them, saying: Blessed are the poor in spirit for theirs is the kingdom of heaven.*† These [words] are the royal food which ought not to be set before the crowd, and therefore *Jesus, seeing the crowds, went up onto the mountain.*† This is the crowd which *berated* the blind man who cried after Jesus at Jericho *to keep quiet.*† 3. This was the crowd that prevented short Zacchaeus from seeing Jesus when he wanted to.† But since he could not go up a mountain he found *a sycamore tree*—that is, something well suited to his stature. *High mountains are for deer, the rock is the refuge of the badger.*† Therefore someone who longs to see Jesus, if he is tall, let him go *up the mountain* to see Him glorified; if he is short let him climb the sycamore to see Him crucified. Now, the sycamore is called the *mock fig*—by this the cross of Christ is very clearly signified.† This is why the Apostle says: *We preach Jesus crucified, to the Jews a stumbling block and to the gentiles folly.*†

†Is 2:3; cfr. Mi 4:2
†Mt 5:2f
†Mt 5:1
†Lk 18:35ff
†Lk 19:2ff
†Ps 103 [104]:18
†Augustine, *Sermon* 174. 3 (PL 38:941–942)
†1 Cor 1:23

4. Someone who wants to see Jesus, therefore, if he is a beginner, let him climb the sycamore to embrace Him as He dies for him; if he is perfect, let him go up onto the mountain to hear Him uttering the secrets of the Father. Let him go up from the crowd, I say, to hear the peace of which the crowd knows nothing. For this crowd presses against Jesus; as the disciples say: *The crowd is shoving against you.*† By a touch he had healed a woman of a flow of blood *and he asked: Who touched me?*† And the disciples [answered]: *The crowd is shoving against you and you ask, Who touched me?*† But the Lord did not ask: Who is shoving me? But: *Who touched me?*† It is one thing

†Lk 8:45
†Lk 8:44
†Lk 8:44f
†Lk 8:45

to touch Jesus and quite another to shove him. Love touches, a crowd shoves. 5. And in our case, brothers, if sometimes we touch Jesus with the hand of holy longing, and if we cling to him for a moment by a [sort of] spiritual glue, a very unruly crowd of worldly thoughts presses forward and shoves against him to keep our heart from experiencing his sweetness. They shove, or—what is greatly to be deplored—they shut him out altogether. *For seeing the crowds* of carnal thoughts, *Jesus goes up onto the mountain*—that is to say, he abandons the distracted heart and goes up into the mind that clings to heavenly things, and in it, as if in his seat, he makes his abode and reveals the secrets of his mysteries.[†]

[†Cf. Is 45:3]

6. *Seeing the crowds, Jesus went up onto the mountain. And when he sat down, his disciples came to him.*[†] For some people Jesus walks; for some, he stands; for some, he sits. When Adam had sinned and strayed from the straight path, the Lord walked *in the afternoon breeze.*[†] With Moses he stood when he said: *You, stand here with me.*[†] With Isaiah he sat. For [the prophet] saw *the Lord sitting on a throne high and lifted up.*[†] He was seated, indeed, when from the hidden depths of his judgement he revealed to [Isaiah] the blinding of the Jews and the enlightening of the nations. And he was sitting with the disciples on the mountain when he instructed them to enlighten those same nations.

[†Mt 5:1]

[†Gen 3:8]
[†Dt 5:31]

[†Is 6:1]

7. Yet *when he sat down, his disciples came to him.*[†] It is not those in the crowd who go up to Jesus, because quite often they are agitated, but it is the disciples, who pursue peace. And this the Lord makes sufficiently clear to his disciples, when he

[†Mt 5:1]

says: *By this shall all men know that you are my disciples, if you love one another.*† Yes, brothers, by this criterion let each person see whether he is a disciple of Jesus. 8. Nor let each examine his own wisdom, evaluation, charitable donations or physical exertions—*If I speak in tongues of humans and of angels*, says the Apostle, *but am without charity, I am nothing.*† No, I say, let him not examine these outer things, but let him explore the love of his heart. For *someone who loves God loves his brother also,*† . Yet only if he loves in the way this same Jesus commands: *This is my commandment, that you love one another as I have loved you.*† Let disciples therefore go up the mountain, let them not only go up but let them go up contemplating, let them go up loving.

†Jn 13:35

†1 Cor 13:1f

†1 Jn 4:21

†Jn 15:12

9. *When he had sat down*, however, *his disciples came to him and, opening his mouth, he taught them.*† What marvelous condescension! *Having in many and varied ways through the prophets spoken to our forefathers in former times, in these latter days God has spoken to us in his Son*† who, *opening his mouth, taught.*† *His mouth*, it says. For to speak to the fathers of old, sometimes he opened the mouths of the prophets, sometimes he used the tongues of angels, sometimes he called on the services of the elements. To speak to us, however, *opening his mouth, he taught, saying: Blessed are the poor in spirit.*†

†Mt 5:1f

†Heb 1:1f
†Mt 5:2

†Mt 5:2f

10. What an antidote this is, my brothers, against the poison with which the ancient poisonous serpent infected the whole human race.† *You will be like gods*, he said.† This is *the golden cup which makes the whole earth drunk,*† purporting indeed by its embellishment to bring happiness

†Rv 20:2
†Gen 3:5
†Jer 51:7

but clandestinely purveying the bitter draught of misery. *You will be like gods.*† A beautiful cup, but poison lurks inside. Well, wretched Adam, made wretched by listening to *You will be like gods,*† become happy by listening to this: *Blessed are the poor in spirit!*† 11. There is a poverty of the flesh and there is a poverty of the spirit. Poverty of the flesh is being without material wealth. Poverty of the spirit is freely abasing ourselves in mind and body for God's sake. In this, someone poor in spirit glories, saying: *I have chosen to be held of no account in the house of my God than dwell in the tents of sinners.*† *Blessed* then *are the poor in spirit,* whom the Lord fills with the Spirit *of fear*†4 and by means of that fear nourishes love.

† Gen 3:5
† Gen 3:5
† Mt 5:3
† Ps 83:11 [84:10]
† Is 2:3.

12. This is the first day of our creation and our re-creation.[5] On it, at the Lord's bidding, light arises for us†—that is, the humility that comes of self-knowledge. For it is humility which divides day from night, darkness from light,† justice from iniquity, the chosen from the reprobate, the damned from the saved. This day begins at evening—that is, at reflection on our weakness—and goes on towards the morning of our restoration.† And just as *the beginning of all sin is pride,*† so all justice begins from humility, which is the first step in the ascent to the kingdom of heaven. *Blessed are the poor in spirit, for theirs is the kingdom of heaven.*†

† Gen 1:3
† Gen 1:3
† Gen 1:5
† Si 10:15
† Mt 5:3

13. But now, the soul that knows herself through humility begins to know God through piety.† At

† Is 11:2

---

4. In this carefully worked out sermon Aelred connects the first seven beatitudes with the seven days of creation and the seven qualities that are mentioned by Isaiah, which are commonly called the seven gifts of the Holy Spirit.
5. Aelred has a similar treatment of the first four beatitudes in Sermon 42.9–14

the Lord's bidding then, *let there be* for her *a firmament* and *let it be called heaven.*† This is [the firmament] of which the Prophet says: *He stretches out the heavens like a skin*†—signifying sacred Scripture. To this firmament then let her lift up her eyes; here let her learn [to know] God. Jesus upbraids the Jews, saying: *You err, knowing neither the Scriptures nor the power of God.*† Christ is indeed the Power of God and the Wisdom of God.† Therefore, someone who does not want to be ignorant concerning *Christ, the power of God,* must strive to understand the Scriptures. 14. Let him be meek, that he may be *quick to listen, slow to speak;*† meek, that he may learn humbly; meek, that he may not resist unseasonably. For in this virtue—as it were on the second day of our restoration—the firmament of the Scriptures most fully appears to us, *dividing the upper waters from the lower*†—that is, angelic knowledge from human. The latter is the lower, the former the upper. This day too begins for us at evening—that is, from an insight into our ignorance—and moves on towards morning—that is, the illumination of divine grace. And it is a step along the way to *the land of the living,*† the land of promise, the land of our eternal dwelling place. For *blessed are the meek, for they shall possess the land.*†

†Gen 1:6f

†Ps 103 [104]:2

†Mt 22:29

†1 Co 1:24

†Jm 1:19

†Gen 1:6

†Ps 26 [27]:13; Ps 141:6[142:5]

†Mt 5:4

15. Now a person who both knows himself and to some extent is waking to a cognizance of God, needs knowledge,† not that which puffs up by pride but that which builds up by charity.† For it is essential that one know how great are the miseries of this life, how great the fear, lest one succumb to temptation; and how great <the sorrow>, lest one grow proud in prosperity. And so *tears will become* one's *bread by day and by night*†

†Is 11:2
†1 Co 8:1

†Ps 41:4 [42:3]

and let him love to weep more than to laugh.

16. So in this third beatitude, as if on the third day, *let the waters which are beneath the heavens*—that is, wandering and earthly thoughts—*be brought together* at the Lord's bidding *into their proper place*[†] and *let dry land appear*[‡] which, collecting the rain of tears, *will bring forth lush green grass and produce grain and trees that bear fruit*.[†] For the earth of our heart, watered with tears, brings forth the fruit of good thoughts. These make our old life flourish anew so that from the new person new fruit may come forth. And this day, no less, begins at evening—that is, with anguish—and moves on towards the morning of divine contemplation. For *blessed are they who mourn, for they shall be consoled*.[†]

[†]Gen 1:9
[‡]Gen 1:11
[†]Gen 1:11

[†]Mt 5:5

17. When a person advances in this way and comes into God's service it is essential that he have the Spirit of fortitude,[†] that he may be steadfast and prepare his state of mind, not for rest, but for temptation.[†] Let him steadfastly pass over favorable circumstances, steadfastly endure adverse circumstances, hungering and thirsting only for justice and in his contemplation scorning all things created. So that this could happen, the Lord in this fourth beatitude, as if on the fourth day, now shows us *a greater light to rule the day*[†]—namely, the example of our Saviour. This enlightens the day—that is, the time of prosperity—lest it be enveloped in the darkness of pride. [He also shows us] *a lesser light and the stars to rule over the night*,[†]—namely, the example of the Church's patience and the endurance of the saints, lest the night—that is, our [time of] adversity—be wholly deprived of light. This day also has an evening—the breadth of temptation

[†]Is 11:2

[†]Si 2:1

[†]Gen 1:16

[†]Gen 1:16

and the hunger for justice—but it moves towards morning—that is, towards prosperity and eternal repletion. For *blessed are they who hunger and thirst for justice, for they will be filled.*† †Mt 5:6

18. Now this person has learned to have mercy on his own soul and so is pleasing to God.† Let him learn [to have mercy] on his neighbor as well. For no one is so just as not to need mercy. And this is the one and only counsel† [that can be given]: someone who wants to receive mercy must have mercy on others. Let the waters, then, at the Lord's bidding, bring forth living creatures†—that is to say, good deeds from good thoughts, not dead but living deeds. *Let him share his bread with the hungry and* bring *the poor and vagrants into* his house. *When he sees someone naked, let him cover him and his body to avert scorn.*† And thus he is permeated with a fifth light as a <fifth> beatitude. It has indeed an evening—reflection on his own need—from which he learns to have mercy on others as he would want for himself, but it moves towards morning—that is, towards the reward that comes from the mercy of God. For *blessed are the merciful, for they shall obtain mercy.*† †Si 30:24 †Is 11:2 †Gen 1:20 †Is 58:7 †Mt 5:7

19. But someone who has already turned away *from evil* and learned to do good is clearly worthy of advancing to understanding.† For those who strive to do good certainly deserve to understand God. This understanding purifies the eye of the heart, so that the person who understands God *through a reflection in a mirror and in an enigma*† will see him quite clearly. In this sixth beatitude, as if on the sixth day, the human person is created, or rather re-created, *to the image of God*,† so that someone who was *made like the dumb beasts* †Is 11:2 †1 Co 13:12 †Gen 1:27ff

by ignorance[†] may be conformed to God by understanding. This day too has an evening—namely, the mirror and the enigma—for it is not able to see clearly, but by purity of heart it moves towards that morning of which the psalmist says: *In the morning I will stand before you, and I will see.*[†] For *blessed are the pure of heart for they shall see God.*[†]

[†]Ps 48:13, 21 [49:12, 20]

[†]Ps 5:5 [3]
[†]Mt 5:7

20. So then, this intelligible world is complete as are all its furnishings.[†] What remains then, but the sabbath? For after the work of these six days, which is not carried out without toil, one comes to rest and peace of mind. Servile fear is banished to be succeeded by filial love.[†] For from being a servant one becomes a son of God, so that one may rest in God and God in oneself. For *blessed are the peacemakers, for they shall be called the sons of God.*[†]

[†]Gen 2:1

[†]1 Jn 4:18

[†]Mt 5:9

21. This is the way,[†] dearest brothers, by which we must return to our fatherland and come to the fellowship of those whose feast we are celebrating today. It was by this laborious way that they went up before us. From this way no persecutions, no hardships, were able to deter them. For they had heard from the Lord the consoling words with which he continues his sermon: *Blessed*, he says, *are those who suffer persecution for justice's sake.*[†] And these: *Blessed are you when men hate you and upbraid you and revile your name as evil on account of me.*[†]

[†]Cf. Sermon 27.21–22 and Sermon 46.15–16

[†]Mt 5:10

[†]Lk 6:22

22. So let there be, dearest brothers, true praise of all the saints on our lips. Let us not praise them with our lips and insult them by our deeds. We praise them truthfully if we do everything

we can to imitate them. Whatever we do freely, we show we love and, although our lips may remain silent, we praise it by our deeds. Let us hasten, dearest ones, to enjoy the extremely pleasant company of the saints and with them contemplate him *who surpasses all the sons of men in beauty*.† Let nothing impede our course, neither indolence nor indecisiveness nor the unparalleled magnitude of the task. 23. To combat indolence, let us set before us the examples of the saints To combat the unparalleled magnitude of the task, let us trust that we will be saved by the grace of God alone. To combat indecisiveness, let us look to the help of the Lord and the unceasing prayer of all the saints for us. For why should we be indecisive, when we have so many fighting right along with us? There are more with us than against us. All we need do is ask our Lord, by the merits of all his saints, to help us as we fight here and with them to crown us with everlasting happiness; [this we ask of] Jesus Christ, our Lord,

    who lives and reigns with God the Father
      in the unity of the Holy Spirit,
   God, through all the ages of ages.
        Amen. Amen. Amen.†

†Ps 44:3 [45:2]

†This final sentence is found also in Aelred's Sermon 45.17

Sermon Twenty-eight
To the Clerics at the Synod

NOW YOU ARE A CHOSEN RACE, *a royal priesthood, a holy nation, and a redeemed people, that you might make known his virtues who has called you out of darkness into his marvelous light.*† That we are a chosen race is a matter of grace. That we are a royal priesthood, a matter of glory. That we are a holy nation, a matter of merit. That we are a redeemed people is a matter of debt. At one time the Hebrews prided themselves on the nobility of their race, saying they were the offspring of Abraham.† Some boasted of their descent from Aaron, others on belonging to the house of David. But you, *O chosen race,* you derive your name 'Christians' from Christ and you have been found worthy through your faith and communion at the altar to become his body and his members. You, I say, have a far happier cause for rejoicing, an incomparably greater reason for boasting. 2. For they derive their origin from the earth; you derive yours from heaven. They pride themselves on the flesh and the propagation of the flesh; you rejoice in the Spirit and in a spiritual generation.† It is to you that the words apply: *To all who received him, he gave the power to become children of God, who were born not of blood nor by the will of man but of God.*† *You have received,* says the Apostle, *not a spirit of slavery leading you back into a life of fear, but*

†1 P 2:9

†Mt 3:9; Lk 3:8; Jn 8:33, 39

†Cf. Jn 3:6

†Jn 1:12–13

you have received the Spirit of adoption of children, in whom we cry 'Abba, Father'. So you are God's children, and not only children but also heirs, heirs indeed of God, coheirs with Christ.† 3. Christians I may call truly happy, truly blessed, ennobled as they are by belonging to such a race as has been adopted as children of God. *For we are,* as the Apostle witnesses, *his very own race.*† Willingly he gave birth to us by the word of his truth that we might be some beginning of his creation .† Well then, *chosen race,* highborn race, beware, I beg you, of a life unworthy of your lineage. Make every effort to prove yourselves not unworthy of your parentage, of him who, with such great and undeserved goodness, in preference to others, *chose you to be his own portion.*† *Keep this glory unspotted,*† for it is better for you to die than to sully your glory with any blemish of baseness.

†Rm 8:15–17

†Ac 17:28

†Jm 1:18

†Ps 32 [33]:12
†Si 33:24

4. The election by which grace comes to us, you must know, is of three kinds. Sometimes wicked persons are chosen from the midst of the wicked, so that they may become good; sometimes good persons are chosen from the midst of the wicked, so that they may become better still; sometimes good persons are chosen from the midst of the good, so that they may reach the summit of perfection. [Take these examples:] The wicked chosen from among the wicked—the Apostle, who tells us of himself: *At first I was a blasphemer and persecutor and inflicted violence, but I received mercy.*† Again: *God set me apart from my mother's womb and called me through his grace.*† And this: *By the grace of God I am what I am.*† The good chosen from among the wicked—Abraham at Ur of the Chaldees.† And indeed the people of Israel in Egypt were chosen as good from the midst of

†1 Tm 1:13
†Gal 1:15
†1 Co 15:10

†Gen 12:1–3

the wicked and were led into the desert to receive the Law and become better still. 5. Good people, too, are are quite often chosen from the midst of the good—as Matthias was chosen from the members of the elect to be advanced to being an apostle.† Barnabas and Saul also were chosen as good from the midst of the good to preach among the Gentiles and reach the heights of perfection.† Similarly *you, too, in your natural condition deserved God's anger, like all those others*† who belong to the mass of the lost, but you were chosen to receive the faith. Then you were taken into the clergy and later still elevated to the priesthood. But since we have now recognized the three kinds of election, it remains for us to inquire as to the cause.

†Ac 1:26

†Ac 13:2

†Eph 2:1, 3

6. For what then were you chosen? To be invested with the glory of the royal priesthood. Behold the dignity of the christian people, behold what Christ's grace has bestowed on us. *Rejoice in the Lord and exalt, you just, and glory, all you of upright heart.*† Blessed be God who has anticipated us *by the blessing of sweetness.*† Not by one blessing only but by two have we been prepared in advance: the kingly and the priestly. Truly, Lord Jesus, truly *you are worthy to receive* glory because for us *you were put to death and you redeemed us for God with your blood and made us a kingdom and priests for our God.*†

†Ps 31 [32]:11
†Eph 1:3; Ps 20:4 [21:6]

†Rv 5:9–10

7. The tribe of Levi was chosen of old to minister to the Lord and the tribe of Judah was chosen to rule the people. The one was raised to priesthood, the other to kingship, but neither of them to both. No one among the ancient people obtained the title and the honor of king and priest at the same time. Rather, when King Uzziah rashly

usurped the functions of a priest, he wasted away with leprosy in punishment for such an outrage.† *But when the time came for mercy,*† for the destitute to be raised from the dung-heap and set on a throne of glory,† *the Mediator between God and the people,*‡ *our Ruler and our Judge,*† *the Lord our lawgiver*† was sent to the wretched to be for us not only the *high priest of good things to come*† but also *King of kings and Lord of lords.*† **8.** He it is whom God the Father *has anointed with the oil of gladness above his fellows,*† whose *name is oil poured out,*† the curdling mountain ,‡ the fertile mountain, the mountain rising above all hills .* In him is every outpouring of grace, all abundance of blessings, so that all who cling to him through faith and love are filed from his plenitude and anointed with his anointing. That is why they are deservedly called *a chosen race and a royal priesthood*† You, however, should regard yourselves as being more properly denoted as a royal priesthood because you rule the people of God and handle divine mysteries.

†2 Ch 26:16–21
†Gal 4:4, Ps 101:14 [102:13]
‡Ps 112 [113]:7; 1 K 2:8 ‡1 Tm 2:5
†Jm 4:12
†Is 33:22
†Heb 9:11
†Rv 19:16

†Ps 44:8 [45:7]
‡Sg 1:2
‡Ps 67 [68]:16
* Is 2:2; Mi 4:1

†1 P 2:9

9. Acknowledge therefore the honor that is yours and honor your ministry. Do not let yourselves be like him of whom it is written: *When honored, man did not understand; he was comparable to stupid beasts and became like them.*† Again: *The stupid man will not know and the fool will not understand this.*† You are kings and as far exalted in rank above earthly kings as the kingdom of heaven diverges from an earthly [kingdom]. They rule human bodies, you govern souls. They bear a material sword, to you is entrusted one that is spiritual. They distribute earthly things, you administer the things of heaven. It is for them to give their subjects temporal goods, it is for you to bestow eternal things.

†Ps 48:21 [49:20]

†Ps 91:7 [92:6]

10. *Now, therefore, you kings, understand; be instructed, you who judge the earth. Serve the Lord in fear*[†] and govern your subjects no less by example than by word. If you want to preside over others in a life-giving way, govern them prudently. Let your life not be out of keeping [with your words], for *the kingdom of God is a matter not of comment but of power.*[†] Govern therefore the senses of your body and the thoughts of your mind. For people's senses and their thoughts are inclined to evil from their *youth,*[†] and, if they are not guarded carefully, death will readily slip in at these windows.[†] 11. Govern *your eyes lest they see vanity, your ears lest they hear of bloodshed, your hands lest they stretch out to wrongdoing, your feet lest they dare to run after evil. Govern your tongue lest it speak falsehood,*[†] for the words of a priest are either true or sacrilegious. If a lie in a priest is sacrilege, what is theft, what is adultery, what is robbery, what is usury, what is hatred, what is murder, what is sacrilege itself? Govern your senses therefore, but, no less than that, govern your thoughts, well aware that *even a secret comment will not go unheeded*[†] and *the schemes of the godless will be brought to account.*[†] For *the Holy Spirit of discipline flees from the travesty of discipline and withdraws from thoughts which are without understanding.*[†] 12. It is a great power, dearest brothers, and it is a great victory to overcome oneself and submit to reason. That is why the Pagan[†] says: *Do you wish to be held in honor? I will give you a great empire. Control yourself.*[1] And our Solomon says: *The patient person is better than the strong and someone who rules his own soul than someone who captures cities.*[†] If you govern

[sidenotes:]
†Ps 2:10–11
†1 Co 4:20
†Gen 8:21
†Jer 9:21
†Ps 118 [119]:37; Is 33:15; Ps 124 [125]:3; Pr 1:16; Is 59:7; Ps 5:7[6]; Ps 33:14 [34:13]; Is 59:3
†Ws 1:11
†Ws 1:9
†Ws 1:5
†Seneca, referred to as *Ethnicus*: pagan, i.e. pre-Christian.
†Pr 16:32

---

1. Seneca, *Epistle 113*, Cf. *Florilegium Morale Oxoniense* 2: *Flores Auctorum*, ed. C. H. Talbot, Anecdota Medievale Namurcensia 6 (1956) 79.

yourselves in this way, you are kings indeed and you are truly reigning already, for *the kingdom of God is within you.*† *The Lord said in the Gospel: The kingdom of God is like this, as if a person cast seed on the earth*† *and so on. And the kingdom of God is within you,*† but now it lies hidden in the seed. Afterwards it will appear in the harvest. Now it is sprouting and growing in might; later on it will flower and bear fruit in blessedness. Well then, kings, well then, priests, *ministers of our God,*† safeguard your royal power, vindicate the dignity of your priesthood by your behavior.

†Lk 17:21

†Mk 4:26
†Lk 17:21

†Is 61:6; 1 P 2:9

13. People are called priests [*sacerdos*] because they 'give holy things' [*dant sacra*]. It is your duty then to give holy things, not to sell them. The grace of baptism and the remedy of penance with the other sacraments are yours to give to the People of God. Above all it is for you to consecrate the most sacred Body and Blood of Christ and deliver them to the faithful. Anyone who handles and receives them *unworthily will be guilty of the Body and Blood of the Lord.*† Therefore, it is written, *many of you are feeble and sick, and many have died.*† You must then, as we have already said, give the Lord's sacraments, not sell them. *Give,* it says, *and it will be given to you.*† And again: *Freely have you received, freely give.*†
14. Woe to wicked priests who expect piety to provide them with an income,† who offer to peddle baptism, confessions, burials, masses, and prayers, and even with Judas the traitor the Body of the Lord. Woe, I repeat a second and a third time, on prelates and subjects who with Gehazi† and Simon Magus† are not afraid to sell and to buy prebends, parishes, holy orders, honors, and church revenues. Let them tremble at the whip

†1 Co 11:27

†1 Co 11:30

†Lk 6:38
†Mt 10:8

†1 Tm 6:5

†2 Kgs 5: 20–27
†Ac 8: 18–24

of the Lord.† Let them tremble and quake at the approach of the dreadful reckoning. Buying and selling spiritual gifts—which is what those doves signifiy—they will indeed be driven out of the Lord's temple with painful retribution. *My house, he says, shall be called a house of prayer but you have made it a robbers' den.*†

15. Truly the children of God who show themselves true kings and worthy priests are always ready not only to impart freely the gifts of the Holy Spirit which they have received freely but also, if necessary, to give their own property and to *lay down their lives for their brothers and sisters.*† Look, you have heard how [we are] a chosen race by grace and how [we are] a royal priesthood to [our] glory. Now it must be stated why it is by merit that [we are] *a holy nation* and by debt that [we are] *a redeemed people*. Indeed, *deceptive is the grace and fleeting the beauty*† which holiness does not commend, which virtue has not brought forth. Therefore for grace to be profitable, for glory to last, there must in addition be the merit of holiness which preserves both.

16. For this is why we were chosen in Christ *before the creation of the world, that we might be holy and unspotted in the sight* of God, *in charity.*† *Be holy, he says, because I am holy.*† So the Lord's minister ought to be holy in body and spirit. For there is a holiness of the body and there is a holiness of the spirit. Holiness of body is the cleanliness of chastity. Wherefore the Apostle says: *For this is the will of God, your sanctification, that you might abstain from fornication, so that each one might possess his own vessel in honor.*† And again he says: *Let fornication or all uncleanness or*

avarice not be mentioned among you as befits a holy people.† Holiness of spirit is zeal for uprightness. Whence David says: *A clean heart create in me, God, and renew an upright spirit within me.*† Let the spirit be upright in examining, upright in judging, upright in punishing. Examination should be careful, judgement should be just, punishment should be tempered.

†Eph 5:3

†Ps 50:12

17. There follows: *A redeemed people.*† That we were created rational humans *to the image of God*† by God our maker, that in him *we live and move and have our being,*† that on all sides we are hedged around by his countless benefits, is all to be ascribed to his goodness and his grace. Therefore, in return for all this we ought to be subject to his commands in all things and obligated for all this to giving him thanks. Who can estimate worthily the heights of glory to which we were raised when he came in search of *the sheep that was lost* and when, finding it, he put it on his sacred shoulders and carried it to the Kingdom of Heaven?† But what is to be valued and marveled at more than anything else is the way in which he redeemed us. 18. For *it was by nothing perishable*, says the blessed Peter, *by gold or silver, that you were redeemed from the empty folly of your way of life, but by the precious blood of Jesus Christ, who was as a lamb without mark or blemish, who loved <us> and washed us from our sins in his blood.*† This act on the part of the Lord was of such a nature and so great that any other of his benefits, as inexpressibly great and numberless as they may be, in comparison with it seem to be little or nothing. *For it was of no use for us to be born if we were not to be redeemed.*† Therefore it was not without good reason that I said holiness pertains to merit but our redemption to debt.

†1 P 2:9
†Gen 1:27

†Ac 17:28

†Lk 15:4–6

†1 P 1:18–19, Rv 1:5

†From the *Exultet*, sung after the blessing of the Paschal Candle

No human being, no angel even, ever could or ever will be capable, therefore, I will not say of requiting, but of admiring worthily or conceiving of that redemption.

19. *That you might make known his virtues,*[†1 P 2:9] it says. Let us know that for this we were chosen, for this we were redeemed, that we might take the pains to make known his virtues. Ths is why it is written: *Be exalted, Lord, in your power, we will sing and hymn your virtues.*[†Ps 20:14 [21:13]] And this: *Praise him for his virtues, praise him for his surpassing greatness.*[†Ps 150:2 [1-2]] Jesus Christ our Lord, the Power[‡*Virtus* is of necessity translated both as 'virtue' and 'power' in this passage.] of God and the Wisdom of God, the supreme Good from whom all good things come, the supreme Power from whom all power derives, he is the *Lord of power, he is the king of glory.*[‡Ps 23 [24]:10] 20. Although he has all the virtues in himself, he indicates that he has three which are special and especially his own. For it is on them that *the whole Law and the Prophets depend*[†Mt 22:40] and in them the rest [of the virtues] are possessed—they are chastity, humility, and charity. These [are the virtues] the Son of God preached by word and showed by example when he lived among us. About the first—which is integrity of body—after mentioning other things about it he said: *Not all can accept this word. Let anyone accept it who can accept it.*[†Mt 19:11-12] And again: These who do not marry and are not given in marriage *will be like God's angels in heaven.*[†Mt 22:30] Of the second he said: *Learn of me, for I am meek and humble of heart.*[†Mt 11:29] And of the third: *This is my commandment, that you love one another. Greater love than this no one has: that he lay down his life for his friends.*[†Jn 15:12-13] 21. As he said, so he did. Not only did he [preserve] his integrity and remain a virgin but also he chose to be born from a virgin. *He humbled himself, he emptied himself, having been*

made obedient to the Father unto death, even death on a cross.† Yet what shall I say of the perpetual love by which he loved us and drew us to himself in compassion,† experiencing the miseries of our death out of charity alone? And you, too, dearest ones, *imitate him as most dear sons and walk in love just as Christ loved us.*† Vest your souls with the ornaments of virtues like these, that you may be worthy to approach the holy of holies.

†Ph 2:7–8

†Jer 31:3

†Eph 5:1–2

22. For the principal vestments in which you go to the altar are symbols for you of these virtues: the alb, stole, and chasuble—which in other terms are called *poderis, orarium* and *planeta*. By the *poderis* understand chastity, by the *orarium* humility, and by the *planeta* charity. The *poderis*, a white vestment reaching down to the feet— whence it is named in Greek *poderis*†—suggests the snowy splendor of chastity, which in the Lord's priest is preserved to the end of life. The *orarium*—which takes its name [from *orare*, to pray]—is a sign of humility, for it is in prayer especially that we humble our souls by confessing our sins and weeping for them. The *planeta*— the outward vestment that covers and smooths everything out—stands for the *charity that sets all things in order* and adorns them. It also *covers a multitude of sins.*† 23. Now let us take a look at this, dearest ones. If someone knowingly and freely presumed to celebrate Mass without an alb,† of what grievous sin he would consider himself guilty? Why then would not any priest or cleric, defiled in mind and body, be much more unclean and profligate if he should handle and perform the most holy mysteries without the vestment of chastity? Similarly, if he attempted to do the same without stole or chasuble,† would he not

†*Poderis* is a greek word derived from *pous, podos*, meaning foot.

†1 P 4:8; Pr 8:30

†*poderis*

†*planeta*

be judged insane or a heretic and a stranger to Christ? O the pathetic blindness of such priests. How much more tolerable it would be to sing Mass without a stole than to approach the altar swollen with pride. It would be far, far more excusable to consecrate the sacraments without a chasuble than to go into the great King's feast without charity, which is the wedding garment.

24. You then, chosen priests and kings, *vest yourselves* in this threefold armor of virtues, so that you may be safe from the threefold plague that is devouring almost the whole world! In the Apocalypse we read about menacing horses which were furiously urged on by a incalculable army of demons as their riders breathed forth from their mouths fire, smoke, and sulphur.[†Rv 9:18] By these three plagues the human race was dreadfully decimated. 25. By 'horses' is signified carnal and proud persons whose hearts harness unclean spirits, not to govern them but to hurl them down and by means of them as many others as possible. From the horses' mouths there comes forth *fire and sulphur and smoke*, killing people because the unscrupulous and profligate are continually, by means of their poisonous advice and conversation, making others drink the plague of vice and the venom of eternal death which the devil gives them to drink within themselves. *For the mouth speaks from the overflowing of the heart and an evil one produces evil from the evil that is treasured in the heart.*[†Lk 6:45]

26. *By these plagues*, then, people are killed, since even those who used to order their lives in accordance with reason incur the penalties of infernal damnation when they recklessly yield to evil blandishments and advice. Whence this saying: *Evil*

conversation corrupts good habit.† And again: *How gladly you bear with fools, being yourselves wise. If someone reduces you to slavery you put up with it.*† By 'fire' the flames of covetousness and avarice are expressed. For the avaricious, set on fire by the brands of their covetousness, never abounding in their abundance, never possessing what they possess, thirst to have more.

†1 Co 15:33

†2 Co 11:19–20

27. By 'smoke' pride is denoted, for smoke *always goes up* and as it goes up it grows thinner and disappears. That is why it is written of the proud: *May they vanish as smoke vanishes.*† And elsewhere: *The pride of them that hate you goes up continually.*† *Pride is always going up* because the proud are always seeking what is higher than themselves, busying themselves with great matters and things too marvelous for them.† They aspire to worldly honors, yearn for positions of dignity. They seek their own glory, can never bear to be subject or to be on an equal footing with others. They look down on everyone, despising their inferiors and envying their superiors. Therefore they are always going up, because by all their efforts and all their attachments they are promoting themselves. The higher they do go up, the more they fade away and disappear like smoke.

†Ps 67:3 [68:2]
†Ps 73 [74]:23

†Ps 130 [131]:1

28. The name 'sulphur' is given to the fetid life of the self-indulgent. This is why the people of Sodom, whose actions were so ignominious and detestable, rightly perished by fire and sulphur. For it is written: *The instruments of a person's sin are the instruments of his punishment.*† Those who delight in the flames of passion and the stench of their own flesh will afterwards, by God's just judgement, be tormented with fire and sulphur.

†Ws 11:17

Let flagrant sinners listen, therefore, to *the beasts that rot in their own dung.*† Let the impure listen and shudder. They have been likened to *stupid beasts*; they are, indeed, far worse than beasts. 29. For beasts live as they were created to live and do not pervert the laws of nature. Whereas these [sinners], corrupt in mind and body, <perverting laws> both divine and human, of nature and of reason, confound the use and order of sex. They befoul their own bodies with monstrous acts of lust and abuse themselves with every sort of lewdness. Let them therefore fear *the bow that is drawn,*† let them fear the torments of fire and sulphur. For as he once rained down fire and sulphur to destroy the people of Sodom, even so, unless they quickly change their ways, the Lord *will rain down* snares on sinners of this sort, inebriating the lustful and the effeminate with the bitterest of drinks. For *fire, sulphur, and stormy winds* will be the portion in their cups.†

30. Those then are the dire plagues by which people are killed. *Alas, alas, Lord God,*† how many men and women, since they came into existence, have perished and daily do perish by these plagues? *Who shall boast that he has a chaste heart?*† Who shall escape immune, not to fall into one of these, if not into all of them? Woe to the human race from these plagues! *Spare, Lord. I beg, you, spare your people and do not give your inheritance up to destruction.*† *Cast not to the beasts the souls that confess you and at the end do not forget the souls of your poor.*† How long will these Furies continue to rage? By them, no sex, no age, no condition, no rank is spared. Only by a euphemism are they called 'Exemptors',† for they exempt nothing.

31. But so great is the frenzy of the ravening wolves that they devour shepherds more hungrily

†Jl 1:17

†. Is 21:15

†Ps 10:7 [11:6]

†Jer 4:10

†Pr 20:9

†Jl 2:17

†. Ps 73:19 [74:21]

†*Parcæ*, usually translated 'the fates'.

than flocks. But if even the physicians are carried off by the plague, what hope will there be for the sick? *For if these things are done when the wood is green, what will happen when it is dry?*† †Lk 23:31
You are salt to the earth, says the Lord, *and if salt becomes tasteless, how is its saltiness to be restored?*† †Mt 5:13
If the shepherds are consumed by wolves, who will chase away the wolves from slaughtering the sheep? But it is not enough [to say] that the shepherds are devoured by wolves; the shepherds themselves are turned into wolves. It is not enough that they do not guard their flocks; they want also to destroy them. *They devour my people*, it says, *as if they were eating bread.*† †Ps 13 [14]:4
Many shepherds have ravaged my people, says the Lord.† And again: *My people is a scattered flock, their shepherds have seduced them.*† 32. Who is to instruct the rich *not to revel or hope in precarious wealth*† when the prelate sets him an example and gives him grounds for pride and avarice? Who will denounce usurers, if the priest himself lends at a usurious rate?† Who will berate fornicators and adulterers, if clerics and priests are procurers and take the lead in profligacy? Oh how disgraceful, how ignominious it is for a physician to hear from his patients: *Heal yourself.*† Or to hear the Apostle's words: *You who teach others, do you not teach yourself? You who preach against theft, are you stealing? You who preach against promiscuity, are you being promiscuous?*† A priest or a cleric who is a loan shark and smoldering with the fuel of avarice or wantonness—what is he but a burning devil?

†Jer 12:10
†Jer 50:6, 17

†1 Tm 6:17

†Cf. Ez 18:8

†Lk 4:23

†Rm 2:21–22

33. If then, dearest brothers, you would be saved from such plagues by the Lord's help, work at fortifying yourselves with the virtues described above. Let charity root out of your hearts the source of all sin—covetousness. Let real humility

hurl down the haughtiness of pride and conceit. Let the blade of chastity and celibacy strike the death-blow to wantonness. If you do this, you will rightly make known the virtues of God. Armed with these [virtues] and at the same time suitably adorned with them, you will safely and worthily, like *children of eternal light*, reach him *who has called you out of darkness into his marvelous light.*[†]
*To him belong honor and glory
for ever and ever.
Amen.*[†]

[†] 1 P 2:9

[†] Rm 16:27

A CUMULATIVE INDEX TO THE FIRST
CLAIRVAUX COLLECTION OF SERMONS
WILL APPEAR IN THE SECOND VOLUME

TITLES LISTING • CISTERCIAN PUBLICATIONS

CISTERCIAN TEXTS

Bernard of Clairvaux

- Apologia to Abbot William
- Five Books on Consideration: Advice to a Pope
- Homilies in Praise of the Blessed Virgin Mary
- Letters of Bernard of Clairvaux / by B.S. James
- Life and Death of Saint Malachy the Irishman
- Love without Measure: Extracts from the Writings of St Bernard / by Paul Dimier
- On Grace and Free Choice
- On Loving God / Analysis by Emero Stiegman
- Parables and Sentences
- Sermons for the Summer Season
- Sermons on Conversion
- Sermons on the Song of Songs I–IV
- The Steps of Humility and Pride

William of Saint Thierry

- The Enigma of Faith
- Exposition on the Epistle to the Romans
- Exposition on the Song of Songs
- The Golden Epistle
- The Mirror of Faith
- The Nature and Dignity of Love
- On Contemplating God: Prayer & Meditations

Aelred of Rievaulx

- Dialogue on the Soul
- Liturgical Sermons, I
- The Mirror of Charity
- Spiritual Friendship
- Treatises I: On Jesus at the Age of Twelve, Rule for a Recluse, The Pastoral Prayer
- Walter Daniel: The Life of Aelred of Rievaulx

John of Ford

- Sermons on the Final Verses of the Songs of Songs I–VII

Gilbert of Hoyland

- Sermons on the Songs of Songs I–III
- Treatises, Sermons and Epistles

Other Early Cistercian Writers

- Adam of Perseigne, Letters of
- Alan of Lille: The Art of Preaching
- Amadeus of Lausanne: Homilies in Praise of Blessed Mary
- Baldwin of Ford: Spiritual Tractates I–III
- Geoffrey of Auxerre: On the Apocalypse
- Gertrud the Great: Spiritual Exercises
- Gertrud the Great: The Herald of God's Loving-Kindness (Books 1, 2)
- Gertrud the Great: The Herald of God's Loving-Kindness (Book 3)
- Guerric of Igny: Liturgical Sermons Vol. 1 & 2
- Helinand of Froidmont: Verses on Death
- Idung of Prüfening: Cistercians and Cluniacs: The Case for Cîteaux
- Isaac of Stella: Sermons on the Christian Year, I–[II]
- The Life of Beatrice of Nazareth
- The School of Love. An Anthology of Early Cistercian Texts
- Serlo of Wilton & Serlo of Savigny: Seven Unpublished Works
- Stephen of Lexington: Letters from Ireland
- Stephen of Sawley: Treatises

MONASTIC TEXTS

Eastern Monastic Tradition

- Besa: The Life of Shenoute
- Cyril of Scythopolis: Lives of the Monks of Palestine
- Dorotheos of Gaza: Discourses and Sayings
- Evagrius Ponticus: Praktikos and Chapters on Prayer
- Handmaids of the Lord: Lives of Holy Women in Late Antiquity & the Early Middle Ages / by Joan Petersen
- Harlots of the Desert / by Benedicta Ward
- John Moschos: The Spiritual Meadow
- Lives of the Desert Fathers
- Lives of Simeon Stylites / by Robert Doran
- Mena of Nikiou: Isaac of Alexandra & St Macrobius
- The Monastic Rule of Iosif Volotsky (Revised Edition) / by David Goldfrank
- Pachomian Koinonia I–III (Armand Veilleux)
- Paphnutius: Histories/Monks of Upper Egypt
- The Sayings of the Desert Fathers / by Benedicta Ward
- The Spiritually Beneficial Tales of Paul, Bishop of Monembasia / by John Wortley
- Symeon the New Theologian: The Theological and Practical Treatises & The Three Theological Discourses / by Paul McGuckin
- Theodoret of Cyrrhus: A History of the Monks of Syria
- The Syriac Fathers on Prayer and the Spiritual Life / by Sebastian Brock

Western Monastic Tradition

- Anselm of Canterbury: Letters I–III / by Walter Fröhlich
- Bede: Commentary…Acts of the Apostles

CISTERCIAN PUBLICATIONS • TITLES LISTING

- Bede: Commentary…Seven Catholic Epistles
- Bede: Homilies on the Gospels I–II
- Bede: Excerpts from the Works of Saint Augustine on the Letters of the Blessed Apostle Paul
- The Celtic Monk / by U. Ó Maidín
- Life of the Jura Fathers
- Peter of Celle: Selected Works
- Letters of Rancé I–II
- Rule of the Master
- Rule of Saint Augustine

Christian Spirituality

- The Cloud of Witnesses: The Development of Christian Doctrine / by David N. Bell
- The Call of Wild Geese / by Matthew Kelty
- The Cistercian Way / by André Louf
- The Contemplative Path
- Drinking From the Hidden Fountain / by Thomas Spidlík
- Eros and Allegory: Medieval Exegesis of the Song of Songs / by Denys Turner
- Fathers Talking / by Aelred Squire
- Friendship and Community / by Brian McGuire
- Gregory the Great: Forty Gospel Homilies
- High King of Heaven / by Benedicta Word
- The Hermitage Within / by a Monk
- Life of St Mary Magdalene and of Her Sister St Martha / by David Mycoff
- A Life Pleasing to God / by Augustine Holmes
- The Luminous Eye / by Sebastian Brock
- Many Mansions / by David N. Bell
- Mercy in Weakness / by André Louf
- The Name of Jesus / by Irénée Hausherr
- No Moment Too Small / by Norvene Vest
- Penthos: The Doctrine of Compunction in the Christian East / by Irénée Hausherr
- Praying the Word / by Enzo Bianchi
- Rancé and the Trappist Legacy / by A. J. Krailsheimer
- Russian Mystics / by Sergius Bolshakoff
- Sermons in a Monastery / by Matthew Kelty
- Silent Herald of Unity: The Life of Maria Gabrielle Sagheddu / by Martha Driscoll
- Spiritual Direction in the Early Christian East / by Irénée Hausherr
- The Spirituality of the Christian East / by Thomas Spidlík
- The Spirituality of the Medieval West / by André Vauchez
- The Spiritual World of Isaac the Syrian / by Hilarion Alfeyev
- Tuning In To Grace / by André Louf
- Wholly Animals: A Book of Beastly Tales / by David N. Bell

MONASTIC STUDIES

- Community and Abbot in the Rule of St Benedict I–II / by Adalbert de Vogüé
- The Finances of the Cistercian Order in the Fourteenth Century / by Peter King
- Fountains Abbey and Its Benefactors / by Joan Wardrop
- The Hermit Monks of Grandmont / by Carole A. Hutchison
- In the Unity of the Holy Spirit / by Sighard Kleiner
- A Life Pleasing to God: Saint Basil's Monastic Rules / By Augustine Holmes
- The Joy of Learning & the Love of God: Essays in Honor of Jean Leclercq
- Monastic Odyssey / by Marie Kervingant
- Monastic Practices / by Charles Cummings
- The Occupation of Celtic Sites in Ireland / by Geraldine Carville
- Reading St Benedict / by Adalbert de Vogüé
- Rule of St Benedict: A Doctrinal and Spiritual Commentary / by Adalbert de Vogüé
- The Rule of St Benedict / by Br. Pinocchio
- The Spiritual World of Isaac the Syrian / by Hilarion Alfeyev
- St Hugh of Lincoln / by David H. Farmer
- The Venerable Bede / by Benedicta Ward
- Western Monasticism / by Peter King
- What Nuns Read / by David N. Bell
- With Greater Liberty: A Short History of Christian Monasticism & Religious Orders / by Karl Frank

CISTERCIAN STUDIES

- Aelred of Rievaulx: A Study / by Aelred Squire
- Athirst for God: Spiritual Desire in Bernard of Clairvaux's Sermons on the Song of Songs / by Michael Casey
- Beatrice of Nazareth in Her Context / by Roger De Ganck
- Bernard of Clairvaux: Man, Monk, Mystic / by Michael Casey [tapes and readings]
- Bernardus Magister…Nonacentenary
- Catalogue of Manuscripts in the Obrecht Collection of the Institute of Cistercian Studies / by Anna Kirkwood
- Christ the Way: The Christology of Guerric of Igny / by John Morson
- The Cistercians in Denmark / by Brian McGuire
- The Cistercians in Scandinavia / by James France
- A Difficult Saint / by Brian McGuire

TITLES LISTING • CISTERCIAN PUBLICATIONS

- A Gathering of Friends: Learning & Spirituality in John of Ford / by Costello and Holdsworth
- Image and Likeness: Augustinian Spirituality of William of St Thierry / by David Bell
- Index of Authors & Works in Cistercian Libraries in Great Britain I / by David Bell
- Index of Cistercian Authors and Works in Medieval Library Catalogues in Great Britian / by David Bell
- The Mystical Theology of St Bernard / by Étienne Gilson
- The New Monastery: Texts & Studies on the Earliest Cistercians
- Nicolas Cotheret's Annals of Cîteaux / by Louis J. Lekai
- Pater Bernhardus: Martin Luther and Saint Bernard / by Franz Posset
- Pathway of Peace / by Charles Dumont
- A Second Look at Saint Bernard / by Jean Leclercq
- The Spiritual Teachings of St Bernard of Clairvaux / by John R. Sommerfeldt
- Studies in Medieval Cistercian History
- Studiosorum Speculum / by Louis J. Lekai
- Three Founders of Cîteaux / by Jean-Baptiste Van Damme
- Towards Unification with God (Beatrice of Nazareth in Her Context, 2)
- William, Abbot of St Thierry
- Women and St Bernard of Clairvaux / by Jean Leclercq

MEDIEVAL RELIGIOUS WOMEN

- Medieval Religious Women / edited by Lillian Thomas Shank and John A. Nichols
- Distant Echoes
- Hidden Springs: Cistercian Monastic Women (2 volumes)
- Peace Weavers

CARTHUSIAN TRADITION

- The Call of Silent Love / by A Carthusian
- The Freedom of Obedience / by A Carthusian
- From Advent to Pentecost / by A Carthusian
- Guigo II: The Ladder of Monks & Twelve Meditations / by E. Colledge & J. Walsh
- Halfway to Heaven / by R.B. Lockhart
- Interior Prayer / by A Carthusian
- Meditations of Guigo II / by A. Gordon Mursall
- The Prayer of Love and Silence / by A Carthusian
- Poor, Therefore Rich / by A Carthusian
- They Speak by Silences / by A Carthusian
- The Way of Silent Love (A Carthusian Miscellany)
- Where Silence is Praise / by A Carthusian
- The Wound of Love (A Carthusian Miscellany)

CISTERCIAN ART, ARCHITECTURE & MUSIC

- Cistercian Abbeys of Britain
- Cistercians in Medieval Art / by James France
- Studies in Medieval Art and Architecture / edited by Meredith Parsons Lillich (Volumes II–V are now available)
- Stones Laid Before the Lord / by Anselme Dimier
- Treasures Old and New: Nine Centuries of Cistercian Music (compact disc and cassette)

THOMAS MERTON

- The Climate of Monastic Prayer / by T. Merton
- Legacy of Thomas Merton / by P. Hart
- Message of Thomas Merton / by P. Hart
- Monastic Journey of Thomas Merton / by P. Hart
- Thomas Merton/Monk / by P. Hart
- Thomas Merton on St Bernard
- Toward an Integrated Humanity / edited by M. Basil Pennington

CISTERCIAN LITURGICAL DOCUMENTS SERIES

- Cistercian Liturgical Documents Series / edited by Chrysogonus Waddell, ocso
- Hymn Collection of the…Paraclete
- Institutiones nostrae: The Paraclete Statutes
- Molesme Summer-Season Breviary (4 vol.)
- Old French Ordinary & Breviary of the Abbey of the Paraclete (2 volumes)
- Twelfth-century Cistercian Hymnal (2 vol.)
- The Twelfth-century Cistercian Psalter
- Two Early Cistercian Libelli Missarum

STUDIA PATRISTICA

- Studia Patristica XVIII, Volumes 1, 2 and 3

CISTERCIAN PUBLICATIONS • TITLES LISTING

Editorial Offices & Customer Service

- Cistercian Publications
  WMU Station, 1903 West Michigan Avenue
  Kalamazoo, Michigan 49008-5415   USA

  Telephone   616 387 8920
  Fax   616 387 8390
  e-mail   cistpub@wmich.edu

Canada

- Novalis
  49 Front Street East, Second Floor
  Toronto, Ontario M5E 1B3   CANADA

  Telephone   1 800 204 4140
  Fax   416 363 9409

U.K.

- Cistercian Publications UK
  Mount Saint Bernard Abbey
  Coalville, Leicestershire LE67 5UL   UK

- UK Customer Service & Book Orders
  Cistercian Publications
  97 Loughborough Road
  Thringstone, Coalville
  Leicestershire LE67 8LQ   UK

  Telephone   01530 45 27 24
  Fax   01530 45 02 10
  e-mail   MsbcistP@aol.com

Website & Warehouse

- www.spencerabbey.org/cistpub

- Book Returns (prior permission)
  Cistercian Publications
  Saint Joseph's Abbey
  167 North Spencer Road
  Spencer, Massachusetts 01562-1233   USA

  Telephone   508 885 8730
  Fax   508 885 4687
  e-mail   cistpub@spencerabbey.org

Trade Accounts & Credit Applications

- Cistercian Publications / Accounting
  6219 West Kistler Road
  Ludington, Michigan 49431   USA

  Fax   231 843 8919

Cistercian Publications is a non-profit corporation. Its publishing program is restricted to monastic texts in translation and books on the monastic tradition.
A complete catalogue of texts in translation and studies on early, medieval, and modern monasticism is available, free of charge, from any of the addresses above.